COLLECTOR'S GUIDE TO
AMERICAN TOY TRAINS

Wallace-Homestead Collector's Guide™ Series
Harry L. Rinker, Series Editor

COLLECTOR'S GUIDE TO
AMERICAN
TOY TRAINS

SUSAN AND AL BAGDADE

Wallace-Homestead Collector's Guide™ Series

Wallace-Homestead Book Company
Radnor, Pennsylvania

Designed by Anthony Jacobson
Manufactured in the United States of America

Library of Congress Cataloging in Publication Data
Bagdade, Susan D.
    Collector's guide to American toy trains / Susan Bagdade and Al Bagdade.
        p.   cm.—(Wallace-Homestead collector's guide series)
    Includes bibliographical references.
    ISBN 0-87069-532-0
    1. Railroads—Models—Collectors and collecting.   I. Bagdade,
Allen D.   II. Title.   III. Series.
TF197.B23   1990
625.1′9′075—dc20   89-51556
                                                                             CIP

Photo on the cover: Trains and accessories courtesy of R.S. Morris. All
items identified by Lionel Corporation catalog number(s) and
approximate year of production. Locomotive and passenger cars: #248,
629, 630; ca. 1926. Station: #127; ca. 1934. Block signal: #078; ca. 1926.
Telegraph poles: #096; ca. 1934. Street lights: #56; ca. 1926. Lamp post:
#57; 1926. Country estate: #911; ca. 1938. Suburban home: #912; ca.
1932. Landscaped bungalow: #913; ca. 1932. Lamp terrace: #922; ca.
1932. Flagstaff: #90; 1932. Automatic crossing gate: #077; ca. 1932.
Silent track bed: #030/031; ca. 1932. Oak trees: #505; ca. 1926. Three-
piece mountain backdrop: #509; ca. 1926.

2 3 4 5 6 7 8 9 0   9 8 7 6 5 4 3 2 1

Contents

Acknowledgments

Harry L. Rinker, our editor and friend, convinced us we wanted to write another book.

Rich Kleinhardt was kind enough to work with us and do the drawings for this manuscript.

This book would not have been possible without the cooperation of numerous train dealers who allowed us to ask tons of questions, gather information, and photograph trains and accessories at their exhibits at train shows.

A special thank you goes to the auction houses in New York. Christie's East and Sotheby's provided us with numerous excellent photographs from their specialized auctions. The authors express grateful appreciation to auctioneers Leslie Hindman of Chicago and Joy Luke of Bloomington, Illinois for allowing us to photograph auction properties during previews.

The Children's Museum of Indianapolis deserves a special note of thanks for inviting us to spend a day taking photographs of their extensive collection and train layout. Robert Shaw of the Shelburne Museum in New Hampshire was kind enough to provide photos from the museum's collection.

We must single out Ron Morris from the Train Collectors Association in Strasburg, Pennsylvania for supplying information and photocopies from the TCA Library. Paul Doyle and Tony Hay were very generous with their time and the information they sent on Hafner and Voltamp.

Additional thanks goes to John Ezzo and Don Speidel who allowed us to invade their private train collections to photograph innumerable examples and who were exceptionally patient in answering all our questions.

Our computer advisor, Tom Stachelski, must be thanked for all his help in teaching us to master our new computer and programs.

From our very own neighborhood, an extra special note of appreciation to Sigurd Nielsen of the Northbrook Camera Shop who was a tremendous help in providing advice, prompt service, and even redeveloping photos that needed adjustments.

Introduction

The toy train market is alive and well. Train shows, often advertised as model train markets, are filled with dealers specializing in tinplate trains. On any given show day, bags containing rolling stock, track, and accessories can be seen tucked under the arms of those who have traveled many miles to add a piece or two to their collections or layouts. The backbone of this field is the many new collectors who are entering the toy train world for the first time. Some are attempting to re-create their first train set, while others have caught the "toy train virus" and may not have narrowed their specific field of interest yet.

This book is aimed at collectors who are just getting their feet wet. By combining terminology, company histories, and practical information about how to shop and where the action is, we feel that this book can serve as a one-volume guide to understanding the toy train market.

When undertaking a book such as this, information can be difficult to obtain, and it is sometimes controversial. Many companies are no longer in existence, and some do not have archives. We have spent many hours over countless cups of coffee with collectors, experts, and "train folk" gathering the information needed for this book. Dates of specific pieces occasionally vary by a year or two, and important characteristics of a specific series of rolling stock may be different in the eyes of various collectors. One may focus on truck designs, whereas others disdain this characteristic in favor of color schemes. However, each relies on the excellent series of books produced by Greenberg Publications and the six-volume Lionel series by Tom McComas and James Tuohy. For the serious collector of Ives, Lionel, American Flyer, or Marx, these are the bibles of the field and are highly recommended by your authors.

Priced examples found at the end of each company history represent pieces that are currently on the market and are

1

graded according to the TCA "excellent" grade unless otherwise noted. Several pieces were obtained from recent auctions and are noted with an "A" before the price. Pricing across the country varies. Most price guides need adjusting yearly, and they should be used only as guidelines for pricing. The same is true with the prices found in this book. They are not an absolute. They are included to give the reader a "feel" for what he might have to pay for a company's products on the open market.

We hope that this book becomes a companion for all those dedicated collectors involved in this most exciting field.

Happy Hunting!

CHAPTER 1

The Forerunners

If one were to ask a group of people what image comes to mind when they hear the word "railroad," some of the following responses could be expected: "A long, slow line of freight cars that holds up traffic." "Noisy, dirty engines pulling old passenger cars that stop at every little town in the country." "An old fashioned, outmoded way of moving freight and people." However, some would picture a large black steam engine puffing smoke with its whistle screaming and drivers flying as it pulls a long string of sleek passenger cars. This was the case during the golden era of steam, but far from what the forerunners looked like.

The earliest self-propelled steam locomotives appeared in the late 1700s and early 1800s. They were quite simple in design. Utilizing wood to fire the boilers, these little oddities were created to pull a string of carriages that more often resembled stagecoach bodies than passenger cars. They were capable of attaining the breathtaking speed of three to six miles per hour. Destinations were limited to where track had been laid. The early puffers were first introduced in Germany and England, and shortly thereafter they made their debut in the United States. Very few toy manufacturers reproduced these pieces, though some examples can be found which were made by craftsmen for the upper class.

Since the westward expansion of the United States was aided by the development of the railroads, the toy manufacturers added train pieces to their inventories. The romance of the railroad became an important factor to these companies. The average person stood in awe at the smoke-belching oddities. The Merriam Manufacturing Company of Durham, Connecticut was one of the first to manufacture painted tin trains around the 1830s. These early pieces rolled on flat, flangeless wheels and were called floor trains. Other companies were soon to follow Merriam's lead. Toy manufacturers such as George Brown of Forrestville, Connecticut who produced three wheel engines; Eugene Beggs; and Althof Bergmann and Company of New York were involved with the manufacture and distribution of American floor trains.

Fabricated from sheets of tinned iron, these trains were painted or lithographed; most were quite fragile compared to the later cast iron or wood pieces. Nearly all of

Fig. 1–1. The simple design and execution of this early lithographed tin floor train by George Brown is typical of the early 1800s floor runners. Note the hearts on the rear wheels. Photo Courtesy of Richard Opfer Auctions

the tin pieces rolled on rectangularly arranged four wheel configurations. They bore little resemblance to the real thing. Smoke stacks and cabs were accentuated out of proportion to the rest of the engine parts. The tin trains usually consisted of a locomotive and a few passenger cars hooked together by a simple hook and eye coupling system.

Tin trains were fairly expensive compared to other toys of the times, and wooden examples were a fairly adequate alternative to those who could not afford the works of Merriam, Brown, or Beggs. The wooden trains were simply left in their natural state or painted in bright colors. Wood engines carried shaped stacks, bells, wheels, and cabs. Some examples were covered with lithographed paper which simulated detail. The paper covering was quite fragile, and finding examples without torn or faded lithography can be a real challenge for the collector. Wooden trains are an important part of any toy train collection. Such companies as Milton Bradley (the game people) and Schieble Toy and

Fig. 1–2. The Ives, Blakeslee Company manufactured this 1883 tin floor train. The surface treatment is lithographed tin, and the large windows in the passenger coaches are punched rather than painted. This reduces the weight and gives the pieces an open, airy feeling. Photos from the Collection of Jim Heath

Novelty Company of Dayton, Ohio produced some interesting examples in wood and paper.

Cast iron toy trains made their appearance around the 1870s, and they were a vast improvement over their tin counterparts. Ruggedly built, they could withstand the rough play they were subjected to by the young engineer. More cast iron examples are available for the collector than the more fragile tin models. Cast iron pieces were usually cast in two separate molds and the parts or halves joined by means of pins or bolts. More realistic in appearance and proportions than the wood or tin locomotives, much of the detail was cast in place. The finished castings were painted and sometimes numbered or lettered to simulate the real trains. Black was the most common finishing color, but sometimes each piece of rolling stock was painted in a different color. Various alloys of cast iron were used and in some cases brass trim was added to the castings for detail. Most examples rolled on driving wheels which lacked driving rods, though

Fig. 1–3. Some toy trains are one-of-a-kind. This c. 1890s wooden train was carved by Herbert Chapman and carries the Swanton, VT railroad name (Chapman's home). The train was constructed from 444 pieces. Photo Courtesy of the Shelburne Museum

Fig. 1–4. Though fairly crude by today's standards, this c. 1890 Carpenter cast iron pull train is highly collectible, especially when found in this condition. Photo Courtesy of the Shelburne Museum

some did possess this feature. Later examples rolled on small wheels mounted on axles that fit inside cast trucks. This gave the piece a simplistic four wheel arrangement, bearing little resemblance to the real steam engine it was meant to copy.

Though more ruggedly built, cast iron trains did tend to fracture when dropped due to the brittle nature of the casting. And paint chipping is inherent in these pieces. Rust was also a major problem and remains a problem for the collector of these examples. Cast iron floor trains were produced through the 1930s, and several manufacturers put motors in their castings and placed them on tracks. These will be discussed more fully in the appropriate chapter.

Coupling was simple, often utilizing hook and eye or cast pin to hole type mechanisms. During the fifty or so years of production, many companies produced their own versions of the push-pull cast iron floor trains. Such manufacturers as Kenton Hardware of Kenton, Ohio; Francis Carpenter of Port Chester, New York; Kilgore Manufacturing Company of Westerfield, Ohio; Hubley Manufacturing of Lancaster, Pennsylvania; and the Pratt and Letchworth Company of Buffalo, New York were important cast iron toy producers with train examples making up a significant part of their inventories. Some

Fig. 1-5. The Stevens "Big 6" locomotive is rather clumsy by comparision to the Wilkins and Kenton examples of the 1880s. The side rod moves when the large rear wheel rotates. Photo Courtesy of Joy Luke Auctions

Fig. 1-6. These two cast-iron locomotives date from about 1890. They are by two of the better known makers of these types of floor trains. The example on the left was cast by Wilkins, and the one on the right is by Kenton. Photo Courtesy of Sotheby's

pieces bore manufacturers' markings in the castings, but many were unmarked. Positive identification often requires locating the example in the company's catalog.

Cast iron examples have been heavily reproduced because of the high collecting price for originals, which often reach into the hundreds of dollars for clean, prime examples. Reproductions are relatively easy to identify as the surface is usually rougher than the originals, and painting is not quite as subtle on the repros. Signs of wear and rust are also good guidelines for establishing authenticity, but these too can be faked. A little water at the right places over a relatively short period of time can produce a false rust pattern that is difficult to recognize as a fake.

To this point, we have discussed toy trains that required the human element of pushing or pulling the train to simulate the motion of the real thing. The incorporation of motors into the bodies brought about a whole new era of locomotion. Trains could speed around a room or on a prescribed course without hands-on operation. George Brown is credited with introducing the clockwork mechanism to American toy trains in 1856. Other toy makers were quick to follow, including the excellent James Fallow and the Blakelee Company of Connecticut. The clockwork mechanism consisted of a series of gears activated by a coiled spring that was wound by means of a key. The key was inserted into the body or smokestack. As the spring unwound, motion was passed through a series of gears to the driving wheels, and thus movement was accomplished. The length of time of

movement and speed depended on the size of the spring and the gear ratios. Some were capable of running nearly an hour on a single winding. The clockwork mechanism was not a new device but was actually incorporated into toys dating back to the sixteenth century. Automated figures utilized the clockwork mechanism to move arms, legs, and heads in a lifelike manner. It was George Brown who first put the movement into American trains.

The early clockwork mechanisms were quite complex and were similar to those used in clocks of the period; hence the name. Because of the intricacy, these delicate movements often broke or needed continuous service. By the turn of the nineteenth century, motors were much stronger and less expensive to produce. Wheels often had to be held while the spring was wound, but later models incorporated an off/on lever that held the gears during the

Fig. 1-7. The clockwork mechanism in this Ives tin, painted locomotive was a step toward self-propulsion. Photo Courtesy of Richard Opfers Auctions

winding procedure and allowed the gears to run free when disconnected.

The first clockworks were mounted in tinplate examples similar to the push-pull floor trains, but by the late 1800s the mechanism was placed in cast iron train frames. In fact, clockwork motors were the principal means of locomotion by the turn of the century. Several companies such as Ives and American Flyer continued to produce clockwork engines along with their regular line of electrics.

Clockworks were free runners, traveling around the floor without any direction in mind. A few companies fixed the pilot trucks in such a manner that the train traveled in circles following the lead of the pilots. Others were attached to a drawing arm that prescribed the path of movement around a circular course. The clockwork mechanism was mounted outside of the train, and the draw bar connected the motor to the engine. As the mechanism unwound, it turned the arm and thus the locomotive in a circular path. The Hubley Manufacturing Company produced such an arrangement in 1892 but mounted the train on a track-like structure. This type of configuration was especially practical for use on a tabletop and simulated the later tracked examples. Clockwork motors are still in use in many of today's toys but seldom found in toy trains. They served as a useful bridge between push-pull and electrified trains.

Somewhat similar to the keywind clockworks were the friction motor examples which were popular from the 1890s to the 1920s. Based on a revolving heavy flywheel that was introduced about the 1880s, the first examples were put in motion by fastening a string to a small wheel. When the string was pulled, the flywheel was sent spinning. The friction motor utilized the flywheel principle but was activated by means of running it on a flat surface. The motion of the flywheel was transmitted to the power wheels when the locomotive was placed on the floor, and the gears on the axles engaged the flywheel. As can be expected, the running time was quite short as friction on the wheels and up through the gears reduced the spinning activity of the flywheel. However, these trains were quite practical because it was not necessary to start the motor with a key—which more often than not became misplaced. One major drawback to the friction drives was that the entire train had to be assembled before the motor could be activated. Once the locomotive wheels were spinning, time was lost trying to place the engine back with the consist.

Toy trains sporting friction motors never seemed to gain the popularity of their keywound counterparts. They are found mounted in cast metal and wood body engines. Clark and Company, and the Schieble Toy and Novelty Company produced a wide range of friction toys in the early 1900s including splendid locomotives fabricated from wood with metal drivers. Both clockwork and friction motors were sometimes connected to devices that produced simulated sparks or whistle tones. These added features usually took their toll on the running time but were good selling points.

The commercial application of the toy steam engine in the late 1800s was the precursor for the steam locomotive. These steam engines were a wonder to watch with their hissing noises and rapid movement. Many contained a driving wheel that could be attached to an action toy by means of a pulley-type belt. When the steam engine was activated, the wheel was set in motion, and this motion was transmitted to the action toy. Ferris wheels turned, figures chopped wood, and miniature workshops swung into action.

The steam locomotive was a natural for the toy train manufacturers. Not only was the running time longer than the keywind or friction examples, but the use of steam power more closely approached the real thing. The trains were placed on tracks, and the wheels were flanged to maintain contact with the rails around curves.

In order to generate steam, water was placed in the locomotive's boiler, and the steam valves were closed. Heat was produced by igniting a wick saturated with flammable spirits or by the use of dry, burnable materials. When the steam reached its peak, the steam valves were opened and the pistons transferred power to the driving wheels putting the locomotive in motion.

In theory this seemed the ideal system, but there were several inherent drawbacks. To begin with, these toys were developed for children to play with, but most came with a warning that a parent should be present during the operation of the train. The use of flammable materials, which saturated the wick or batting, produced a potential fire hazard—especially in the hands of a youngster. Failure to open the steam valves when the steam was headed could result in enough steam pressure to cause an explosion. In addition, clogging of the steam lines could result in safety hazards for the young and adult engineer alike. As the steam condensed back into water, puddles usually formed behind the locomotive. These steamers were affectionately known as "puddlers" as a result of the steam condensation.

In spite of all of the dangers, the steam locomotive was a wondrous sight to behold as it puffed around the track with the driving rods and drivers spinning. Some really fine examples came from the shops of Beggs of Paterson, New Jersey in the 1880s, and the Weeden Manufacturing Company which issued the "Dart" in the late 1880s. Weeden's expertise in the manufacturing of quality toy steam engines was

Fig. 1-8. The Weeden "Dart" was America's answer to steam propulsion. Fired by alcohol, these puddlers traveled across the floor pulling a full complement of cars. Note the Dart name under the cab window. Photo Courtesy of Beute & Son

a natural for their entrance into the steam locomotive field. Their popularity lasted into the early 1900s. Locomotives were fabricated from sheet metal utilizing the strength of the material to handle the steam pressure in a satisfactory manner.

Steam locomotives were quite realistic in appearance which added to their popularity. Owing to the complexity of construction, their initial cost was quite high compared to clockwork and push-pull models. Examples occasionally surface for the collector, but a word of caution is in order. Before pouring water into the boiler and firing it up, a careful examination of the working parts might prevent an unexpected explosion. Rust, dirt, and clogged pieces can turn an interesting piece into a potential bomb. Careful cleaning and checking of the parts is necessary. There has been a resurgence of interest in the steam locomotive, and several model toy train companies are issuing examples of the steam classics.

The advent of electricity was a boon to the toy train industry. For the first time a train's speed and direction could be controlled from a distance which simulated reality more closely. Electricity did not replace completely other forms of locomotion as many companies such as Ives and Marx companies produced clockwork trains in addition to their electric lines. Keywind examples were often less costly to produce and continued as an inexpensive alternative to electric. Some manufacturers produced similar trains in clockwork and electric models such as Marx's M10000 streamliners. However, electric trains cap-

tured the imagination of the young consumer and became the dominant form of locomotion by the 1920s–30s. Such giants in the field as Lionel and Gilbert-American Flyer built their reputations on electric examples.

Before examining the various electric power sources, it is important to understand how an electrified locomotive operates. In its most simplistic form, positive or "hot" current is fed into one rail of a track. If one thinks of electricity as water flowing in a narrow pipe, a fairly good image of how current flows can be derived. Electric collectors in the form of metal strips or contacts pick up the positive electric charges and pass them through the motor. The electric current activates the motor when the current passes back out of the motor into a second rail of the track called a ground rail. This flow of electric current is called the negative current. In some cases, the wheels pick up the electric current directly from the track either from the tender which is then wired to the locomotive motor or through the drivers. In such cases, the wheels must be insulated from the metal body to prevent shorting or electric shocks when touched. By reversing the polarity or flow of the current, the motor could reverse in the opposite direction, and the locomotive would travel in reverse. The electric motors were geared to the driving wheels.

It should be apparent from this discussion that an electric power source must make contact with the tracks to complete the circuit of power source to the motor and back to the power source.

The amount of electrical current to the motor must be monitored in order to control the motor and thus the locomotive's speed. Without a monitor somewhere in the circuit, the locomotive would be either moving or stationary and only one speed could be generated. This device is known as a rheostat and its function is to filter the amount of current to the motor at any given time.

By the late 1800s when American electric trains made their debut, very few homes were wired for electricity. Those that were wired featured overhead light sockets as the terminus for the electric power. The wall outlet was still years away from practical home use. Realizing this, toy manufacturers produced self-contained electrical sources for the home railroader. The wet cell was one of the first of these self-contained electrical sources, and it consisted of a series of glass jars, metal electrodes, and battery acid. As one can imagine, these were very dangerous in the hands of the young engineer. The acid was very corrosive, and spills or splashes could result in burns on the skin as well as holes in the family carpet. The wet cell's life expectancy was limited, and acid and electrodes had to be replenished periodically. Those who had the luxury of indoor lighting could combine the house current with the wet cells and thus recharge these batteries automatically.

The dry cell batteries were much cleaner and less dangerous. When hooked together and tied to the track, they produced a continuous source of electric current without the danger of corrosive mate-rials. The dry cells also had a limited life expectancy, and replacement of one or a series was necessary as signs of decreased power began to show in the form of slow locomotive response to the available current. Carlisle and Finch of Cincinatti, Ohio marketed their electric trains in sets which included the dry cell batteries about the late 1890s. Replacements were available for a nominal cost.

Other sources of electric power included a hand cranked dynamo featuring a large wheel and handle which, when turned, produced electric current. The major drawback to this system was the manual power needed to operate the train. Arm weariness quickly could overcome the interest in the train layout. A curious alternative was the use of water power. Connected to the faucet, electric current was generated as the water passed over a series of turbine-like blades. Occasionally these devices appear at flea markets and provoke a series of guesses as to their function.

The introduction of the rheostat into the electric circuit brought about the speed control of the train. By placing this device between the power source and the locomotive's motor, electric current could be portioned out to the motor in increments. This device was the basis for the modern day train transformer.

The standard automobile battery also provided current for many train sets, but these were cumbersome and required the same care as the wet cell jars. These alternatives were available at auto parts stores, catalog houses, and service stations.

The ultimate controlling device is the

transformer. Usually packaged as part of a train set, they were manufactured in sizes that provided sufficient power for the appropriate train and possibly a few accessories. The transformer gathered electric current from the house source, converted it to the proper cycle for the train (AC or DC), and portioned it out to control the speed. Some carried circuit breakers that stopped the engine motor completely at any point, and others contained reversing switches that changed the direction of the flow of current and thus the direction of the locomotive.

One final source of electric power should be mentioned. Several manufacturers utilized small batteries which fit into the locomotive or tender and produced current for the life of the battery. Neither engine speed nor direction could be controlled efficiently without hands-on operation. These examples were inexpensive alternatives to the standard transformer and were popular after the second world war. Most were incorporated in plastic train sets as weight reduction was important in maintaining the length of service of the batteries as well as the limited amount of electric current they were able to produce.

Fig. 1-9. The transformer is one of the several forms of electric power. These two examples include a 1946 Gilbert-American Flyer on the left and a 1939 Lionel piece on the right. Photo Courtesy of Nelson's Auctions

Priced Examples

Sets

Early American painted tin floor runner, locomotive with two pilot wheels, two drivers, tender, two coaches — A-$247.00

Ives "Vulcan," painted tin, two pilot wheels, two drivers, clockwork, tin tender, two coaches with "Central R.R. of N.J." on coaches — A-$2,970.00

Locomotive, American painted tin, lithographed "UNION" on boiler, two pilot wheels, two drivers, clockwork, painted tin tender and coach — A-$440.00

Wilkins painted cast iron floor runner, locomotive with two pilots, four drivers, tender, gondola, two coaches with four wheel trucks — A-$170.00

Locomotives

George Brown, painted tin "HERO" on boiler, two pilot wheels, two drivers, floor runner, 10 inches long — A-$7,700.00

Early American painted tin, lithographed ``AMERICA'' on boiler, two pilot wheels, two drivers, clockwork — A–$632.00

Ives (Whistler), painted tin, large bell, filigree pilots and drivers, clockwork, $11\frac{1}{2}$ inches long — A–$6,050.00

Weeden steam locomotive, alcohol burner — A–$135.00

CHAPTER 2

Terminology: Speaking Like A Pro

It is important that collectors and dealers meet on a common ground to discuss their favorite subject. This involves the use of the proper terminology whether they're talking about toy trains or the real thing. Many of the terms are interchangeable, but some refer only to the toy train.

The term **prototype** has several meanings in the train world. Strictly speaking, it refers to the full size train or its components. Therefore a toy train engine would be designed and executed in scale from the prototype. The toy train manufacturers' research departments also produced models that are known as prototypes. Some are design fantasies and never reach the marketplace, while others are master models on which the production pieces are based.

A train, whether it is a toy or a prototype, is composed of two basic units: an engine or motive device, and a string of rolling stock called a **consist**. The consist can be either freight or passenger cars or

Fig. 2–1. Though maintaining a steam locomotive profile, this stubby, little locomotive is hardly prototypical. Photo from the Collection of John Ezzo

any combination of these. Freight cars are also referred to as **goods** cars and include such pieces as box cars, tank cars, gondolas (low-sided carriers), hoppers (high-sided carriers), flat cars, and the inevitable caboose or rolling work office of the train— usually the last car on the consist. The caboose is seen in many variations including the standard version with a cupola on the roof looking down the consist, or a bay window version that allows for vision down the side of the train. A work caboose is a specialized freight car with a forward

Fig. 2-2. The classic caboose carries a cupola on the roof. Photo from the Collection of Alan Gilbert

Fig. 2-4. Flat cars were often converted for other uses such as this Lionel Auto-loader. Many variations of this car exist along with reproduction automobiles. Photo from the Collection of John Ezzo

open section to receive such items as a crane boom. This is referred to as a **crane tender**.

In addition to the standard freight cars, there are many pieces that were specialized in their design. **Reefer-refrigerator** cars carried perishables. **Searchlight**, **crane**, and **stock cars**, as well as many variations of the flat car which were altered to carry such loads as automobiles on several levels, all saw service in both the toy and prototype trains.

A specialized set of cars carries the initials MOW that translate into maintenance of way. These cars were used for keeping the track clear for fast moving

freight and passenger trains. MOW rolling stock included such unique cars as cranes, crane tenders or work cabooses, and flat cars that carried rails, ties, etc.

Most toy train manufacturers designed rolling stock that mirrored prototype cars. However, some freight cars were purely the imagination of the toy train designers and would never have seen service on a real railroad.

The action car was also part of most toy manufacturers' inventories. Freight cars that dumped logs or coal, launched missiles, or moved cattle through various

Fig. 2-3. The wrecker caboose features a forward open section to receive the crane boom and hook. Photo from the Collection of Anita Hoban

Fig. 2-5. The wrecker crane was a popular piece of rolling stock. Its function was to correct problems that might arise along the road such as derailed freight or passenger cars. Photo from the Collection of John Ezzo

Fig. 2-6. Some "action" cars bore little resemblance to any prototype but were designed to increase the play value of a set. The #3410 Helicopter-car was such a piece of fanciful rolling stock. Photo from the Collection of John Ezzo

pens were produced to gain an edge on the competition and increase play value.

Passenger cars can be classified into three distinct types: baggage, coach, and observation. There are several variations of these basic cars: a **combine**, which incorporated two functions such as mail or baggage and coach; a domed top on a coach called a **Vista Dome** car; and a sleeping car, commonly referred to as a **Pullman**. The Pullman car in reality is any passenger car that was manufactured by the Pullman Coach Company, but by common consent, it refers to any coach in a passenger consist.

Each piece of rolling stock can be broken down into fundamental units. They consist of a body, frame, coupling device, and set of trucks which carry the wheels. In some cases, the body and frame are, for all practical purposes, the same piece as in a flat car.

One of the most misunderstood parts of the rolling stock is the **truck**. To the lay person it is the wheels, but to the train buff the wheels are only one part of the truck.

Closer examination reveals that it consists of a frame, a series of springs to cushion the ride, one or more axles, wheels attached to the axles, and a bolster that joins it to the frame. The axle-wheel combination is called a **wheelset**. The axles terminate in **journal boxes** or journals that contain bearings and lubricants which allow the axle to roll freely.

Each piece of rolling stock is joined to the next and to the engine by means of a coupling device or **coupler**. Early couplers were merely locking devices that held the cars together. As young engineers became more demanding, manufacturers were sent back to the drawing board to find ways of uncoupling cars automatically. Uncoupling devices fall into two categories—

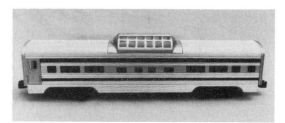

Fig. 2-7. Vista Dome passenger cars featured a second deck with windows for panoramic views of the countryside. Photo from the Collection of John Ezzo

Fig. 2-8. These three freight cars illustrate three different types of trucks.

mechanical and electrical. The mechanical ones required that the couplers pass over a device in the track that physically lifted and separated the couplers and thus the cars. A disadvantage to the mechanical couplers was that they always (or nearly always) uncoupled when passing over the segment whether uncoupling was wanted or not. In some cases, it required passing back and forth over an uncoupling segment to separate the cars.

Early trucks were separate devices, each mounted on the chassis as independent units. With the development of some of the automatic uncoupling systems, some couplers were joined to the truck as a single unit. When the truck rotated on its axis, it carried the coupler with it. The combination helped maintain a constant height for the coupler which facilitated the coupling process. This type of truck is known as a **talgo** truck.

Electric uncoupling was selective. This type of uncoupling also required a separate, specialized segment of track, but the process could be accomplished on demand. By pressing a distant controller, a young engineer could activate an electric or magnetic impulse that caused the couplers to open and disengage. By reversing the direction of the train, the couplers reengaged. This was a major step in the development of the coupler mechanism. Many manufacturers strove for the perfect automatic coupler.

Nothing excites the imagination more then the power unit of the train—the locomotive. As discussed in the previous chapter, prototype engines were powered by steam, diesel fuel, or electric motors. By examining the various parts of a typical steam engine, it will become apparent that many of these features are consistent with all types of locomotives. Some engines were shrouded in steel plates to produce an Art Deco type streamlined appearance. The New York Central Commodore Vanderbilt and the Mercury are two examples of this type of treatment. The basic working mechanism remained the same. Fig. 2-9 shows a typical steam locomotive with many of the key parts labeled.

Wheel configuration is an important factor in describing an engine. The pilot truck helps guide an engine into a curve smoothly, and, conversely, the trailing truck guides the cab and tender in a similar manner. In between these rotating trucks are the power wheels or **drivers**. Not all locomotives possess pilots and trailers but usually, the larger the engine, the more the need for these trucks. A numerical string is the most accepted method for describing wheel configurations. These refer most frequently to steam locomotives. The first digit details the total number of pilot wheels even if none are present. The last digit details the trailers. Anything in between refers to the drivers or power wheels. The following examples will illustrate this point.

4-6-2   4 pilots, 6 drivers, 2 trailers
0-4-0   0 pilots, 4 drivers, 0 trailers
4-6-6-4 4 pilots, 2 sets of 6 wheel drivers, 2 trailers

The ability of an engine to begin movement and maintain it is called **traction**. It is

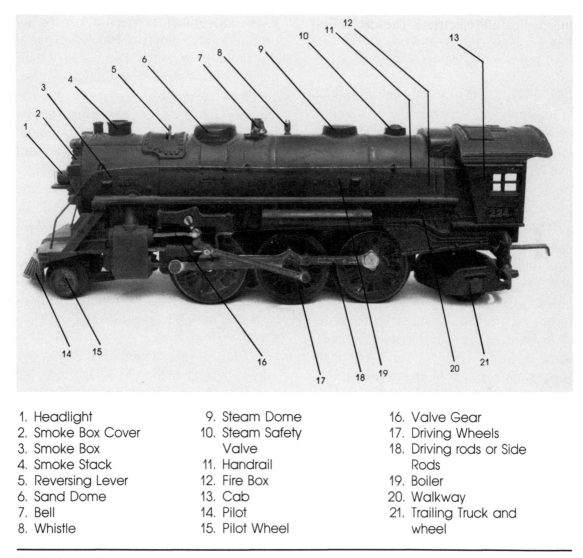

1. Headlight
2. Smoke Box Cover
3. Smoke Box
4. Smoke Stack
5. Reversing Lever
6. Sand Dome
7. Bell
8. Whistle
9. Steam Dome
10. Steam Safety Valve
11. Handrail
12. Fire Box
13. Cab
14. Pilot
15. Pilot Wheel
16. Valve Gear
17. Driving Wheels
18. Driving rods or Side Rods
19. Boiler
20. Walkway
21. Trailing Truck and wheel

Fig. 2-9. Labeled parts of a steam locomotive.

a direct function of the weight of the engine and rolling stock. The lighter or smaller the engine, the less the traction. Toy train manufacturers overcame this difficulty in a variety of ways. The most common method was to place rubber tires on the non-electric pick-up drivers. The tires resemble rounded rubber bands and fit snuggly on the wheel next to the flange. It is important that the collector identifies which engines came with these traction tires as they tend to be lost over a period of time and should be replaced for proper operation. Lionel introduced ''Magne-Traction'' which will be discussed in the appropriate chapter.

Wheel configuration does not play as

important a role in identifying the diesel engines, as these are more recognizable by their profiles and distinctive body shell features.

Trailing behind the steam locomotive is an important separate piece of equipment. The **tender** is exactly what the name implies. It tends to the needs of the locomotive by providing fuel such as wood, coal, or oil to fire the boilers; and it supplies the water necessary for the manufacturing of steam. Several toy train companies produced matching tenders for their locomotives, and it is important for the collector to mate the proper tender to the right engine. Other companies such as the Louis Marx Company provided a wide range of tender styles in order to create variety. However, some of Marx's tenders also were made specifically for certain engines.

Diesel engines were produced in a wide range of styles, but only a few actually

Fig. 2-10. The tender provided fuel and water for the locomotive. Marx collected a lot of mileage from its basic tender by changing the road names.

were reproduced by the train manufacturers. Lionel's diesel inventory was one of the more impressive. Diesels had their heyday during the 1950s through the 70s, but their forerunners were part of the toy industry dating back to the 1930s with the introduction of Lionel's Hiawatha and the M-10000 series produced by Lionel and Marx. Four major companies manufactured diesel prototypes during the 50s, 60s, and 70s and these included the EMD or Electro Motive Division of General Motors, Fairbanks-Morse, General Electric, and the American Locomotive Company or Alco. Each of these manufacturers produced distinctively styled diesel locomotives that have become identified with the specific companies.

Those of special significance to the toy train collector are the EMD ''E'' and ''F'' streamlined units, the GP road switchers affectionately called ''Geeps,'' and the SD unit which is slightly longer then the Geeps but similar in profile. The ''E'' and ''F'' units are broken down into A and B units. The A units were the forward or streamlined section which carried the cab,

Fig. 2-11. The GP-9 or "Geep" diesel was the workhorse of many railroads. Lionel modeled its #2349 diesel in O 27 Gauge and released it in 1959. Photo from the Collection of John Ezzo

whereas the B units were powered, but lacked the cab and acted as helpers in long consists.

Often trains were linked by back-to-back A units listed as AA. This allowed a train to reach a destination and return without having to turn around. When B units were used, the designation would be AB or ABA or combinations of these units depending on the need for pulling power. For practical purposes, the toy train companies fabricated some A and all B units without power. These are called **dummy** units but gave the illusion that the entire complex was powered.

The standard road switcher, commonly called the **cow** was modeled after EMD's road switchers. The prototype can be found with a B unit called a **calf**. The calf was not modeled by any major toy manufacturer, but is found in the repertory of the scale HO trains.

General Electric manufactured a series of road and industrial switchers that also were reproduced by the toy train companies. These are known as the "U" series or **U-Boats** and include the U36B and

Fig. 2-12. The Alco AA units were both powered in the prototype, but the unit on the right is a dummy while the left unit is powered. The overall effect is similar to the prototype. Photo Courtesy of Joy Luke Auctions

U36C. In addition, a 44 ton industrial switcher also road the rails.

Fairbanks-Morse's powerful Trainmaster was beautifully reproduced by Lionel and is one of the classics of the toy manufacturer's series. It was designed as a large engine and is most impressive when viewed in comparison to other road diesels. The ABA units of Fairbanks C-lines were also brought to toy train size by Lionel.

The FA units produced by Alco were modeled by the toy companies, and both A and B units were scaled down. The FA differs from the EMD F units mainly in the profile. The sharp nose is one of the distinctive features of the FA and it differs from the rounded, smooth nose of the F units. American Flyer chose the Alco PA as the flagship of its diesel line. The PA with its long thin nose and A and B units is a handsome series.

A third type of locomotive was also modeled by the major toy producers. They were called "traction" engines, and the prototypes are powered by electricity rather than steam or diesel propulsion. Electric power often was supplied from overhead wire systems called **catenaries**. It was similar to the old trolley car motive arrangement. Electricity passed from the catenary wires to **pantographs** mounted on the top of the engine and down to the motor. Though most early Lionel, Ives, and American Flyer engines carried pantographs on the body shell, they were ornamental in nature, and electricity for motion was provided through the rail. Lionel's model GG1 featured pantographs that could be used in a catenary system as well as receiving power from the customary source.

The term **tinplate** has become synonymous with toy trains and to the collector, it differentiates the scale model train from the toy. However, by definition tinplate refers to a manufacturing technique that was frequently used in the production of early toys of all kinds. Large sheets of tinned iron or steel were painted or lithographed, cut, folded, and assembled to produce engines and rolling stock. Lithographed sheets usually carried all of the details, such as ladders and rivets, in printed form. At times, additional detail was added through embossing, whereby the end result was an elevated surface that highlighted the detail. Painted tinplate pieces frequently had detail added as secondary, three dimensional items. Ladders, doors, etc. were added after the piece was assembled and painted. Both lithographed and painted tinplate were surface treated with the color and were subject to scratch-

ing and chipping, especially in the hands of a child.

Painting and printing tinplate was an inexpensive method of mass producing train pieces, but other more sophisticated techniques were also employed. **Die casting** is a technique whereby molten metal was poured into a mold and the finished product trimmed and painted.

The molds were often detailed, and this was passed on to the positive shell. Thus such items as hinges, rivets, railing, and ladders were cast in relief as part of the shell. Pieces could not be lost when added to painted tinplate shells. Both tinplate and die cast shells were then affixed to a frame or chassis. Die casting was the technique of choice for steam locomotives and some rolling stock such as flat cars where detailing was important. Instead of adding detail as a separate step, it was cast in place. The ease of adding detail brought the toy train closer to scale.

With the introduction of plastic to industry, toy train manufacturers utilized this material extensively, especially in the 1950s through the 70s. Pre-colored plastic was injected into molds and highly detailed, lightweight castings were produced at a low cost. The coloring was added to the plastic prior to injection and became part of the body. This saved an additional step when compared to the metal die cast process, and the color was not subject to chipping or scratching. Engine shells and a large variety of rolling stock were produced using this technique. Die casting and plastic molding are popular methods of

Fig. 2–13. The Rectifier received electric current from the overhead pantographs. Lionel's version was a superb example of this locomotive. Photo from the Collection of John Ezzo

manufacturing scale model railroad pieces, but tinplating was only associated with the toy train world.

Collectors tend to shy away from plastic molded pieces as the heft and weight of tinplate and die cast pieces are more appealing. However, the plastic molded engines and cars have a charm of their own and are an important part of any collection.

By using the terms found in this chapter, you will find yourself speaking like a pro.

CHAPTER 3

Tracking Down The Gauges

In order to bring consistency to the toy train world, the use of gauges was one method adopted for standardizing toy train size. To appreciate gauging fully, it is important to first analyze the train track on which gauging is based.

Prototype train track consists of a pair of rails that are mounted on wooden members called **ties** and fastened to the ties with spikes. Between the rails and ties is a gravel material called **ballast** that helps maintain the ties in position and also acts to shed water from the area. Toy train tracks usually lack this ballast, though scale modelers often include it in their track laying. Sitting on top of the rail is the **railhead**, and it is on this piece the wheels of the locomotive and rolling stock travel.

Toy train track was fastened most frequently to the tie by means of metal foldover tabs. When a three rail system was utilized to provide electricity for power, the center or power rail was insulated from the metal ties. Other power

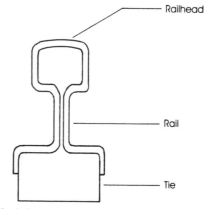

Fig. 3–1. Rail parts.

rails also need insulation to avoid shorting. In some cases plastic ties were used as a method of isolating the power rails from the nonpower rails. The shape of the railhead differs from manufacturer to manufacturer. Some produced thin, knife-edged railheads such as those from Carlisle and Finch, others produced shaped or wide railheads. The wider the head and conversely the wheel, the better the traction and thus the less tendency for derailment.

Some railheads were flat, while others were rounded. The shape of the railhead often conformed to the manufacturer's train wheels and was one of the factors that prohibited some manufacturers' products from running successfully on another's rails.

To keep the train from sliding off the rails, flanges were used on the inner section of the wheels. The flange kept the wheel in contact with the rail. Some companies' flanges were quite large, whereas others were barely discernible. High flanges required tall rails, and this often negated the use of tinplate trains on scale track which was lower in profile.

When trains were picked up off the floor and placed on rails, the earliest examples were continuous pieces that were either pre-formed or assembled into ties by the operator. Carlisle and Finch offered

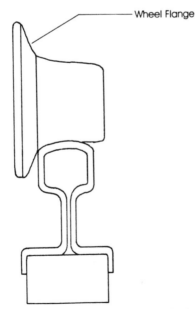

— Wheel Flange

Fig. 3–2. Flange at inner section of wheel.

long pieces of rail that fit into slotted cross-ties to form running track. Continuous track limited the operator to the configuration of the single piece of track. Ovals and circles were the order of the day. The introduction of sectional track provided flexibility in the design of the rail system. Individual pieces could be purchased and added at a later date to alter the configuration and increase play value. The system could be dismantled easily and put away without major effort.

Sectional track consists of small, individual curved or straight sections of rail with the ties attached. The sections were joined by means of metallic pins for electrical continuity or fiber pins for electrical insulation, for example, where an accessory requires a break in electric current. Sectional track allowed for the inclusion of crossings and switches or points which increased the interest in the layout. Both two and three rail tracks were manufactured in sections.

With this working knowledge of track anatomy, it is a short hop to understanding gauging. **Gauge** refers to the distance between the two outside running rails. American gauges utilize the dimension from the inside of one running rail to the inside of the opposite. This measurement is transferred into a number or letter that is called gauge, and all track that falls within this measurement is within that gauge.

Early European gauges were usually measured from the railheads. This could be a problem when trying to compare them to American gauges as the railheads differ in size and shape, depending on the manufac-

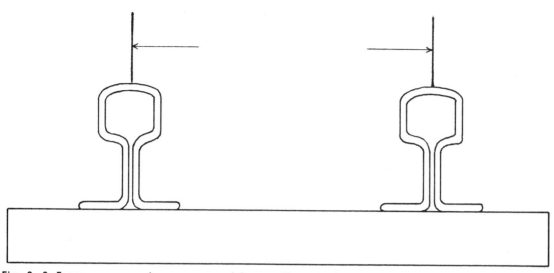

Fig. 3-3. European gauging, measured from railheads. Compare with Fig. 3-4.

turer. Some were rounded, others were ovoid in cross-section. The general rule of thumb is to subtract 2–3 millimeters or about 1/8 inch from the railhead dimensions to find the equivalent American gauge. This subtraction brings the dimension to the inside of the railheads.

The larger gauges were used almost exclusively by European manufacturers, especially for their steam powered locomotives. Gauges 2 through 4 were quite unwieldy for the home railroad and found little favor in the United States. During the late 1800s, placing a number on a gauge did not necessarily insure that it met the proper measurement requirements. In some

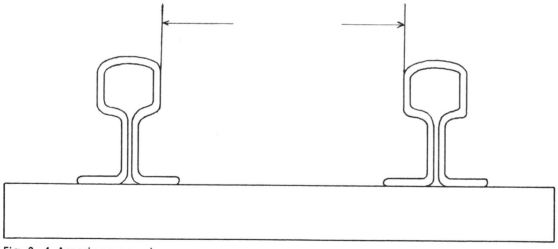

Fig. 3-4. American gauging.

cases, one company's Gauge 4 would be equivalent to another's Gauge 3. The larger gauges were gradually controlled to more manageable sizes such as Gauge 1 and Gauge O. The following chart lists the measurements of the larger gauges and is included as a basis for comparison. They are measured from the insides of the railheads.

European Gauges

Gauge 4	=	$2\frac{7}{8}$ inches
Gauge 3	=	$2\frac{1}{2}$ inches
Gauge 2	=	2 inches
Gauge 1	=	$1\frac{3}{4}$ inches
Gauge OO	=	$\frac{3}{4}$ inch

From this chart, it is apparent that some American manufacturer's gauges were compatible with European gauges. Lionel's $2\frac{7}{8}$-inch was compatible with the European Gauge 4, and Carlisle and Finch's and Voltamp's 2-inch gauges were comparable to the European Gauge 2. The gauge dimensions are for reference only, as several companies used their own systems. As an example, Bassett-Lowke and Bing Gauge 4 was equivalent in size to Marklin's Gauge 3.

American gauges were generally smaller and more manageable. As mentioned, they were measured from inside the railheads and are presented for comparison with the European gauges. Lionel's Standard Gauge was trademarked by the company and is equivalent to Ives and American Flyer's Wide Gauge.

American Gauges

Standard or Wide Gauge	=	$2\frac{1}{8}$ inches

Gauge 2	=	2 inches
Gauge 1	=	$1\frac{3}{4}$ inches
Gauge O	=	$1\frac{1}{4}$ inches
Gauge S	=	$\frac{7}{8}$ inch
Gauge HO	=	$\frac{5}{8}$ inch

It should be apparent from this chart that S Gauge is actually half of Gauge 1, and HO Gauge is half of Gauge O. The present scale G made popular by the German firm of Lehmann or LGB is equivalent to Gauge 1 or $1\frac{1}{3}$ inches between the running rails. The large scale Delton Locomotive Works, REA, Kalamazoo, Bachmann, Lionel, and

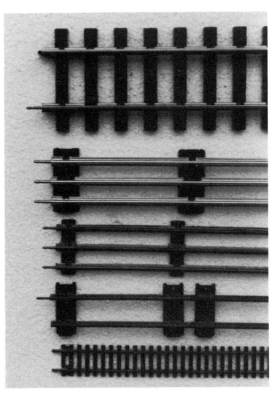

Fig. 3-5. This photo shows a comparison of gauge sizes. The top is the large Gauge 1 and in descending order are Super O, O 27, S, and HO.

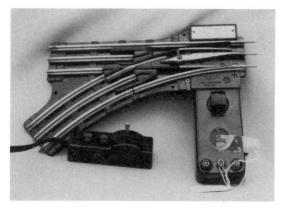

Fig. 3-6. The switch or turnout moves the train from one section of a layout to another. Some were mechanical, while others, such as this electric Lionel example, were operational from a distance by means of a switch machine. Photo Courtesy of Nelson's Auction

RO Trains also travel on Gauge one track. Anything less than the accepted dimensions for each gauge is known as **narrow gauge** and is designated with an "n" along with the gauge such as On, Sn and HOn. These narrow gauges apply more to scale modeling and are rarely found in toy trains.

When all of the track is placed together no matter what the gauge, the end result is known as a **layout**. Switches or turnouts that shift the train off of the mainline onto a siding or secondary route can be operated manually or electrically from a distance. The power source usually was a transformer, though other types of electric gen-

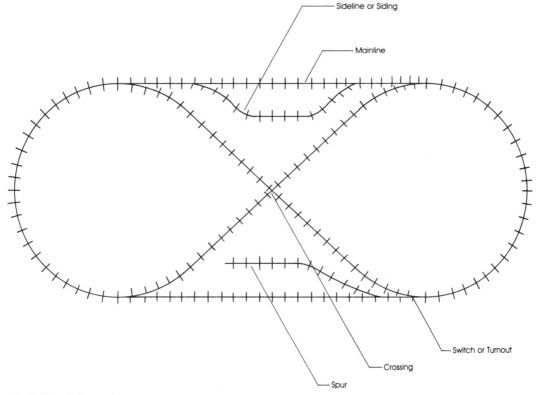

Fig. 3-7. Track layout.

eration have been used. Electric current passes from the transformer to the track through a series of wires that fasten to the track by means of solder, screw posts, or removable snap-on attachments. These basic elements are common to the toy train. The scale modeler utilized significantly more sophisticated equipment that is beyond the scope of this book.

The term **scale** is one that has been overworked and often misapplied by the toy train industry. In its strictest sense, it defines the proportions of an engine or piece of rolling stock within a specific ratio of dimensions to the prototype for each gauge. The dimensions apply to elements of the piece which include length, width, and height, and, to the scale modeler, include all accessory pieces as well as trucks and couplers even down to the paint job. The following chart lists the standards for proper scale set by the National Model Railroad Association.

Scale	Model		Prototype
G	1″	=	24″
I	1″	=	32″
O	1″	=	48″
S	1″	=	64″
HO	1″	=	87.1″

The scale letters correspond to the appropriate track gauges with the exception of G scale which rolls on Gauge 1 track. Thus the relationship of scale and gauge is established, and it is quite interdependent.

Toy trains from the late 1800s can best be described as "non-scale" trains be-cause they bore little resemblance to anything that actually rode the rails. Prior to the 1920s, the scale model industry which is so large today was in its infancy, and the major American manufacturers continued to concentrate on trains that were operationally sound with little regard to scale. In fact, scale and toy trains were at the opposite ends of the spectrum. However, the terms "scale" and "gauge" were often used interchangeably in a vast grey area during this period. This was a misnomer as one term had very little to do with the other at that time. It was not unusual for a toy train manufacturer to introduce a "scale" train set when it actually was a vague facsimile of the prototype. Other terms such as "semi-scale" and "scale-like" also found a place in the descriptions of these trains.

One merely has to look at Marx's Bunny train or Lionel's Mickey Mouse train to understand what a non-scale train

Fig. 3-8. Scale modeling includes detail on the floor as well as the rest of the piece of rolling stock. The Marx piece on the bottom is devoid of any detail, while the Atlas piece above is approaching scale. Photo from the Collection of Joel Kaufmann

might be. Imagine if you will the prototype of such a train where a rabbit crouching on its haunches pulled a string of cars into Grand Central Station in New York. These trains may possess the proper dimensions to fall within the scale definition, but that is where the similarity ends. These two trains were selected as extreme examples, but many early examples still could not be classified as anything other then non-scale.

The present day scale modeler may at times look with scorn at tinplate trains because of their lack of realism, but in fact they were the pioneers for the scale modeling industry. Because of the scarcity of supplies, the scaler often reworked toy trains to increase their scale appearance. Trucks, couplers, ladders, undercarriages, and paint jobs were changed to reflect this trend. Some of these hybrids appear at antiques shows and flea markets and can cause confusion to the neophyte collector when they carry a Lionel or American Flyer nameplate but do not match anything in the company's inventory for the period.

Today's scale trains possess detail that was unheard of during the infant years of the toy train industry. Brass engines that feature scale piping, grab irons, rivets, and the like cause the toy engine to pale by comparison. Rolling stock also exhibits exquisite detail down to the springs on the trucks, proper bulkheads for the period, as well as couplers, ladders, and brake wheels. The sophisticated scaler is usually quite proficient in weathering these pieces to add additional realism. At the present time, scale model railroading appeals more to the adult railroader who possess the skills and patience to bring the examples to full bloom.

Toy trains could be handled quite roughly by the young engineer without great cause for concern. The high rail profile associated with toy trains and the relatively large wheel flanges also kept the toy train from being classified as a true scale item to the purist, but its successful operation by a small person was the bottom line. Good traction and rail stability were of prime importance to successful sales.

During the 1930s, the major toy manufacturers began leaning toward a two-rail direct current system that was more realistic than the alternating current three-rail system commonly used up to that time. Most house current to this point was alternating in nature. The AC motor mounted in the locomotive cycled in opposite directions at a rapid rate. Reversing this system to allow the locomotive to travel in a reverse direction was difficult and required special electrical fixtures. The units were known as the E-units and were developed by Ives and sold to Lionel. Direct current, or DC, worked with a fixed magnet in a continuous cycle. Reversing was simplified by merely reversing the field in the fixed magnet.

It was during this period that Lionel and American Flyer became increasingly aware of the public's interest in "more realistic toy trains," and from their drawing boards some very commendable examples began to take shape. Lionel's and American Flyer's Hiawatha locomotives (the passenger cars departed from the prototypes), Lionel's City of Portland, and Flyer's aluminum example of the stainless steel Zephyr are good examples of these companies' assault on the high walls of scale modeling.

The culmination certainly was Lionel's magnificent O Gauge Hudson locomotive, a true collector's gem. The short-lived OO Gauge of the late 1930s both in two and three rail systems was another step in the direction of true scale. Marx's and American Flyer's $\frac{3}{16}$ of an inch to one foot scale was also an attempt to answer the mounting demand for more realism in toy trains. The full extent of their involvement in scale will be discussed in the appropriate chapters.

Prototype modeling became increasingly important to the toy train manufacturers and many relied on the original blueprints of the prototypes for the design and fabrication of their trains. Scale was the order of the day, and it was here to stay.

CHAPTER 4

The Beginning Years of Lionel

"Lionel, more than a toy— a tradition since 1900"

Joshua Lionel Cowen started the Lionel Manufacturing Company with Harry C. Grant in 1900. The company made "electrical novelties". Cowen's first train was actually an "animated advertisement" that was designed for shop windows to attract the customers' eye to small objects for sale. This "Electric Express" consisted of open, motorized gondola cars with wooden frames that circled the tracks in shop window layouts. Much to Cowen's surprise, customers were more interested in the train than the merchandise it was supposed to promote.

In the age of electric trolleys, Cowen's second train was a street car modeled on the City Hall Park prototype with a metal frame body enameled with gold pinstriping. The body was made by Morton E. Converse and Company in Massachusetts. The cars made for Lionel were maroon, green, and yellow and had "City Hall Park" on one side and "Union Depot" on the other. Early trolleys were made with brass wheels and no coupler pocket, while the later ones had cast wheels and a coupler pocket.

By 1902, Lionel produced his first in a long series of train catalogs. This tremendous merchandising device became known as a "wish book" in later years. Needless to say, this first catalog was modest in size and featured only sixteen pages with black and white photographs. Lionel introduced his first accessory, a bridge, that same year. He realized that accessories would play a tremendous role in train layouts. This bridge, a two foot long suspension type, was an exact copy of actual railroad suspension bridges.

Four large dry cell batteries ran the first trains. They were wired together and attached to the track by brass connectors and could run for 10 to 15 hours. Even in the very early years, Lionel trains were merchandised as a special treat for birthday or Christmas because they were expensive by comparison to other makers.

Much was made of the father-son connection. Trains were advertised showing proud fathers building train layouts for eager boys. Girls were never a part of the picture.

When electricity became more widespread in homes, the first of the Lionel electric engines was marketed. It was #5, based on an electric tunnel locomotive used by the Baltimore and Ohio Railroad in 1903. These replicas usually were painted maroon with a black roof and base. They did not have a trailer. At this time the open gondolas were made of metal instead of wood, and a new car, a cast iron motorized

Fig. 4-1. Much of Lionel's advertising was geared toward the father-son relationship. Reprinted with the Permission of Lionel Trains, Inc.

derrick with a crank mechanism to load the gondola car, was added to the line. "Play value" was emphasized so that the child could actually work the devices and be involved in the workings of the train set up. Mario Caruso became supervisor in 1904 and ran the factory in an excellent manner leaving Cowen free to do what he did best—sell the merchandise.

The first Lionel trains ran on a two-rail track which had a $2\frac{7}{8}$-inch wide gauge. This was wider than the standard 2-inch used by the other train manufacturers of the time. This gauge was used from 1901 until 1905. Examples in $2\frac{7}{8}$-inch gauge are extremely rare, and none had catalog numbers stamped on them. New collectors would probably have an impossible time locating these pieces, though some do surface occasionally at house sales.

Numbers that are used here preceding the name of a car refer to Lionel catalog numbers. Other $2\frac{7}{8}$-inch gauge cars from this period included the #800 Boxcar called the "Jail Car" due to the bars on its windows. It had "Metropolitan Express" rubber-stamped on the sides. It was maroon and had a matching #900 trailer. The #1000 passenger car in $2\frac{7}{8}$-inch gauge was also maroon with a black roof and frame and had names of the various railroads on it. It had a #1050 trailer to accompany it. Trailers in $2\frac{7}{8}$-inch gauge refer to a locomotive with the motor removed.

By 1906, Lionel produced a three rail track with the current in the insulated center rail. Lionel was the first manufacturer to use this three-rail track in America, and other manufacturers adopted it.

Gauge size was reduced to 2⅛-inches, and Lionel called it Standard Gauge; it was used until 1939. It actually measured 2¼-inches between the rails. Standard Gauge was divided into two periods. The Early Period refers to 1906–1923, while the Classic Period falls between 1923–1939. Early Period paint colors reflected the actual drab colors used by the existing railroads of the times and had rubber-stamped lettering. During the Classic Period, first drab colors were used, but after World War I, they utilized bright colored paints with metallic pigments such as chrome yellow, bright blue, emerald green, and vermilion red. Copper and brass trim also were used with brass and nickel number and name plates.

The 1906 Lionel catalog advertised a wide variety of rolling stock including an electric trolley car, the No. 1, that is highly coveted by collectors. Two other trolleys, two steam locomotives, a Pullman sleeper, seven different freight cars, and a baggage car comprised the line. Cars utilized the names of major railroads of the times such as the New York Central, Harlem River Railroad, and Pennsylvania Railroad. Transformers also were introduced to control the speed of a train. These were a big improvement over batteries.

Trolleys in Standard Gauge were outstanding sellers for a number of years since they were the primary means of city transportation at the time. 1910 was the peak year of trolley production. Thirteen different powered trolleys and interurbans were offered in the catalog that year. Lionel's trolleys copied the prototypes and even had figures of people that could sit on the

Fig. 4–2. Both electric profile locos on the lower shelf are identified by rubber stamping, while the steamer on the top shelf carries brass plates. Photo Courtesy of Christie's

seats. Most had "Electric Rapid Transit" stamped on the side. Two color combinations were used most often.

The No.1 was the smallest of the Lionel trolleys. The size continued to increase over the years trolleys were made. These examples had open platforms. One version made for the Maryland Electrical Company was marked "Curtis Bay." The No.8 trolley was an exact copy of the "Pay As You Enter" cars in use throughout the country. It was made from 1909–1915, and was the largest trolley Lionel made. There were no trailers made for these trolleys.

The Lionel Manufacturing Company moved its factory to New Haven, Connecticut in 1910. Several years later trolleys were eliminated from the catalog, because they did not lend themselves to use with accessories that would eventually comprise from 35–40 percent of Lionel's total sales.

Every year the offerings in the Lionel catalog expanded to meet the ever growing desires of Americans obsessed with railroads. In the 1912 edition, buyers were offered four different models of electric engines, two steam locomotives, passenger cars in a variety of sizes, and an assortment of trolleys. Rheostats were added to dry cell batteries to regulate the speed of trains, while new, improved transformers were in use for homes already wired for electricity. Cowen liked to involve his family in the business—his son Lawrence's picture was seen on advertisements, boxes, and train catalogs.

With the factory and number of employees continuing to expand, Cowen

found the New Haven location inconvenient. He moved the factory to Newark, New Jersey and soon after that, when more room was needed, to nearby Irvington. In 1915, O Gauge trains, which were 1¼-inches wide, were introduced to compete with Ives who had been using this gauge since 1910. O Gauge trains were less expensive to produce, utilized less room, and eventually dominated toy train production in America.

Lionel also had competition from German made trains prior to World War I, but the war stopped the flow of these German trains to the United States and gave Lionel another opportunity to come to the forefront. Lionel also had important government contracts during the war to produce signal and compass equipment. Not much train production was carried on during these war years, though some basic freight and passenger sets were offered. The "Pullman Deluxe" was the best train of the period with a #42 electric engine, a coach, and a baggage car comprising the set. Mostly Lionel concentrated its efforts on its lucrative war contracts.

In 1918, the Lionel Manufacturing Company became the Lionel Corporation with Joshua L. Cowen as President. Collectors distinguish cars before 1918 as "manufacturing" cars and cars after 1918 as "corporation" cars.

Coupler types are necessary to help determine the dating for Standard Gauge equipment. From 1906–1914 they used short and long straight hooks; 1910–1918 short and long crinkle hooks; 1914–1925 hooks with ears; 1924–1928 combination latch, and 1925–1942 the latch, according to *Greenberg's Guide to Lionel Trains*.

The first Standard Gauge locomotives had cast iron wheels or drivers with thin rims. There were thick-rimmed iron wheel versions by 1912. In the 1920s die cast wheels had steel rims and red spokes. 1934 was the first year steel-rimmed wheels with black spokes were introduced.

Another method of determining the dates various pieces were made is by the motor construction. The super motor was introduced in 1923. It featured large gears on one side. In 1925 gearing was changed, and the small gear super motor was made. A Bild-A-Roo motor came about 1927. It could be assembled with a screwdriver.

Early steam engines in Standard Gauge were cataloged from 1906–1926 and were modeled after engines being used by east coast railroads. They were made of stamped sheet metal, had pilots, red painted window trim, and lettering rubber-stamped in gold. They were identified as N.Y.C. & H.R.R.R. (New York Central and Hudson River Railroad), Pennsylvania Railroad, B.& O.R.R.(Baltimore and Ohio Railroad), and P.& L.E.R.R. (Pittsburgh & Lake Erie Railroad). Some more expensive locos were made in brass and nickel and had no lettering.

All the early steamers at Lionel had hand reverse levers and were painted black, except for the brass locos. Numbers were not on the locomotives, only in the catalog. The #5 appeared first in the 1906 catalog and was available until 1926. It was the smallest and least expensive of the early engines and was designed to pull medium and large passenger cars and the #10 Series freight cars. There are many variations of the #5 with different numbers and

Fig. 4–3. Nickel and brass were used to fabricate Lionel's Standard Gauge #7 locomotive and tender (top). The #29 olive colored day coaches (bottom) were joined by crinkle couplers. The set dates about 1924. Photo Courtesy of Christie's

features. The #5 that carries the B.& O. lettering with a four wheel tender is most desirable.

Lionel's largest loco of the times was the #6 issued from 1906–1923. The #6 Special was a nickel and brass version and was twice as expensive as the standard #6. The #6 Special was changed to a #7 in 1910. Many reproductions exist that were made by the McCoy Manufacturing Company. Large bells were used on locos from 1908–1914, and smaller bells were seen from 1912 through 1926. Headlight varieties included the slide-on from 1908–1911, the pedestal from 1912–1918, and the strap headlight from 1918–1926. In 1928 die cast headlights with red and green panels were utilized.

Lionel modeled its early electrics on the S–1 prototype electrics used by the New York Central railroad. According to Tom McComas and James Tuohy in

Lionel: A Collector's Guide and History, Volume III, Standard Gauge "early characteristics included a ''square'' cab, thin-rim drivers, script lettering and Monitor roofs with slide-on headlights. Collectors have come to call a separate piece of metal that was soldered to the regular roof of early period locos a Monitor roof. The numbering system on early electrics is confusing since some coincide with the year produced and others do not.

One of the most popular engines is the four-wheel version of the #33 introduced in 1913 and made through 1924. It was sold in sets with the #100 Series freights and #35 and #36 Series passenger cars. A variety of colors were utilized, including dark olive, black, grey, maroon, red, dark green, and others, but olive green and black were most common. A special version made for Montgomery Ward was midnight blue and came with the #35 and #36

Fig. 4-4. The thin rim Standard Gauge #5 steam locomotive is highly prized by collectors. This 0-4-0 configured example first appeared in 1907. Photo Courtesy of Christie's

Fig. 4-5. Four pilot wheels were added to the #6 thin rim steamer (top). The rolling stock (bottom) includes the earliest #15 Caboose, #13 Cattle Car, and #14 Boxcar, all of which date from 1908. Photo Courtesy of Christie's

Fig. 4-6. Devoid of any paint on the body shell on this #54, 0-4-4-0 electric profile, it featured red wheels, ventilators, and pilots. It measures 14 inches long. Photo Courtesy of Sotheby's

Series passenger cars. The #33 featured a round cab. Most had New York Central markings, but some had C. & O. (Chesapeake and Ohio) markings. Before 1916 the #33 had the U-frame and cast iron wheels. After that a straight frame and die cast wheels were used. Some Lionel locomotives were marked for various stores such as F.A.O. Schwartz, Macy's, Montgomery Ward, and Sears, Roebuck and Company.

The #42 round cab became Lionel's symbol. One could see it on boxes and in the catalogs. It was a prime example of toy trains of the time. This loco was a big piece, $15\frac{1}{2}$ inches long, 4 inches wide, and 6 inches high. It could pull twelve or more #10 Series freight cars and came in a variety of colors. Modifications were made during the years it was made. In 1921 the #42 became the first twin-motored loco Lionel made. The #42 is considered the most significant loco of Lionel's Early Period. Sales were tremendous during this Early Period. Locos such as the #42 helped Li-

onel become the biggest manufacturer of toy trains in the United States.

Square cab versions of electric locos are more desirable for collectors than round cab types. Various colors designate different years so collectors can date the locos by that information. All square cab electrics made in 1910 were green on the exterior. Maroon was the inside and primer color. In 1911 the inside color was changed to green. By 1912 almost no primer was used.

Early Period passenger cars that have knobs on the roof were the first made. These passenger cars were made of separate pieces of stamped metal soldered together. Hook couplers were used, and numbers were stamped on the ends. An accessory lamp kit was sold in 1911 to illuminate the cars. The #29 Day Coach was made from 1908–1921. It was the first passenger car made for sale at Lionel, was

Fig. 4–7. The #38 Standard Gauge electric profile locomotive is typical of the 1913 pieces that were being manufactured by Lionel. The body is painted black with red and brass trim and rubber-stamped identification. Photo Courtesy of Joy Luke Auctions

Fig. 4–8. Mojave was a popular Lionel color. This set headed by the #42 loco pulled a #419 Combine, #418 Parlor, and a trailing #490 Observation. Photo Courtesy of Sotheby's

designed for commuter trips, and was fashioned with open ends. About 1910 Lionel started manufacturing large passenger cars. There were the #18 Pullman cars, #190 Observation cars, and #19 Combine cars which were either Baggage-Pullman cars or Baggage-Parlor cars.

The best freight cars of the Early Period were the #10 Series. They were introduced in 1906 and made through 1926, but the earliest ones are the most desirable. In 1914 Lionel began to paint cars by dipping them rather than spray painting. Rubber stamping replaced embossing on the bottom of the cars in 1918. "Lionel Corporation" and catalog numbers were rubber-stamped in gold on dark-colored cars and in black on light cars. Before this they bore the "Lionel Mfg Co." mark.

The #10 Series consisted of the #11 Flatcar, #12 Gondola, #13 Cattle Car, #14 Boxcar, #14 Harmony Creamery Special Boxcar, #15 Tank Car, #16 Ballast Dump Car, and #17 Caboose. The #11 Flatcar never had a load with it. Most of these cars had no lettering. The #12 Gondola came in red, brown, grey, and maroon. Some were marked "Lake Shore," some "Rock Island." The #13 Cattle Car came in various shades of green. The #14 Boxcar came in red, yellow, orange, and darker orange. The Harmony Creamery Car was purchased from Lionel for a special promotion. It was dark green and had a #14 on the bottom of each car. The #15 Tank Car came in red, wine, and brown. The #16 Ballast Car had levers to release the load it carried, and it came in red, grey, brown,

wine, and dark green. The #17 Caboose came in brown, wine, and the red example with awnings which is the most desirable.

The #100 Series represented the bottom of the line freights in the Early Period at Lionel. They were smaller than the #10 Series and consisted of five cars which were the #112 Gondola, #113 Cattle, #114 Boxcar, #116 Ballast, and #117 Caboose. The entire set was discontinued in 1926.

Classic Period refers to Standard Gauge trains made by Lionel from 1923 until 1942. These later trains had more authentic detailing, came in brighter colors, and had more brass and nickel trim. The #402 was the first electric locomotive of the period and was introduced in 1923. Steam engines were not made until 1929 in the Classic Period, and the #390 was the first. The S-Class New York Central locomotives were the models for Lionel's electrics along with the Milwaukee Road bipolars and the Pennsylvania's BBB-style electrics.

The #8 and #8E were the smallest and least expensive electric locos made by Lionel and were made from 1925–1932. Maroon and olive green were the most ordinary colors. From 1928–1936 Lionel made the #9, #9E, and #9U. The #9 had manual reverse, #9E had electric reverse, and #9U came in kit form. "U" refers to "you build it" in Lionel terms.

One of the most desirable electric locos from the Classic Period was the #381 (the largest engine) made from 1929–1936. The #408E was introduced in 1927 and was used to pull the top of the line State Set. It

Fig. 4–9. Lionel's #9E locomotive carries a "Build-A-Loco" plate along with the identification number. The two-tone green "Stephen Girard" cars match the color scheme on the locomotive. Photo Courtesy of Christie's

was made in tan, mojave, apple green, and tan with a brown roof. Some of the #408E's were repainted a dark green shade at the factory to replace the #381.

Steamers were not introduced until 1929 because electrics were easier to make. They had fewer moving parts and less de-

tail. Lionel made the boilers of stamped metal and the frames and steam chests of pot metal. For trim they used brass, copper, and red paint. No actual prototype steam locomotives were used as models for these Lionel steamers. Earlier versions used brass and copper trim while later ones

Fig. 4–10. In 1929, Lionel released this splendid Standard Gauge passenger set painted in apple green. The brass plates identify the electric profile as #408E and coaches consist of a #419 Combine, #418 Pullman, #431 Diner, and a #490 Observation. Photo Courtesy of Christie's

Fig. 4-11. Note the graceful lines on Lionel's #385E "Washington Special" locomotive. This specimen dates about 1934 and is fitted with copper trim. Photo Courtesy of Christie's

had nickel trim. The #390/390E were a good start for Lionel. At first they pulled the Blue Comet but were replaced by the #400E.

The #400E is the loco used with the top of the line sets after being introduced in 1931 and was made until 1939. The engine was used in sets with the Blue Comet, State cars, and the #418, #419, and #490 Series passenger cars. It also pulled the #200 Series freights. The most difficult to find is the black model with nickel trim. The tender supplied with this loco was the twelve wheel Vanderbilt type, the #400T.

Classic Period passenger cars with the big names are the most important Lionel Standard Gauge examples. Early passenger cars were trimmed in brass; transitions

Fig. 4-12. Green was a popular color in the Lionel rainbow. The #390E locomotive and tender are painted in this color, and the 1926 set on the lower shelf is covered in olive with maroon trim. Photo Courtesy of Christie's

used a combination of brass and nickel trim, and the later cars have all nickel trim.

State Cars by Lionel were the most elaborate toy train passenger cars that were mass produced in the United States. Each car was 21 inches long, 7 inches high, and had tremendous detail including hinged roofs, revolving armchairs, lights, and hinged toilet seats. They were first made in 1929 and called the "Transcontinental Limited." Each car was named after a state, hence the State Set name. Pullmans were the #412 California, #413 Colorado, #414 Illinois—the Observation was the #416 New York. Cars were green with darker green roofs and lighter apple green window trim. The #408E pulled the four car State Set and the #381E pulled a three car State Set. Different versions were made of the State cars through 1935 including a brown State set pulled by a brown

#408E. All of the brown versions are difficult to find.

1930 saw the introduction of Lionel's Blue Comet named after a Jersey Central train that went to Atlantic City. At first the Blue Comet was pulled by the #390E in blue followed by a two-tone #400E in blue. The cars were named after comets: two Pullmans, #420 Faye and #421 Westphal; and Observation #422 Temple. These cars were a little smaller than State cars. The Blue Comet was made until 1938, but individual cars were sold until all inventories were depleted.

The "Stephen Girard" #424, #425, and #426 Series were the smallest of Lionel's name cars and were made from 1931–1938. The cars were about 6 inches shorter than State cars. The #424 Pullman Liberty Bell, #425 Stephen Girard Pullman, and #426 Coral Isle were light

Fig. 4-13. The car on the top shelf is an example of a combine car. The forward section carries baggage and the aft section carries passengers. Each of the coaches rides on 6 wheel trucks. Photo Courtesy of Sotheby's

Fig. 4-14. The top-of-the-line Standard Gauge "State" Set derives its name from the state plates mounted on the sides of the cars. Photo Courtesy of Christie's

Fig. 4-15. The Standard Gauge "Blue Comet" is considered one of Lionel's finest achievements. These later coaches were trimmed in nickel. Photo Courtesy of Christie's

green with dark green roofs and cream window trim.

In the Classic Period, the #200 Series freights replaced the earlier #10 Series and became the top of the line freight cars. The #500 Series were smaller and less expensive than the #200 Series and replaced the earlier #100 Series. According to McComas and Tuohy, "most collectors break the 200 and 500 Series cars into three categories: early cars (1926–1932), transi-

tion cars (1933–1936) and late cars (1937–1940)." Differences in these periods are related to trim such as ladders, handrails, plates, door handles, and brakewheels, and whether it is brass or nickel or a combination of both. Also color, journals, and brakewheels must be considered to determine date.

Comprising the #200 Series were a #211 Flatcar, #212 Gondola, #213 Cattle Car, #214 Boxcar, #214R Refrigerator,

Fig. 4–16. The 1920s #200 Series Standard Gauge freight set offered a wide variety of cars from a working floodlight and dumper to a log carrying car. Photo Courtesy of Christie's

#215 Tank, #216 Hopper, #217 Caboose, #218 Dump, #219 Crane, and #220 Floodlight. The #211 Flatcar came only in black. After the first year it had a wood load. The #212 Gondola came in green, grey, and maroon, and some non-regular production colors. The #213 Cattle Car first came in mojave with a maroon roof. Later other combinations were used. The #214 Boxcar was made in various colors as was the #214R Refrigerator. The #215 was made with and without the Sunoco decal. Dark green was the only color used for the #216 Hopper. The #217 Caboose came three different ways during the three periods. The #218 Dump Car was an "action" car since the side opened to re-lease the load. The #219 Crane Car was popular because it was quite large and moved in all different ways—controlled by three knobs at the rear of the car. The #220 Floodlight was the last car introduced in the series.

The #500 Series had similar cars to the #200, but they were smaller and less expensive. They were first made in 1927. There were ten cars in the series, and all were brightly colored. The #515 orange Shell Tank Car is the most difficult to find in this series.

Accessories were plentiful for Standard Gauge layouts, but more emphasis was placed on play value rather than accuracy regarding size or color combinations.

Some accessories were sold for use with both O Gauge and Standard Gauge trains. During the late 1930s, accessories comprised about 25 percent of Lionel's total sales figures.

Early accessories made before 1936 had brass trim and were green, cream and terra cotta. The later examples had nickel trim and were painted cream, red, and silver. Some examples include the #444 Roundhouse Section made from 1932–1934, the #840 Power Station, and Lionel villages such as the #921. Also there were tunnels, towers, street lamps that copied lamps in New York City, and the #300 Hellgate Bridge based on the prototype that crossed the East River in New York. It came in green and cream in 1928, while a later version was silver, ivory, and red.

Priced Examples

Sets

#8 locomotive, #337, 338 passenger cars, original boxes and factory box	$595.00
#10 locomotive, Log Car, #514 Refrigerator Car, #513 Cattle Car, two #512 Gondolas, #517 Caboose	$350.00
#33 locomotive, #112, 113, 114, 116, 117 freight cars, restored	$650.00
#38 locomotive, four freight cars, original boxes	$475.00
#385E locomotive and tender, #1766, 1767, 1768 passenger set, c1934	A–$2,100.00
#390E locomotive and tender, three #516, 517 coal train	A–$2,200.00
#390E locomotive and tender, #420, 421, 422 passenger cars, "Blue Comet," original boxes and set box	A–$6,200.00
#392 locomotive and tender, gunmetal, #424, 425, 426 Girard passenger set	A–$3,600.00
#400E locomotive and tender, #212, 219, 217, 220 work train, original box	A–$5,500.00

Locomotives

#8E, 0-4-0, electric, restored	$395.00
#9E, 0-4-0, electric, orange	A–$1,100.00
#9U, 0-4-0, electric, orange	A–$1,600.00
#10E, 0-4-0, electric, 1932	$395.00
#10 interurban trolley and trailer	$650.00

#42, electric, peacock with red trim, 1919 $650.00

#381, State $3,900.00

#384E, mint condition $600.00

#385E steam with tender, 1933 $695.00

#400E and tender, gun metal, original box   A–$1,700.00

#1835, steam, 1932 $950.00

Rolling Stock

#12 Gondola Car, red, restored	$150.00
#13 Cattle Car, green, restored	$150.00
#15 Tanker, restored	$150.00
#114 Boxcar, restored	$125.00
#211 Log Car, restored	$195.00
#213 Cattle Car, restored	$375.00
#214 Boxcar, restored	$395.00
#218 Dump Car, mohave, nickel journals	A–$250.00
#219 Crane car, green, original box	$395.00
#511 Log Car, restored	$75.00
#513 Cattle Car, restored	$195.00
#514R Reefer, original box	$225.00
#515 Tanker, "Shell", restored	$195.00
#517 Caboose, red and green	A–$85.00
#520 Floodlight Car	A–$220.00

Accessories

#45N Gateman	$95.00
#77 Crossing Gate	$95.00
#78 Operating Traffic Signal, restored	$150.00
#107 Direct Current Reducer	$150.00

#120L Tunnel	$50.00
#122 Passenger Station, restored	$175.00
#126 Illuminated Station	$195.00
#155 Illuminated Freight Shed	$350.00
#280 Bridge, restored	$75.00

CHAPTER 5

The Years Prior to World War II at Lionel

After the cessation of World War I, train production at Lionel went full steam ahead. Many trains, plus a great variety of elaborate accessories were made. These post-war years were a wonderful time for electric toy trains in America. People were prosperous, the economy was booming, and many new inventions made consumers eager to purchase trains and add accessories such as crossing gates, tunnels, bridges, signals, warning bells, flashers, semaphores, and transformers that could shift engines into reverse. Lionel used flashy promotions and lavish catalogs to whet the public's appetite. These attractive "wish books" were given away free for the asking.

By 1921 Lionel had already made more than one million train sets. Construction techniques were well established because Lionel held many patents and numerous innovative devices were used first by them. Advertising campaigns were being spread all across the country bol-

stered by magazine layouts and ads in the comic sections of Sunday newspapers. During the 1920s, Lionel became the most successful toy train company in the world.

Lionel was truly unprepared for the stock market crash and the subsequent Depression. Naturally there was a big drop in sales and profits during the Depression. Families no longer had the excess money to buy the elaborate train set-ups to please their children for Christmas, birthdays, or any other occasion. With rent and food money being scarce, there was certainly no money for a frivolous expense like toy trains.

Arthur Raphael, Lionel's general sales manager introduced the "department store specials." These were Lionel sets with different combinations of cars or different paint colors than those which were listed together as sets in the catalog. They were sold less expensively by department stores like Macy's, Sears, and Montgomery Ward. Lionel had to handle these "specials'' carefully in order not to jeopardize the relationship it had with the smaller, independent toy dealers who sold their Lionels at retail price. Even these less costly models could not stop the drop in profits Lionel experienced in the early 1930s.

During the Depression, Lionel brought out one of its greatest steam locomotives, the Standard Gauge #400E which was $2\frac{1}{2}$ inches long and featured copper trim and red spoked wheels. Elaborate passenger sets of this period included the famed Blue Comet from 1930-1939, pulled by the #400E, which was dropped when Lionel stopped making Standard Gauge.

Another innovation of the 1930s period in toy train manufacture was the introduction of plastics that were made in a process that resembled metal die casting. Plastics were placed into the mold in a powder form and pressure and heat were applied. Bakelite was the first plastic used by Lionel.

1934 was a year of great financial difficulty for the Lionel Corporation. One savior was the introduction of the Mickey Mouse and Minny Mouse handcar which sold for $1 with a circle of track, and it is credited with saving the company from bankruptcy. Lionel's handcar had a powerful wind-up motor and ran on a 27 inch diameter track. Before they were even cataloged, 250,000 were sold. The Mickey Mouse handcar came in red, green, and orange and was almost 10 inches long. A Santa Claus handcar came out in 1935 and featured Santa and a Christmas tree instead of Mickey and Minny Mouse. Another ver-

sion that was made for several years had Donald Duck and Pluto.

A Mickey Mouse Circus Train was issued with a red #1508 clockwork Commodore Vanderbilt engine and a #1509 Mickey Mouse action stoker tender. A diner, a circus car, and a band car comprised the rest of the four-wheel lithographed circus set; it came with track and a cardboard layout that formed a circus tent. Another piece was a statue of Mickey Mouse as circus barker. This set sold for $2.

Actually the streamlining of its trains is really what brought Lionel out of receivership and back to its former profitable status, just as it did for the nation's railroads. As cars, highways, buses, and even airplanes had become more plentiful and available in the United States, the nation's railroads had experienced a decline in the Depression years of the 1930s. The era of streamlining brought the railroads back to a state of prominence, and Lionel followed right along with accurate, detailed replicas of steam and diesel trains. Lionel's Flying Yankee was based on the Burlington Zephyr, the diesel City of Portland by Lionel was modeled after the Union Pacific's M–10000 streamliner. The steam Hiawatha was based on the Milwaukee Road's version, and the Commodore Vanderbilt steam loco was designed after the New York Central's first steamer ever streamlined and used on its Twentieth Century Limited passenger trains. "Streamliners were not coupled together in the conventional manner, but were linked by swiveling vestibules that made

Fig. 5–1. The Mickey Mouse Circus Train (bottom) was issued with accessories that are rarely found with the train. Powered by a clockwork motor, the locomotive was "fueled" by a figure of Mickey shoveling the coal from the tender. The steamer on the top shelf is fueled from a Vanderbilt tender. Photo Courtesy of Christie's

Fig. 5–2. The Flying Yankee was based on the Burlington Zephyr and was finished in chrome. Photo Courtesy of Christie's

them look like sleek one-piece trains'' according to Ron Hollander in *All Aboard!*

Hollander also calls 1935 "the year of the whistle" since reproducing an "authentic-sounding steam whistle" was an event of major importance. Each of the streamliners that Lionel copied from the major railroads was made with whistles.

One of Lionel's most popular accessories also appeared for the first time in 1935, the automatic gateman who emerged from

his shed waving his illuminated lantern as a train passed. The Lionel Corporation was emerging from the Depression quite successfully and had its first profitable year in 1935 due to these new developments. Another benefit for Lionel after the Depression was protective tarrifs which restricted foreign imports; this made American toys more profitable. The European toy trains could no longer compete with the American lines.

As leisure time became more available to American workers with the shorter work week, many adults turned to scale model railroads for entertainment. Here every piece was "in scale" in the layout. These train enthusiasts were no longer playing with toys that children used, but recreating actual model railroads. For these collectors, Lionel produced an intricately detailed version of the New York Central's Hudson-type steam locomotive in 1937 that was accurate in every detail. This die cast steam engine was Cowen's pride and joy and was considered the best piece ever made by Lionel.

With the success of the Hudson, Lionel went on to produce cheaper die cast engines. According to Ron Hollander, "the die casting process, in which molten metal was forced under high pressure into the cracks and crannies of hardened steel dies, produced highly detailed locomotives. Pipes, rivets, compressors, air tanks, and even a miniature locomotive builder's plate (BUILT BY LIONEL) were all cast into the engine in one piece." These loco-

motives were painted black like their counterparts on the actual railroads.

In 1938 Lionel's OO Gauge was introduced, and the Hudson was duplicated in this new gauge. Lionel marketed the gauge until 1942 when toy production was halted for the war effort. The scale Hudson in OO Gauge was #001E. Its tender was the #001T and was made with and without a whistle. In freight cars they made the #0014 yellow Boxcar, #0015 silver Sunoco Tank Car, #0016 grey Hopper, and #0017 red Caboose.

The OO Gauge line was enlarged in 1939 to include full and semi-scale sets as well as sets for both two and three rail track. There was not much difference between the full-scale and semi-scale cars. Forty-two inches was the diameter for the two-rail track while the three-rail track was 27 inches. These trains were made until 1942. According to a 1940 Lionel catalog, "OO Gauge is especially desirable for men and boys who have small quarters in which to work." The track measures $\frac{3}{4}$ inch between the running rails.

During the mid 1930s, many new de-

Fig. 5-3. With the increased interest in scale model railroading, Lionel offered scale-like cars that contained considerably more detail than their previous offerings. This caboose features simulated wood sheathing on the body. Photo from the Collection of John Ezzo

Fig. 5-4. Lionel introduced its OO Gauge line in 1938, and it was available until 1942. The set was headed by the #001E 4-6-4 Hudson locomotive. Photo from the Collection of Don Speidel

vices were introduced by Lionel to make toy trains more realistic and lifelike. In 1938 we see the first automatic uncoupler where the rolling stock can be separated at a touch of a button. Cars that performed tasks such as dropping barrels, dumping coal, and moving logs added to the realistic effects.

Accessories became more action oriented as opposed to static ones that just stood by the side of the track. Remote control was a major innovation of the times because it allowed the train operator to control his layout from a distance by pushing buttons, switches, or levers. Remote control was a great feature that helped to sell trains because it made the setups more realistic. The downside was that the child used his imagination less and made more use of the wonderful new mechanical devices.

Standard Gauge train manufacture was discontinued in 1939. Lionel started to concentrate its efforts toward obtaining lucrative war contracts. By 1941 they were involved in the war effort in a major way, and even stopped train production entirely for the years 1942–44. To keep the attention of American children focused on trains, Lionel manufactured a "paper train" as a substitute for the real thing. This cardboard train and track set consisted of 250 pieces; it was a freight set designed from an O Gauge train set. The paper train was very difficult to put together. The wheels were flanged and rolled on the paper track by means of wooden axles. Accessories such as gates, workmen, and signals also were included, in addition to a selection of rolling stock. The set contained the #224 loco, #2224 tender, #2812 red Gondola, #61100 yellow Automobile Car, and #47618 red Caboose.

In 1944 Lionel issued "The Lionel Planning Book" to aid American boys in planning their train layouts for when World War II would be over and train production would commence once again. In the meantime, the war was extremely profitable for The Lionel Corporation.

O Gauge

1915 was the first year that Lionel cataloged a complete line of O Gauge trains. Electric locomotives were modeled after the New York Central's electric S-type cabs. The #700 Series were the first early O Gauge electric engines. Three engines were made that first year, the #700, #701, and #703. The first two were made in dark green, had hook couplers, pedestal headlights, and cab windows trimmed in red. They had cast-iron wheels, and the ventilators were painted gold. The #703 was larger in length and width and had a hand reversing unit. Other details were the same.

In the following year, the engines in the #700 Series had die-cast wheels with nickel rims. None of these had Lionel markings. These engines are difficult to find today. In 1917, the numbering system used by Lionel changed, and the #700 Series became the #150 Series. One major difference was that the #150 Series had strap headlights instead of the pedestal ones from the #700 Series. The #152 was made from 1917–1927 and was painted in dark green, olive green, light grey, or dark grey.

Lionel's early passenger trains were very sturdy since they were made from a single piece of tin for the whole car body, except for the roof. The single piece made up the sides, floor, and ends of the car; and tabs folded into slots to fasten the car. Lionel soldered the joint where the tab met the slot, while other manufacturers did not do this. Lionel also patented and utilized a single piece of shaped metal the length of the car behind the side wall of the car to form the window trim and to make doors. They used this technique on all their prewar O Gauge trains.

Passenger cars associated with the early electric period in O Gauge include the #600 Pullman, #602 Mail, #610 Pullman, #612 Observation, #603 Pullman, #604 Observation, #629 Pullman, and #630 Observation. These #600 cars came in dark green and brown through 1918 and in maroon after that. The #600 was also the smallest of these passenger cars.

From 1915–1923, Lionel made the #601 Pullman and #602 Mail cars in dark green and orange. The largest of the early passenger cars were the #610 Pullman and #612 Observation. They were made from 1915–25 and featured double windows with transoms. They first were issued in dark green, and then also in mojave and maroon.

These cars were used in top-of-the-line sets.

The #610 passenger series was revised completely in 1926 with changes in windows, air tanks, railings, and such. By 1928 "Lionel Lines" appeared on the sides of each car instead of a railroad name because Lionel felt this was a better selling feature.

1920 saw the introduction of the #603 Pullman and #604 Observation cars made through 1925. Usually they were in orange. The #629 Pullman and #630 Observation cars appeared in 1924 and were carried over into the later electric period. First they were dark green and had hook couplers; then they were in orange or red with latch couplers.

From 1924–1934 the #710 Pullman and #712 Observation were top-of-the-line passenger series cars for Lionel. For the first few years they were made in orange with a matching orange #256 engine. Red was the main color in 1930, and the cars came with the #260E Locomotive. Blue was the color change for 1933 and 34, and then the series was discontinued. Sometimes Lionel colors are not what they appear to be in the catalog. Collectors frequently sent items to the Lionel service department for repairs, and then cars were repainted with colors the company currently was using without paying attention to the original color. Sometimes a collector will think he has found a rare color variation, when in truth he has found only a factory repaint.

Smaller freight cars from the early electric period were 5 $\frac{1}{2}$ inch long and came with less expensive sets, while 7-inch cars came with more expensive sets. Small cars included the #800 Box, #802 Cattle, #801 Caboose, and #901 Gondola, and were made from 1915–25 with hook couplers, no journals, and road names rubber stamped on the sides. Large freight cars of the period included the #820 Box, #821 Cattle, and #822 Caboose. These also had hook couplers, no journals, and road names rubber stamped on the sides. They also were made for the ten year period from 1915–25.

Later electrics in O Gauge were made from 1924 until 1936 when the last ones were cataloged. Changes in the later electrics include latch couplers, brass number inserts, and an automatic reversing unit. Colors were brighter, glossier and showed greater variety. These electrics more closely resembled real locomotives. Additional details and trim were used too.

The #256 was the largest O Gauge engine made by Lionel in the prewar period and the only one with two motors. The engine was advertised as the "Twin Motor," was introduced in 1924, and had "Lionel" rubber-stamped on its side. Other features included spoked wheels, brass window inserts, combination latch couplers, and metal-stamped headlights. Several years later they changed to cast headlights, disc wheels, roof trim that was brass, and latch couplers. A brass nameplate was added in 1927, and brass trim was used on the roof in the form of two brass whistles which replaced the single nickel ventilator. Changes continued during the years this engine was made. Orange was the color for the #256 engine.

Fig. 5-5. The #256 electric profile locomotive was the only prewar locomotive featuring twin motors. This piece was painted a distinctive orange. Photo Courtesy of Beute & Son

In 1924 the #253 was added and ran until 1936. It was 9 ¾ inches long and came in a variety of colors. After 1931 it was made with an automatic reversing unit and became the #253E. While this engine was packaged in sets with the #603, #607, #610, and #613 passenger cars and the #800 Series freight cars, it was also used in some department store specials. The train made for Macy's in New York had a brass plate that said "Macy Special" and was numbered #450. On the bottom was an R.H. Macy Co. nameplate, and "Macy Special" was rubber-stamped on the three #610 passenger cars.

Another engine, the #254 was introduced in 1924 and was modeled after a Milwaukee Road electric. This was also used for the Bild-a-Loco engine in 1928, but was called 4U in the catalog. The U stands for "You build it." A boy was supposed to be able to learn about electricity and mechanics by constructing his own engine from the kit. An orange #254 also was used in a Macy Special with three orange #605 Series cars.

Other electric locos were made during

the period. The #248 was cataloged from 1927 until 1932 in various color combinations. This was the engine used with the lowest price sets so it is readily available to collectors. The loco was $7\frac{5}{8}$ inches long and was the smallest of the prewar electrics.

The first of the O Gauge steamers was made in 1929. The #257 and #258 came in black, had copper and brass trim die cast frames and metal-stamped boilers. In 1931 Lionel made two larger engines, the #261 and #262 in black with red spoked wheels and copper trim. The #262E was made in 1933 and then was used with uncataloged department store specials. These and other early steamers were made from the designers' imaginations, while later ones were modeled after real prototypes.

The #260 series were the largest of these early steamers and included the #260E, #263E, and #255E. The tenders were die cast, had stamped metal frames and were named #260T. In succeeding years, there were various color changes to the engines and tenders.

The O Gauge Hudson came out in 1937 after several years of research. A tremendous amount of detail was used for this

Fig. 5-6. The #260E was part of the #260 Series which was the largest of the early steamers. This example carried a pair of flags on the front of the smoke box. Photo from the Collection of John Ezzo

#700EW. It was really designed for collectors and model railroaders rather than as a toy train for children. It even came with a walnut display stand. It is the most sought after Hudson by collectors today. The Hudson was 15-inches long and was cataloged from 1937 until 1942 as an engine and tender set. A kit version of the Hudson was offered by Lionel beginning in 1938. Actually six different kits were needed to complete the Hudson engine.

Continuing the trend towards realism, Lionel used the Pennsylvania's B-6 0-6-0 switcher as a prototype for its switcher in 1939, numbered it #701 and made it until 1942 along with its tender the #701T.

Die cast steamers made by Lionel were moving in the direction of realistic designs. In 1936 there was the streamlined Torpedo #238E. In 1939 Lionel stopped using the letter ''E'' to indicate a reversing unit, since they assumed that the train buyers knew that all of Lionel's trains had reversing units. Some other steamers of the period include the #224, #225, #226E, #228, and #239.

With their production of diesels and streamliners, Lionel led all other toy train manufacturers in this class of trains, though they were slower than others in producing steam engines. Lionel's three car M-10000 was modeled on the Union Pacific's version made in 1934. Lionel coupled its cars together in a very similar way to the real train. To simulate the one unit look of the train, Lionel's designers invented a new coupling system using vestibules to retain the smooth, sleek look. The

The Chicago-based Hafner Company worked exclusively with keywind trains dating back to 1914. This wall of Hafner trains spans the 38 years of their existence. *Photo Courtesy of the Children's Museum of Indianapolis*

Lionel's Blue Comet was produced in an O Gauge and Standard Gauge version. This O Gauge model frequently appears at toy train shows in a wide range of conditions. *Photo from the Collection of John Ezzo*

The American market was very lucrative for European train manufacturers prior to World War I. This Bing electric profile locomotive is dressed in American colors and heralds to appeal to this market. *Photo Courtesy of Mike Hill's Hobby Shop*

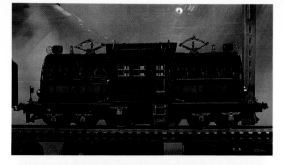

This Standard Gauge electric profile locomotive represents the ultimate in craftsmanship. It was the lead piece in Lionel's popular States set. *Photo Courtesy of the Children's Museum of Indianapolis*

Though it doesn't follow the colors of a prototype power station, Lionel's version is one of its most popular and sought-after accessories. *Photo Courtesy of the Children's Museum of Indianapolis*

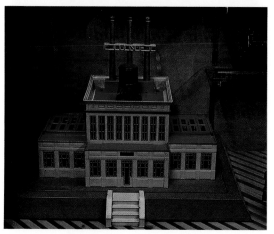

American Flyer's top-of-the-line Wide Gauge President's Special was headed by the 4–4–4 electric profile locomotive. Note the brass eagle on the platform. *Photo Courtesy of Mike Hill's Hobby Shop*

The roundhouse and accompanying turntable are the heart of any busy train lay-out. Locomotives are serviced in the facility and returned to duty via the turntable. All of the trains are post-war Lionel pieces. *Photo Courtesy of the Children's Museum of Indianapolis*

Many collectors enjoy watching their trains in action. The layout affords the opportunity of putting the trains and accessories in real railroad situations. *Photo Courtesy of the Children's Museum of Indianapolis*

Fig. 5-7. The scaled Hudson locomotive was the ultimate in detail. It came complete with its own walnut stand. Photo Courtesy of Sotheby's

Fig. 5-8. The 0-6-0 scale switcher required O72 track for proper operation. Photo from the Collection of John Ezzo

Fig. 5-9. The "Torpedo" first appeared in 1936 and is one of the more recognizable O Gauge Lionel locomotives. The presence of a reversing unit was indicated by the letter "E" in the cataloged #238E for this streamlined example. Photo from the Collection of John Ezzo

M-10000 cars were the longest O Gauge cars made by Lionel and required a new track with a wider turning radius. They referred to this track as "072". The M-10000 made in 1934 came in canary and brown, and also in aluminum finish. The engine was #752E, the center coach #753, and the end car #754. The following year they were offered with and without whistles. Other versions were made through 1941.

Lionel introduced the Hiawatha in 1935 for both passenger and freight sets. The engine was #250E, the tender #250TW. Passenger cars were the #782 Front Coach, #783 Center Coach, and #784 End Coach, and they were made until 1941. A freight set was offered in 1938 with the #2800 Series freight cars and the new automatic couplers.

In smaller streamliners, the Commodore Vanderbilt was introduced in 1935 and first headed a three car red Comet set, with two #603 Pullmans and a #604 Observation, a freight set with three #651 Series cars, and a set called The Silver Streak by collectors due to its chrome-plated Flying Yankee cars. Blue Streak passenger sets came out in 1936 and ran through 1938. The Flying Yankee came out first in 1935 in all chrome with a black roof on the power car. Several versions were made which ran through 1941. Next on the scene was the City of Denver in 1936 which came in a four car set.

Fig. 5–10. Lionel's version of the M–10000 streamliner was released in silver, canary yellow, and brown. The cars were the longest that Lionel made and required O72 track to navigate the curves. The lower level train incorporated a whistle. Note the vestibule and coupling method developed to give these trains a sleek appearance. These trains are affectionately referred to as the "banana" trains by collectors. Photo Courtesy of Christie's

The Blue Comet was brought into the line in 1936, and most had the new box couplers of the period. This train is highly prized by collectors of prewar Lionel examples. Automatic box couplers were introduced in 1938, and a "2" was added to this series to designate the new couplers. Major design changes were made in these #2613 cars, and the color was changed to green with a darker green roof.

Large freight cars made by Lionel in the period from 1926–1942 followed the #820 Series cars. There were ten different

nonoperating freight cars in the series. Between 1926–35 they had 800 number designations and latch couplers. Brass trim and nameplates were used, and they came in bright colors. By 1936 the box couplers replaced the latch couplers, and nickel journals replaced copper ones. Nameplates and trim also changed to nickel, and different paint colors were used. The automatic couplers were used in 1938, and the cars had 2800 numbers, while those with manual couplers retained the 800 numbers. Comprising this series were the #811 and

Fig. 5–11. The Blue Comet is highly prized by collectors. This O Gauge version was headed by the #263E loco with its Vanderbilt tender. Photos from the Collection of John Ezzo

#2811 Flatcar, #812 and #2812 Gondola, #813 and #2813 Cattle Car, #814 and #2814 Boxcar, #815 and #2815 Tanker, #817 and #2817 Caboose, #816 and #2816 Hopper, #814R and #2814R Refrigerator Car, #810 and #2810 Crane, and the #820 and #2820 Floodlight Car.

Smaller freight cars were made starting in 1923 that were derived from the old #800 Series cars. In this grouping there were the #803 Hopper, #804 Tank Car, #805 Box, the #806 Cattle, #807 Caboose, #831 Flat, #902 Gondola, and #809 Dump cataloged through 1931. These four-wheel versions had similar changes to the larger freight cars. A #650 Series of small eight-wheel freight cars came out in 1935 that were similar to the four-wheel cars except for the altered frames.

In operating freight cars Lionel made three small and three large cars in the prewar years. The small ones include the #3659 operating Dump Car in red, #3652 operating Gondola in yellow, and #3651 operating Lumber Car in black. All these operating cars came with automatic cou-

plers. Large ones were the #3811 operating Lumber, #3859 operating Dump Car, and #3814 operating Merchandise Car in brown with three "Baby Ruth" boxes.

To go along with the scale Hudson and switcher, Lionel made four scale model freight cars in 1940, the #714 Boxcar, #715 Tank Car, #716 Hopper, and #717 Caboose. These were designed for the scale modeler market as opposed to the toy train collector. The cars came in kit form too with a "K" added to the Lionel numbers.

Semi-scale freight cars also were made in 1940 and were designed to run on T-rail track. They had box couplers, O Gauge wheels and trucks and were similar in design to the scale cars. These cars were pulled by the semi-scale #763E Hudson.

During the prewar period, accessories played an important role and had significant space in the catalogs each year. O Gauge accessories had the same number as Standard Gauge ones, but had an O before the number. "N" after a number meant that the accessory was useful for both gauges.

In O Gauge, the first coupler used was the hook coupler, just like Standard Gauge. By 1924 the latch coupler was used. A combination version was in use in 1924 and 25 that connected with hook and latch couplers. The manual box coupler appeared in 1936, followed by the automatic box coupler in 1938. This automatic version underwent many changes during the prewar era; constant adjustments were made until the war. After the war, the automatic box coupler was not made again.

Fig. 5–12. Large series freight cars such as this #812 Gondola and #817 Caboose were cataloged from 1926 to 1942. These early examples carry brass plates and latch couplers. Photo Courtesy of Nelson's Auctions

During the manufacturing period for O Gauge trains, three different kinds of O Gauge track were made. All were the same 1¼-inch width, but the variations regarded the weight and diameter of the track. Regular O Gauge track was heavyweight tin and made a 30-inch diameter circle. 027 track was lighter weight, slightly closer to the ground, and formed a 27-inch circle. For the streamliners, Lionel made the 072 track which made a 72-inch circle. Two versions of this size were made, the regular tubular type and the solid T-shaped resembling actual railroad track. T-rails were used for scale locomotives and cars.

Although war production provided The Lionel Corporation with substantial income and was beneficial to the United States' war effort, those connected with the factory were eager to return to toy train production after World War II was over.

Priced Examples

Sets

#250 electric locomotive, (2) #603 Pullman, #604 Observation	$200.00
#253 electric, #607 Pullman, #608 Observation, 1925–32	A–$125.00
#262E steam, tender, #805 Boxcar, #803 Hopper Car, #801 Caboose, 1933	$140.00
#616 "Flying Yankee", (2) #617 passenger cars, #618 Observation, 1935	A–$250.00
Commodore Vanderbilt locomotive, tender, (2) #2640 Pullman, #2641 Observation, 1938	$155.00

Locomotives

#201 steam switcher, 0–6–0, mint	$2,900.00
#224 steam, 2–6–2, like new	$275.00
#226E with 12 wheel cast tender, like new	$600.00
#238E Torpedo, 4–4–2, restored	$595.00
#248 electric 0–4–0, red, restored	$195.00
#259E steam, 2–4–2, very good	$95.00
#262 steam, 2–4–2	$275.00

Rolling Stock

#813 Stock Car	$75.00
#2810 Crane Car, original box	$175.00

CHAPTER 6

World War II to the Present at Lionel

Lionel's war contracts ended the day after the United States dropped the atomic bomb on Hiroshima. Not wanting to waste a minute since Christmas was a few short months away, Lionel rushed to retool to have some trains available after the long war had deprived America of its toy trains. This early post-war period was a tremendous boom time for the Lionel Corporation. Because there were no toy trains available during the war, Americans had tremendous desires for trains and could not wait to purchase them for their existing layouts or to start their children collecting trains.

The public had a great deal of money to spend on luxury items such as toy trains from the prosperous wartime economy. The baby boom provided many new consumers for the trains, and advanced technological improvements made everyone eager to start, or add, to their train layouts.

Although no trains were actually made during the World War II years, Lionel ex-

ecutives had been planning their post-war designs and their extensive marketing strategies. They hastily assembled one set, the #463E for that first Christmas season. It consisted mostly of leftover prewar rolling stock and had a #224 die cast steam locomotive, a #2466W whistle tender, a #2458 all metal double door Automobile Car with the old prewar #2758 marked on it, a #2555 single dome Tank Car with its old #2755. The only all new car was a #2452 Pennsylvania black plastic Gondola that had an injection molded plastic body and a #2457 sheet metal illuminated Caboose in O Gauge.

Since the public was so eager for new trains, the early post-war period was the perfect time for Lionel to introduce a new coupler system that was incompatible with the earlier prewar couplers. However, they did manufacture coupler adapters to accommodate their customers' earlier purchases. Understanding that more realistic trains would increase sales even more, Li-

63

onel continued its move in that direction. Knuckle couplers and die cast trucks were to play a major role in the realistic approach since the prewar box couplers and tinplate trucks did not fulfill the new requirements for realism. The automatic knuckle couplers were quite difficult to operate and had to be redesigned completely by the middle of 1946. Injection molded plastics provided an inexpensive means of bringing realism to toy trains since the process resulted in highly detailed car bodies.

Another technique that provided a competitive edge for Lionel in the early post-war period was the operating smoke device developed in 1946. Lionel used a small pill in the engine's stack where it was heated by a GE bulb that also functioned as the headlight. When it became hot, it produced smoke. In subsequent years, a high resistance wire replaced the bulb.

The engine where the smoke was used first was Lionel's version of the Pennsylvania Railroad's PA S-2 direct drive steam turbine that came out in 1946. It had a double worm drive (which was two driving axles instead of one), twenty wheels, and the special smoke lamp that was to be an

Fig. 6-1. Passenger cars built in the years following World War II, such as this 1948 O27 coach, featured knuckle couplers and diecast trucks. Photo Courtesy of Nelson's Auction

astonishing success. In O Gauge this turbine was the #671 and was exactly the same in 027 gauge but was #2020. By the following year the design was changed to a single worm drive. These turbines went through a series of changes and were eventually discontinued in 1956.

Another innovative aspect where this locomotive was used was in an "electronic" freight set. Two tiny radio receivers in the #467W tender and one in each of the four freight cars plus an additional "transformer" (that was actually a radio transmitter) came with the set. Radio frequencies were transmitted along the track to make actions such as engine reversing, whistling, uncoupling, and unloading to occur. This "electronic set" was quite advanced for 1946 and expensive even for the prosperous post-war period. The development of this set was actually an outgrowth of Lionel's wartime technological developments. It was produced for four years, but did not sell well.

Other turbines included the #726 Berkshire, which was the biggest locomotive Lionel made in 1946. It was changed extensively the following year. The #746 Norfolk and Western made in 1957 was the model of the railroads' Class J Northerns. This was the only Northern example Lionel ever made and came with the #2046 tender. The Norfolk and Western is a highly collectible post-war steamer.

Magne-Traction was introduced on Lionel's engines in 1950 for steam, diesels, and electrics. Magnets were utilized to provide better traction, more pulling power, and to keep trains from leaving the rails at

Fig. 6-2. The sleek lines of the Class J Northern in Norfolk and Western colors is one of the prized post-war locomotives. Photo from the Collection of John Ezzo

higher speeds. Due to the shortage of materials during the Korean War, engines were made without Magne-Traction for several years, but it returned in 1954.

Lionel's main merchandising tool had always been its wonderfully detailed color catalog that came out each year to whet the appetite of boys and their fathers for the newest developments in Lionel trains. However, after the war, there was a tremendous paper shortage, and Lionel was unable to secure enough paper to print the huge numbers of catalogs it required. Their advertising manager decided to insert the 1946 catalog in an issue of *Liberty* magazine. Lionel purchased 16 color pages in the November 23rd issue of *Liberty* to reach the 6 million readers of the magazine. This was the largest purchasing of advertising space in a magazine ever bought at that time. *Liberty* also provided a cover illustration detailing a father and son playing with Lionel trains. A huge success for Lionel, this advertising coup gave them a company record in both sales and production, just one short year after the war.

In 1946 all the Lionel locomotives were steam engines. Cowen was especially

attached to steam, but soon he realized that with the modernization of the country's actual railroads and Lionel's continued desire to provide realistic trains, they would have to modernize their locomotive production and produce diesel engines too. But in 1946 and 47, Lionel's first two years of post-war production, steamers still dominated. The Pennsylvania Railroad's streamliner GG-1 Electric designed by Raymond Loewy was chosen as the prototype for Lionel's first electric locomotive made after the war to head a fleet of passenger and freight trains. The first GG-1 #2332 appeared in the 1947 catalog. It had a die-cast body in Brunswick green with the gold striping and lettering of the Pennsylvania Railroad and was made in O Gauge. Although it was not made exactly to scale in order to accommodate the 30-inch diameter of O Gauge track, it was very accurate in all other details. It had a single motor, coil-operated couplers, and very realistic movable and operational pantographs. It was also the first locomotive

Fig. 6-3. The GG-1 had several variations including this example with five gold stripes on a green body. Two motors were incorporated in the body. Photo from the Collection of John Ezzo

with a horn to imitate the air horn of the GG–1 instead of a steam whistle.

In 1949, the GG–1 was overhauled and its number changed to #2330. Two motors were utilized, Magne-Traction was added, the body was die cast, and twelve drive wheels were in place. The wheels were sintered iron rather than zinc, since zinc wheels could not be used with Magne-Traction. A 1955 variation showed the GG–1 as #2340 in Tuscan red with gold striping as part of the Congressional Set with the #2543 William Penn Pullman, #2544 Molly Pitcher Pullman, #2542 Betsy Ross Vista Dome, and #2541 Alexander Hamilton Observation. Variations of the GG–1 were cataloged through 1963 which was its last appearance.

Lionel made several other electrics during the post-war period including General Electric's EP–5 Rectifier built for the New Haven Railroad. The rectifier-type loco converted alternating current into direct current. Much heat was generated by this process. Rectifiers had the advantage of being able to have more horsepower in a smaller space than motors that ran on alternating current. Lionel's EP–5 was the #2350 New Haven from 1956.

For the 50th golden anniversary of the Lionel Corporation, the factory produced the #773 Hudson. Unable to duplicate all of the details from the 1937 #700EW Hudson (due to costs), this was still a fine engine. Of course there was smoke which had not been available previously, plus Magne-Traction. The tender was #2426W which was die cast and had a Bakelite coal pile. Since it did not sell too well, it was discontinued after the anniversary year, but later re-released in the mid 1960s. The #773 Hudson came in a set with the three Livingston Pullmans, the #2625 Irvington, #2627 Madison, and #2628 Manhattan. This is one of the most valuable post-war passenger sets since it only was made for one year. The passenger cars had people silhouetted in the windows.

Lionel's catalog was probably the most influential of all the sales devices used to promote toy trains. Children waited eagerly for its appearance each year, and it did much more than provide a list of trains and accessories. The child's imagination

Fig. 6–4. The Congressional cars derive their names from the patriotic plates located on the sides of the cars and include two Pullmans, a Vista Dome, and Observation car. Frequently, sets are found with the #2530 Railway Express Baggage car. However, this was not part of the original set, but mates well with the Congressional cars. Photo from the Collection of John Ezzo

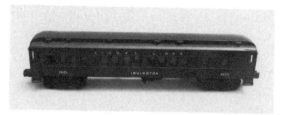

Fig. 6-5. The Irvington Pullman was a classic design and is part of a superb set of coaches. Photo from the Collection of John Ezzo

could go wild as he plotted his role as chief engineer of his very own railroad. Each and every decision was something to agonize over and dream about to make sure the best choices were made whether children were spending their allowances, their paper route money, or were choosing Christmas or birthday gifts. The artists' renderings on each catalog page illustrated the trains in action with steam puffing, in various dazzling layouts of operating cars and working accessories.

Fig. 6-6. The covers of Lionel's catalogs were designed to excite the imagination of the youngster. This 1959 example is crisscrossed with flying missiles. Reprinted with the Permission of Lionel Trains, Inc.

The descriptions went beyond a child's wildest imagination by using tremendous hype and numerous exaggerations. In these early post-war years when Americans were thrilled to have their families back together again as a unit, the message conveyed through the catalog was "with a Lionel in the house, your child's future is secure."

Along with each Lionel piece, there were excellent operating and repairing instructions. Lionel became the largest toy company in the world and achieved supremacy over both Marx and American Flyer. The catalog was one important reason why. Additionally Lionel had other superior marketing techniques, fine quality control, great engineering in its designs, and truly made an outstanding product. Lionel's three-rail track was also better than American Flyer's two rail track and provided electrical flexibility.

Lionel produced an enormous array of operating cars that was unequaled by other train companies of the period. The most famous one was the 1947 #3472 Automatic Refrigerated Milk Car. This car had an actual milkman who moved the milk cans

Fig. 6-7. The 1956 O Gauge Budd Car is a fine example of Lionel's supremacy in engineering design. Photo Courtesy of Nelson's Auction

between the car and the loading platform. The young Lionel operator controlled this milkman by the push of a button. Another successful operating car was the #3656 Cattle Car in orange that had the car, corral, and nine head of cattle to maneuver.

Trackside accessories had many clever operating aspects to their performance and could create a world in miniature in a train layout. For example, the newstand had a puppy dog running around a fire hydrant while the newsboy offered the paper. Crossing signals of all types flashed warnings to both trains and pedestrians in a busy Lionel world. The Lionel automatic gateman was an accessory made for fifty years from 1935–1984. It was the first accessory to utilize a human figure in action. It has been the most imitated accessory Lionel ever made. Human figures became permanent fixtures in Lionel layouts after the huge success of the automatic gateman.

Despite the fact Cowen preferred electrics and steamers to diesels, he realized diesels were the future for American railroads as well as for Lionel. In 1948 when Lionel finally introduced its first diesel, it was a resounding success. The flashy red, silver, and yellow Santa Fe became the largest selling engine in Lionel history, and it ran in various formats for 18 years. Since this dazzling new diesel was modeled on the actual Santa Fe and New York Central F–3 made by General Motors' Electro-Motive Division, Lionel got the railroads and GM to jointly finance the new dies and retooling required for Lionel to produce the F–3 in exchange for their names on the new diesel engines. This provided great advertising for the companies since Lionel's products were exceptionally popular and their catalogs and ads reached millions of eager consumers. GM had its emblem on every F–3 diesel whether it had Santa Fe or New York Central markings. The #2333 Santa Fe had brilliant colors, while the #2333 New York Central F-3 was more subdued in two-tone grey with white striping.

There was a wealth of details on these diesel locomotives including celluloid windows covering portholes, simulated turned aluminum horns on the roof, and grab irons on the front of the loco. The F–3 was the first twin-motored loco in O Gauge after the war. There were many changes in the ensuing years including Magne-Traction and a change to styrene plastic. The first F–3 in 027 gauge was the Texas Special in red, white, and silver, and that was a single motored unit.

Called the Super Speedliner, the first post-war streamlined passenger set in O Gauge came out in 1952 headed by the

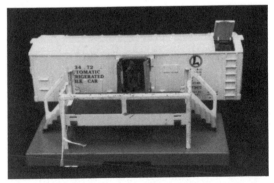

Fig. 6–8. The automatic Refrigerated Milk Car was one of Lionel's most popular "action" cars. Photo Courtesy of Nelson's Auction

Fig. 6-9. The #2343 AA F-3 diesels were the lead pieces in the Super Speedliner. Photo Courtesy of "The Antique Trader Weekly"

#2343 Santa Fe AA, followed by a #2532 Silver Range Vista Dome, a #2531 Silver Dawn Observation, and Pullmans #2534 Silver Bluff, and #2533 Silver Cloud. Another superior set with the #2383 Santa Fe AA was the 1958 Super Chief set with aluminum cars with red stripes comprised of the #2530 Railway Express Baggage Car, #2563 Indian Falls Pullman, #2562 Regal Pass Vista Dome, and the #2561 Vista Valley Observation. The last of the O Gauge passenger sets of the post-war era headed by the #2383 Santa Fe AA was the Presidental set with the #2522 President Harrison Vista Dome, #2523 President Garfield Pullman, and #2521 President McKinley Observation made from 1962-1966.

Lionel's model of the Fairbanks-Morse Trainmaster was the largest loco made after World War II. Made in 1954, the dies were partially paid for by Fairbanks-Morse in exchange for having its logos on all models. The first was the #2321 Lackawanna with a grey body, maroon striping, and yellow trim. This twin-motored plastic body loco was close to true scale in size. It was the first Lionel diesel to use a stamped, sheet metal frame. The previous ones were die cast. After 1954, all Lionel diesels had sheet metal frames because they were cheaper to produce. The FM coupler was a mechanically operated

Fig. 6-10. The Jersey Central version of the FM Trainmaster (top) is the most desirable of these large locomotives. The F-3 Southern ABA (bottom) was released in 1955. Photo Courtesy of Christie's

knuckle coupler activated by a magnet in an uncoupling section of the track. Other FM locos were the #2331 Virginian introduced in 1955, and the #2341 Jersey Central in 1956. FM's were made from 1954–1966.

General purpose GP–7 and GP–9 road switchers which were yard switchers outfitted with road trucks and increased power were made by Lionel from 1954-1966 in nine different road names. They had sheet metal frames and hand rails, Magne-Traction, operating couplers at both ends, and horns.

Lionel's model of the Alco FA was introduced in 1950. It was the first of the two unit diesels in 027 gauge, was smaller than the F–3, and was made in the yellow, grey, and red markings of the Union Pacific Lionel #2023. The Alco Union Pacific set included the #2481 Plainfield, #2482 Westfield, and the #2483 Livingston. Known as the Anniversary Set, it was produced in Lionel's fiftieth year and is the most desirable of the 027 post-war era. Lionel used many other Alcos in uncataloged department store specials.

The peak year for sales for Lionel was 1953 when $32.9 million worth of trains and accessories were sold. The years between the end of World War II and the Korean War were years of quality as well as quantity. Lionel products continued to be outstanding sellers because of the attention paid to providing action in operating cars as well as accessories.

An interesting set that one should take note of is the girls' train that was first cataloged in 1957. It consisted of a pink steam engine and freight cars in pink, light green, yellow, lilac, and a blue caboose. It sold poorly during the two years it was offered. Girls were not that interested in having their own train, especially in pastel colors.

Some inexpensive starter freight sets

Fig. 6–11. This 1960 A.T. & S.F. switcher featured a ringing bell. The detail included the well-shaped horn, stacks, and handrails. Photo from the Collection of John Ezzo

Fig. 6–12. The 50th anniversary was celebrated in O27 with the release of the grey and gold-yellow colored #2023 AA diesels and New Jersey stamped passenger coaches. This set is truly a collector's item. Photos from the Collection of John Ezzo

Fig. 6-13. The Lionelville trolley was a throwback to the early trolleys that helped launch the company. Photo from the Collection of John Ezzo

made from 1948–52 were the Scout Sets, an outgrowth of the earlier Winner and Lionel Junior Sets. These freight cars had plastic couplers that were not compatible with other freight cars.

The Lionel Boxcar Series was introduced in 1953, the #6464 series, were 11-inches long and were exceptionally popular with collectors. They were longer and higher than earlier boxcars and came in many road names, colors, and numerous variations. In 1954 they started producing multi-colored boxcars with the casting done in the named railroad's color scheme.

Other freight cars included oil tank cars, crane cars, such as the Bucyrus Erie, gondolas, hopper cars, operating box cars

where a man came out of the door, and automobile boxcars. There were flatcars that carried different types of lumber loads and automatic coal dump cars, searchlight cars, and both operating and nonoperating stock cars. The most popular of these stock cars was the operating cattle car that came out in 1949 and was made for seven years. Refrigerator cars were also made in nonoperating and operating styles. The most successful of these was the Automatic Refrigerated Milk Car (that was mentioned before). It was the first Lionel car to have a human figure in action.

Over sixty different varieties of flatcars were made carrying loads from bulldozers to airplanes. Action cars were designed to keep children actively involved with the operations of the railroad

Fig. 6-15. Far from a prototype, the track cleaning car served an important function. The pads on the bottom distributed cleaning fluid located on the top of the car. Photo Courtesy of Nelson's Auction

Fig. 6-14. The popular #6464 Series boxcars contained some rather rare examples such as the Alaska Railroad car. Photo from the Collection of John Ezzo

so they would not become bored. One very unusual car was the #3435 Aquarium made from 1959–62. The action consisted of fish swimming by the windows when the switch was activated.

Cabooses represented a home on wheels for the actual train crew, and Lionel examples came in a variety of styles and colors. The most popular style Lionel made was a model used by the Southern Pacific railroad from 1947–69. Lionel used many different road names on the SP style caboose. Other varieties of cabooses were made with accessories such as lights, smokestacks, tool boxes, window inserts, and operating couplers at both ends.

Fig. 6-16. Action cars such as this operating helicopter car were designed to capture a child's attention, and most were quite unusual. Photo from the Collection of John Ezzo

Fig. 6-17. Lionel's cabooses were the backbone of the freight fleet. Photo Courtesy of "The Antique Trader Weekly"

Operating accessories continued to be a big seller for Lionel during the post-war years. A sizable portion of each catalog always described the features of these accessories in glowing terms. For a reasonable amount of money, budding engineers got much play value from accessories such as the operating barrel loader, the ice depot with a worker who pushed blocks of ice into a refrigerated produce car, the log conveyor, the oil derrick, the coal elevator, the lumber mill, and the dispatching billboard, to name just a few. There were numerous stations, switching towers, water towers, motorized turntables, fork lifts, and bridges such as the Bascule Bridge. In addition to the popular gateman house, Lionel made crossing gates, flashing signals, semaphores, street lamps, and other types of signals to control traffic in the railroad yard and layout.

Lionel added a new track size called Super O in 1957 with a circle diameter of 38 inches as opposed to the 31 inches of O Gauge. Manual and remote control switches were available in Super O through 1966.

Although Lionel made some of its best trains during the second half of the 1950s, sales were not as strong as in the earlier part of the decade. Times were changing rapidly in America, and railroads were again in a decline. Air travel was becoming more available and more popular. Airplanes captivated the imaginations of boys who were once enamored with trains. Families moved around frequently due to job changes, and large train layouts became difficult to move or to store. People had smaller homes or apartments and larger families after the war. As a result, HO Gauge increased in popularity, while O Gauge sales decreased dramatically. Although Lionel started to produce HO Gauge examples in 1957, they really manufactured this gauge too late to make significant inroads. An economic recession from 1957 through 1959 added to the decline in sales and overall Lionel profits.

Lionel entered into an agreement with Rivarossi, the Italian manufacturer of high quality HO Gauge trains, to have him make HO trains for Lionel which Lionel would distribute under its own name. For Lionel, this meant not having the expense of making HO dies. For Rivarossi, it meant a wider distribution for his train products in the United States. In 1957, Lionel announced these HO trains in a flyer with the current catalog. During the first year of production, the cars were stamped "Rivarossi" on the bottom, and the trains offered closely resembled Lionel's O Gauge line.

But in reality, Lionel had waited too long to enter the HO field. Many train manufacturers were already well established in HO Gauge. It was a disadvantage to have their trains manufactured abroad. Even though Rivarossi made a good product that was selling well, he could not keep up with the demand. Lionel was never able to catch up to the other producers.

Sales continued to decline at Lionel, and internal problems were becoming more severe. Cowen retired from actively running the company, and his son Lawrence wanted to get out of the toy train

business. The company decided to expand the HO line in an effort to obtain a larger share of the scale model hobbyist market, but lessened the quality of the product. Athearn, an American train manufacturer made the locomotives for Lionel, while Rivarossi continued to make the rolling stock.

Producing a cheaper train was not the solution to Lionel's problem in HO Gauge. Since HO Gauge appealed mostly to the adult market that demanded quality examples which were accurate in all details, collectors were not very interested in what Lionel was offering. Athearn made an F-3 diesel locomotive in a variety of road names along with a Virginian rectifier and a GP-7. The main problem was that these locos had a very poor quality motor, and they broke down constantly. Athearn also made rolling stock for Lionel.

A decision was made in 1959 to put more money into HO Gauge even though sales were continuing to decline due to both the poor product and the economic recession of the late 1950s. Lionel chose to manufacture its own HO line and needed new tooling to do this. They acquired the Hobby Line, a small HO manufacturer, and used their dies for the new freight cars and yard engine. In 1959, Lionel made the Santa Fe loco, the Texas Special loco, and Alaskan Alcos, yard switchers, and such, plus boxcars, hopper cars, cattle and poultry cars, tank cars, and a circus car in rolling stock.

During the years 1960-66, Lionel made most of its own cars. Many items reflected the military and space motif that was of interest. Some cars had operational rockets and missiles. In the 1960 catalog, they announced "A First in HO—Brand New Action Packed Operating Cars." They made the #0319 Operating Helicopter, #0847 Exploding Target Car, #0850 Missile Launching Car, #0300 Operating Lumber Car, and #0301 Coal Dump Car. However, these held no real interest for serious HO collectors who were seeking scale size examples and authentic details.

In 1961 HO cars continued to stress play action cars. Fifteen different train sets were made. In the following year, smoke, headlights, and whistles were reduced to HO size. By 1963 slot racing sets came to the forefront, and trains became even less popular. Continuing to lose money, Lionel tried to cut costs. In 1964, the catalog was produced on less expensive paper, and the HO line was limited to six pages. Only four pages were allotted to HO in 1965. HO was discontinued all together in 1966.

Passenger cars for the 1961–1966 period with new Lionel tooling were models of the streamlined cars made by the Budd Company of Philadelphia. They had heavy plastic shells and two road names were utilized: Santa Fe and Pennsylvania.

By 1964 some new boxcars came from a Lionel die. Operating rolling stock included the #0039 Track Cleaning Car, #0357 Cop and Hobo Car, #0366 Operating Milk Car, and #0370 Operating Sheriff and Outlaw Car. Tank cars, hopper cars, gondola cars, and cabooses also were made.

Some of the more interesting accessories included operating examples such as the #0494 Rotating Beacon, #0140 Banjo Signal, #0282 Crane, and #0197 Radar Antenna. Military accessories such as the #04480 Missile Firing Range were made too. The ever popular #0145 classic Automatic Gateman was made through all the years of HO production. Scenic accessories also were available for HO layouts.

With the recession causing people to have less money to spend on trains, and Lionel's gimmicky cars not appealing to collectors, they continued to lose money on HO Gauge.

Internal problems plagued Lionel in addition to their financial troubles. Cowen sold his stock in 1959, and Roy Cohn's group brought the controlling interest in the company. Their answer was an extensive diversification program to expand into areas other than trains. Many trains were removed from the line to make way for cheaper examples. Even pieces from the museum were sold, and personnel cuts were made. In the few short years after the takeover by Roy Cohn's group, the company was in a shambles, and it experienced tremendous losses. However, it still managed to offer a line of trains each year.

Roy Cohn sold out in 1963 to an investor who sold out the same year to an investment group. Joshua Lionel Cowen died in 1965. In 1969 Ronald Saypol, a Cowen relative, took over. Soon after that Lionel was out of the train business. They entered into a licensing agreement in 1969 with the conglomerate General Mills who made games, toys, and models in addition to cereals. General Mills purchased the Lionel name, trademarks, and manufacturing equipment and made the trains themselves.

Model Products Corporation was the name given to the General Mills division that made the Lionel trains. Though this name was only used for three years, through 1972, most collectors use MPC to refer to all Lionel trains made from the year 1970 on. With the molds, dies, and tools purchased from Lionel, they moved from the Hillside plant to a new location in Mt. Clemens, Michigan. Production began in earnest on toy trains in April of 1970.

Fundimensions was the name General Mills gave to the division that made Lionel trains after Model Productions Corporation. The Lionel line increased in both quantity and quality each year after being taken over by General Mills. Fundimensions incorporated many of the best aspects of the older Lionel trains in their new products, and frequently they duplicated some of the 1950s trains. Once again there were steam locos in heavy diecast metal, whistles, smoke, Magne-Traction, and the wonderful automatic gateman.

Fig. 6–18. This O27 Fundimensions NW2 yard switcher carried nonoperating plastic knuckle couplers and a hand-reversing mechanism. It was cataloged from 1971 to 1974. Photo Courtesy of Nelson's Auction

For the 75th anniversary of the original company, Fundimensions decided to more closely associate themselves with the original founder Joshua Lionel Cowen and all he represented. A special anniversary train utilized old Lionel ads and catalogs. Again in 1980, Fundimensions manufactured a series of six boxcars making use of historical information about Lionel on the cars' sides.

Fundimensions used this slogan "not just a toy, a tradition" to connect itself to the original Lionel manufactory where Cowen played such a significant role. These new trains were very well done with excellent painting and striping. The catalogs still depicted the trains being made, but no longer employed those elaborate scenic layouts that captivated the imaginations of boys everywhere and put them in the roles of railroad engineers.

From 1970–1980, the Lionel Division of General Mills made GP–7s and GP–9s in 21 different road names. They made more of these diesels than any other engines during that period. Without Magne-Traction, these diesels did not run as well nor pull as many cars as the pre–1966 Lionels. These new engines had nylon gears which were less expensive and quieter.

During the early years that General Mills manufactured Lionel trains, the trains did not undergo year by year technical changes that had occurred in the past. Only one production run was done that usually consisted of about 6000 pieces for a top-of-the-line loco. An item would appear in the catalog in the second year only if there was any remaining inventory. Previously, a Lionel item could remain in the line for as long as it sold well. For example, the Santa Fe F-3 ran for 18 years with numerous opportunities for variations on the repeated production runs.

In GP 20s, the #8352 Santa Fe was the first new diesel made in Mt. Clemens. It was not made from an earlier diesel, was not popular with collectors, and was made from 1973-75.

For the first ten years that General Mills took over, they made F-3s in ten different road names. In an attempt to bring back collectors items, six of those F-3s were the rarest of those originally made. Essentially these new F-3s were the same as the 1950s models, but they had no horn nor Magne-Traction. The motor and power truck were the same, but the idler and pinion gears were nylon. The most detailed F-3 made in Mt. Clemens was the #8952 Pennsylvania that had nearly as much detail as the 1950s model. One F-3 that is especially sought after by collectors is the #8562 Santa Fe F-3 from 1976 due to its excellent decoration.

In 1974, the first engine casted from an all new die came out in Mt. Clemens. It was the U36B, a General Electric U-boat. The first one was the #1776 Seaboard Coastline Bicentennial done in a Bicentennial theme. In the same year, they came out with the #8470 Chessie at the head of the Grand National freight set. The following year they made the #7500, the 75th anniversary set which utilized different Lionel logos from the various production years. The first SD-18 was the #8855 Milwaukee Road that headed a top-of-the-line freight set in

1978. The loco was a lengthened version of the GP-9.

When the FM units were made, Lionel produced the #8951 Southern Pacific and the #8950 Virginian Limited Edition items. Only the original runs were made. Since the demand was high for these pieces, collectors were unhappy more were not available. In 1982 the SD-40, a scale length modern diesel was added to the line in various railroad names.

Alcos of the Fundimensions era were also made for mid-range sets as the earlier ones from the 60s had been. The first of the new Alcos was the #8020 Santa Fe from 1970. Lionel switchers of the 1970s were also similar to the cheapened versions of the 1950s switchers.

In electrics, General Mills reissued the GG-1 in 1977 as the #8753 Pennsylvania. In this unit the Magne-Traction was not as strong so the pulling power was not as great, and there was no horn. Again this was a Limited Edition model so only one production run was made. Fundimensions made several other GG-1's, all of which are highly desirable.

Other electrics included rectifiers such as the #8659 Virginian made in 1976 along with a hopper, boxcar, and caboose to go with it. This loco also had no Magne-Traction and no horn. Pantographs were improved, and cars ran better on overhead catenary wires.

Essentially the large steamers made in the early years of Fundimensions were remakes of the small Hudson-type steamers of the 50s. One new feature on these steamers was the "Mighty Sound of Steam" developed in 1970. The biggest steam engine of the period was the #8600 New York Central which headed the Empire State Express Set in 1976. It also headed the #8702 Southern Crescent and the #8801 Blue Comet; both had the Sound of Steam and smoke. Responding to demands from collectors, Fundimensions issued a #773-style New York Central Hudson #8406 in 1985. Another scale Hudson came out in 1988. The #18002 New York Central is gun-metal grey and has spoked wheels. This loco commemorates the 50th anniversary of the New York Central system.

The small steamers from this period came mostly in sets. The #8141 Pennsylvania from 1971 was the first cataloged steamer to have the "Mighty Sound of Steam." For the first department store special set made in Mt. Clemens by Lionel and sold by Sears, there was the #8043 Nickel Plate made in 1970. It did not have smoke or the sound of steam.

Since the desirable Irvington dies were not in existence, Lionel decided on a compromise passenger car and produced the Milwaukee Special in 1973 with two pullmans and an observation car. The Broadway Limited, with the same consist in Pennsylvania cars, came out the following year. The Capitol Limited Set with Baltimore and Ohio cars followed in 1975. None of the cars were available separately.

Â new Blue Comet was made in 1978 with three cars that were the same as the original Standard Gauge version, plus three additional cars. These were the first cars to have six wheel trucks that were die-cast metal instead of plastic.

In 1979, Fundimensions reissued the large aluminum cars from the Congressional Limited. These cars had a polished aluminum finish and were featured with the Pennsylvania F-3 twin motored diesels also made that year. The set was comprised of two passenger cars, a Vista Dome car, and an observation car. Later, a diner car, a combine, and another passenger car were added. These proved exceptionally successful for Fundimensions. A Burlington Zephyr Set followed in 1980 led by a chrome-plated twin F-3 diesel. An even more outstanding set was made in 1981 with the J class Norfolk and Western steam engine and six aluminum Powhatan Arrow passenger cars painted deep maroon with black roofs, gold lettering, and striping. Other successful passenger sets followed.

During the years 1970–79, Lionel made boxcars in 65 different road names and numerous variations. Since boxcars were sold in sets, collectors had to purchase an entire set to get the desired car. The first boxcar made in Mt. Clemens was the #9202 Santa Fe in red with white lettering in 1970.

Fundimensions made the #9301 Operating Post Office Car from 1972–1985. At the touch of a button, a man tossed out a sack of mail from an opening door. Other operating boxcars revived in the 80s included the horse transport car, the operating giraffe car, the cop and hobo car, and the icing station refrigerator car to name a few. In large cars they have reintroduced several operating milk cars and cattle cars.

A new boxcar for 1976 was the all plastic Hi-Cube boxcar with large sliding

Fig. 6-19. Some rather unique pieces of O Gauge rolling stock were manufactured during the Fundimensions era. This quad hopper carries the Sun-Maid Raisin logo and is molded in plastic. Photo from the Collection of John Ezzo

doors. Ten different ones were made with various railroad names. A Mickey Mouse Hi-Cube Series with Disney logo and characters along with a 50th birthday car for Mickey was also made for one year in 1978 and then reintroduced from 1982-84.

After buying molds from Pola of Germany, a European toy train maker, Lionel came out with the first Standard O cars in 1973. Though these cars were well made, they were not too popular. They made a small assortment of full-scale cars including a reefer, boxcar, and gondola in several road names. They were discontinued in 1976, but have recently been made again to go with the #8406 scale Hudson.

Lionel made five different types of cabooses in Mt. Clemens from 1970-80. Essentially they were the same as those made from the 1946-69 period. The Continental Limited Set in Norfolk and Western markings from 1982 featured an unusually large, scale-length, square-cupola caboose with 027 passenger style die cast trucks and two operating couplers.

HO trains were made by

Fundimensions from 1974 through 1977 and were not very successful.

In accessories, only the more ordinary ones such as crossing gates, stations, lamps and such were made during the 1970s. The elaborate action accessories that played such an important role in Lionel's development and marketing strategies were not made. One noteworthy accessory was the #2125 Whistle Shed from 1971. The building was white with a brown base, green roof, and light. A group of buildings in kit form including the Rico Station was made from 1974-77; these new accessories were made in Germany, but were discontinued because of expense. In 1980, Fundimensions brought back the #454 Sawmill as #2301. They also made 0 Gauge switches. By 1982 the animated newstand and icing station were again being made. For the next few years, some newly revived action accessories appeared on the scene.

In the 1987 offerings, there were more revival accessories and some new ones too. Many accessories were reintroduced in new and brighter colors to appeal to

Fig. 6-20. This HO Gauge diesel contains standard HO horn-hook couplers. The bottom plate indicates it was manufactured in 1976 and is part of the Fundimensions line. Photo from the Collection of Alan Gilbert

collectors. Even the operating gateman that had been made for fifty years, in one form or another, reappeared after a two year hiatus.

General Mills decided to consolidate its toy manufacturing operations in 1983, including Fundimensions, Kenner Toys, and Parker Brothers Games, and moved to Mexico. This was a most unsuccessful move for Lionel. Production was unable to meet demand there. Lionel became a division of Kenner-Parker Toys, Inc. in 1985, and production of trains moved back to Mt. Clemens. The next year, Richard Kughn, a real estate entrepreneur from the Detroit area, fulfilled his childhood dream and formed a corporation which purchased Lionel Trains and formed Lionel Trains, Inc.

Innovations for 1987 included the introduction of the Lionel Large Scale Line in 1/24th scale, which is about twice the size of O Gauge. Lionel continues to manufacture the 027 Gauge Traditional line including train sets, locomotives, a variety of rolling stock, accessories, and power and track for beginners to enjoy and experience the world of model railroading.

In addition, the Collector Line includes the Large Scale Trains and the American Flyer S Gauge trains. Lionel Classics, which are direct reproductions of the metal Lionel trains from the 20s and 30s, were reintroduced in 1988.

Another outstanding innovation is Railscope. This is "a locomotive with a tiny video camera mounted inside. It lets you view your train layout from an entirely new perspective: inside the train"—just as an engineer inside the cab would see it. "Railscope is a breakthrough in microelectronic technology. As the train proceeds down the track, an electronic signal is transmitted in a series of pulses via the rails. These pulses form a clear, crisp black and white picture." Railscope is made for HO, O, Large Scale, and American Flyer S Gauge.

Lionel now uses the phrase "trains to grow up with, not out of" on its boxes. Trains are being manufactured by Lionel for kids and "big kids" because adults do not want to give up their trains. Since Richard Kughn has taken over at Lionel, the company appears to be well on its way back to being a very successful and profitable manufacturer of trains and related products.

Priced Examples: O Gauge

Sets

#665 steam 4-6-4, tender, #6112 Gondola, #6473 Horse Car, #36180
Hopper Car, Caboose, 1954 .... $170.00

#681 steam 6-8-6, Pennsylvania tender, #LV25000 Hopper Car, #X6014
Boxcar, #1302 Caboose, 1950 .... A–$175.00

#726 steam 2–8–4, tender, #2422 Chatham Pullman, #2432 Clifton Vista Dome, #2421 Maplewood Pullman, 1946 — $330.00

#736 steam 2–8–4, Pennsylvania tender, (2) #2422 Chatham Pullman, #2432 Clifton Vista Dome, #2423 Hillside Observation, 1950 — $330.00

#2343 F3 AA diesel, #2533 Silver Cloud Pullman, #2532 Silver Range Vista Dome, #2530 Baggage, #2531 Silver Dawn Observation, 1950 — $475.00

#2343 Panama Limited F3 AA diesel, #2532 Sioux Vista Dome, #2533 Black Hawk Pullman, #2534 Illini Pullman, #2531 Land of Corn Observation, 1950 — $320.00

#2360 GG–1 Pennsylvania, #2542 Betsy Ross Vista Dome, #2543 William Penn Pullman, #2544 Molly Pitcher Pullman, #2541 Alexander Hamilton Observation, Congressional Set, 1955 — A–$2,400.00

Mickey Mouse set, Mickey engine, Mickey Hi-cube, Goofy, Dumbo, Donald Duck, Cinderella, Peter Pan and caboose, 1977 — $850.00

Locomotives

#400 Budd car, like new	$395.00
#2322 Virginian Trainmaster, blue, 1956	$375.00
#2340 GG–1, maroon, 5 stripe version	$550.00
#2350 Rectifier, New Haven	A–$175.00
#2368 F3 AB diesel, Baltimore & Ohio, 1956	$220.00
#8851 F3 AA diesel, New Haven	$90.00

Rolling Stock

#3356 Horse Car	A–$40.00
#3435 Aquarium Car, 1959	$90.00
#3464 operating Boxcar, A.T. & S.F., 1956	$15.00
#3620 Searchlight Car, 1954	$20.00
#3656 Cattle Car	A–$40.00
#3662 operating Milk Car and stand, 1955, excellent	$69.00
#3927 Track Cleaning Car, 1956	$60.00
#6414 Evans Auto Loader with 4 autos, 1955	$50.00
#6456 Hopper Car, Lehigh Valley, 1948	$7.00

#6464–425 Boxcar, New Hampshire, 1956	$30.00
#6817 Flat Car with scraper, 1959	$16.00

Priced Examples: 027 Gauge

Sets

#1688 steam, tender, #6468 Boxcar, #6425 Tanker, #477618 Caboose	$A–$44.00
#1862 steam 4-4-2, tender, passenger car, baggage car, horse car, The General Set	$250.00
#2026 steam 2-6-2, tender, #6032 Gondola, #6656 Cattle, #X9066 Caboose, 1952	A–$40.00
#2034 steam 2-4-2, tender, #6042 Gondola, #X6014 Boxcar, #LV25000 Hopper Car, #634656 Hopper Car, #1007 Caboose	$50.00
#2035 steam 2-6-4, tender, #6062 Gondola, #6100 Boxcar, #6462 Pipe Car, #6257 Caboose, 1950	$50.00
#2055 steam 4-6-4, tender, #6462 Gondola, #X6014 Boxcar, #477618 Caboose	$110.00

Locomotives

#211 Alco AA, Texas Special	$50.00
#610 switcher, Erie, 1957	$85.00
#627 44 ton switcher, Lehigh Valley, 1956	$125.00
#2033 Alco AA Union Pacific, 1952	$100.00
#2041 Alco AA Rock Island, 1969	$100.00

Rolling Stock

#52 Fire Fighting Car, 1958	$210.00
#3472 operating Milk Car and stand, 1949	$49.00
#7706 Sir Walter Raleigh Boxcar	$10.00
#9268 NP Caboose	$11.00
#9301 Mail Car	$14.00
#9324 Tank Car	$11.00
#9725 MKT Cattle Car	$10.00

Accessories

#128 animated Newstand, 1957	$100.00
#364 Lumber Loader, 1948	A–$50.00
#397 Coal Loader	A–$75.00
#445 operating Switch Tower, 1950	$70.00
ZW 250 watt Trainmaster transformer	$100.00
ZW 275 watt Trainmaster transformer	$150.00

CHAPTER 7

The American Flyer Story

The American Flyer story is actually a story with two parts spanning two eras. The first period includes the formative years of the company and its role in the Wide and O Gauge market. The second period begins with the acquisition of the company by Alfred Carlson Gilbert. Though post-Gilbert periods exist, these two earlier eras had the most significant impact on the company and should be considered as such.

Originally founded as the Edmonds-Metzel Hardware Company in Chicago, Illinois, Flyer became known as The American Flyer Manufacturing Company in 1910. A glance at the Chicago Business Directory at the Chicago Historical Society shows that American Flyer Manufacturing Company produced "miniature railways." Under the control of W.O. Coleman and later his son W.O. Coleman,

Jr., and Henry Hafner, (the clockwork specialist who was later to start his own clockwork train company in 1914), Flyer produced toy trains for thirty-one years.

Quality control of the products was not consistent, and cataloging also was a problem since some items were cataloged as one item but bore a different number when released from the factory. Pictures did not always match the end product. However, some truly splendid examples were created from the Flyer shops. In spite of these wonderful examples and the loss of the European competition after the first world war, Flyer never attained the prominent position in the train world that was occupied by Lionel. Though the company did work in the above mentioned gauges, O Gauge material is encountered more frequently on the open train market.

O Gauge

The American Flyer Manufacturing Company began producing clockwork locomotives about 1907. Generally, they were non-prototypical and featured 0-4-0 wheel configurations. They can best be described as little stubby shaped cast iron pieces, though a few examples were fabricated from sheet metal rather than cast. The tenders were generally little four wheel trail-behinds, often of stamped sheet metal. Clockwork locomotives were manufactured exclusively until about 1918 or 1919 when American Flyer turned its attention to electric powered examples. Even when electric powered locomotives moved to the forefront, A.F. continued to manufacture the clockwork examples until the mid 1930s. Many were included as part of packaged sets.

Changes in the length and type of the boiler were the most distinctive differences in these pieces. Some featured battery operated headlights and ringing bells. They were quite distinctive and though few car-

Fig. 7-1. This O Gauge cast iron #15 clockwork steamer has a brake lever in the form of a loop protruding from the cab. Photo Courtesy of Joy Luke Auctions

Fig. 7-2. These two clockwork locomotives date about 1920 and are typical of the stubby, non-scale appearance of these early cast-iron pieces. The "New York Express-Chicago" #515 passenger car is also typical of the rolling stock manufactured to accompany these locos. Photo Courtesy of Christie's

ried any numbers, and the driving rods were rather simple affairs, they served as the forerunners for the more elaborate electric powered examples that saw many years of service at American Flyer.

The first electric steamers were basically reworked clockwork locomotives. The top-of-the-line cast iron clockwork body was fashioned to receive the electric motors as these bodies were large enough to accommodate the mechanism. This reworking existed for about ten years with most examples lacking any consistent number identification system. Electric current was received from the middle rail by means of roller pickups that traveled in contact with this rail. These reworked clockwork bodies were used until 1931 when completely new designs were inaugurated.

The electric profile locomotive first was cataloged in 1920 and was a major part of American Flyer's locomotive line until 1934. Both cataloged and uncataloged examples were manufactured in painted and lithographed versions. Some of the electric profile engines headed sets sold through the catalog or for the mail order companies such as Sears and Wards, while some were sold individually. They were introduced to challenge Lionel's successful line of electric profiles.

Flyer's electric profiles fall into three general categories based on the shape of the body shell. The box cab type is basically a squared rectangular form set upon the chassis. The steeple cab in profile features a raised center cab section with tapered front and rear motor sections. The center cab or St. Paul electric is somewhat similar to the box cab variety though the cab sits higher than the motor sections and instead of squared corners, there is a more rounded contour to the motor segments.

The basic body types were lithographed or painted, and a specific model often was decorated in either technique in order to add additional variety to the line. Wheel configurations were 0-4-0 with the exception of the 1922 top-of-the-line #3020 which featured four wheel pilot or pony trucks at each end. This gave them a 4-4-4 wheel configuration. To compliment the #3020 electric profile locomotive, Ameri-

Fig. 7-3. Box cab.

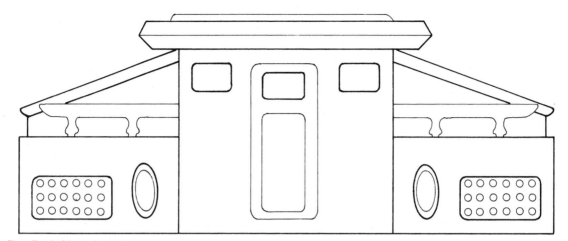

Fig. 7–4. Steeple cab.

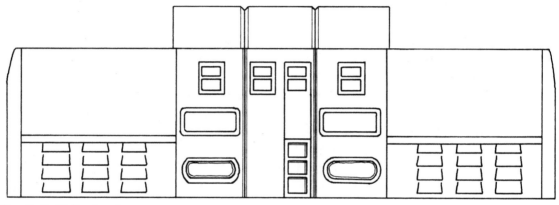

Fig. 7–5. St. Paul cab.

can Flyer released a series of 9½-inch long passenger cars consisting of a Pullman, Mail and Observation cars #3003, #3002, and #3004 in the 1922 Flyer catalog. They are known as the Illini and Columbia Series. Columbia was lithographed in Tuscan red or brown sides, and the Illini was lithographed in shades of green. These were beautiful cars when used in conjunction with the #3020. Early cars of this series

carried a latch type coupler found on the #3020, but later examples had variations of the slot and tab. Air tanks can be found on the frames, but later versions had the tanks removed. All rolled on two sets of four wheel trucks.

Fig. 7–6. Flyer's top-of-the-line O Gauge #3020 was issued from 1922–25. It featured a unique latch-type coupling system. Photo from the Collection of Don Speidel

Fig. 7–7. The #3020 was the lead piece for the Illini Set which consisted of a series of coaches with green body shells and air tanks under the frames. The latch-type coupler was uni-directional as can be seen in this photograph. Photo from the Collection of Don Speidel

The distinctive feature on these electrics was the overhead pantograph which was purely decorative. Some models such as the #1093 had a single pantograph with a non-working bell mounted at the opposite side. Some examples such as the #1096C had pantographs and non-working headlights cast as single units mounted at each end, whereas others had working headlights as individual pieces such as model #3116. The locomotives nearly always carried identifying numbers

Fig. 7–8. The set box from the O Gauge Illini Set is nearly as collectible as the train set itself. The cover design was used in much of American Flyer's advertising. Photo from the Collection of Don Speidel

rubber-stamped, lithographed, or on plates mounted on the sides of the body shell.

Coupling was accomplished using tab and slot couplers except for the #3020. The most common methods of reversing were manual and track activated automatics which tripped a reversing lever extending from the frame of the locomotive. Remote reversing also was employed, however many of the less expensive or simple models had no reversing capabilities.

Steam locomotives got a big boost in 1931. New body shells were designed for receiving the electric motor power units. The old method of reworking clockwork bodies took a back seat to the new designs. A new wheel configuration featuring a two wheel pilot truck was added in this same year. These were the first Flyer steamers with other than the 0–4–0 configuration. Electric contact was made by means of the roller pickups. The eight wheel Vanderbilt tender was previewed in 1931.

From 1931 through 1939, the majority of the steamers were very similar in design, with minor variations in boilers, cabs, and the presence or absence of such items as copper fittings, valve gear, and wheel arrangements. Flyer's #3302 locomotive came off the drawing board in 1931 and featured many ideas that were used in future steam locomotives. Sporting a 2–4–2 wheel configuration, it possessed a manual and remote control reversing device, cast valve gear, drivers, and a glowing red light in the firebox. Some models carried a ringing bell.

Electrical pickups varied during this nine year period. Roller types first were used and replaced with sliding shoe and

Fig. 7-9. Trimmed in copper, this O Gauge steamer is typical of the 1930s American Flyer electric locomotives.

sliding pickups. Some models featured several different pickups during their life span. The 2-4-2 configuration became the standard until the Depression when the company went back to the 0-4-0 arrangement on the cheaper models.

One of American Flyer's most beautiful steamers was released in 1936. Cataloged as #1681, the Hudson was their first six wheel driver locomotive. It featured a one piece die-cast boiler and separate cast fittings. The Hudson carried a remote whistle in the tender. The wheel configuration was 2-6-2, but the trailing truck appeared to carry two axles. This false truck

was quite realistic in appearance. A more realistic tender was added to the locomotive the following year. The Hudson #1681 lasted until 1939 when it became #449.

Sheet metal was used to construct the streamlined 0-4-2 "Torpedo" in 1936. The following year the locomotive was #1686, was wheeled 2-4-4, and was painted a gun metal color. It also had a remote reversing unit. Variations exist in this streamliner including the #43226 which had cut-out skirts over the driving wheels. Several eight wheel box type tenders trailed behind the Torpedo.

A single unit locomotive-tender cast in aluminum was modeled after the Burlington streamlined Hudson in 1936. This curious locomotive carried four driving wheels and a four-wheel truck on the tender section. It is one of the most desirable Flyer O Gauge locomotives.

1938 was a banner year in locomotive design and execution. The 0-6-0 die cast switcher with remote reversing which wore #429 under the cab window was in-

Fig. 7-10. Flyer's 1936 O Gauge #1771RW Set was headed by the #1681 2-6-4 Hudson locomotive and featured green enameled passenger cars with "American Flyer Lines" lettering. Photo Courtesy of Christie's

troduced. It was actually cataloged as #431, one of the interesting inconsistencies found in American Flyer trains. The 2–4–4 and 2–6–4 die-cast #424 and #427 were introduced in that year and the following year. However, the #4622–4 Atlantic 4–4–2 and the #4622–6 Pacific 4–6–2 die-cast locomotives came with fairly complex valve gear and driving rod combinations. Both of these later examples came with cast aluminum tenders.

During the years following the Depression, many locomotives were manufactured which were not numbered or cataloged. Some were cast, while others were produced from sheet metal. Power was supplied from electricity or a clockwork mechanism. The majority were rather unspectacular.

The major toy manufacturers issued low priced toy train sets from time to time. American Flyer was no exception. The Hummer Line was first marketed in 1916 and continued for about ten years. The Hummer name appeared on many of the passenger cars which were headed by simple 0–4–0 sheet metal clockwork locomotives. One die cast version was issued about 1925. The tenders were simple little sheet metal cars. Passenger coaches were equally simple four wheel lithographed pieces, some without floors. These had wheel-axle combinations attached to journal projections from the lithographed sides. Coupling was by means of a hook and eye unidirectional system. Later passenger coaches had road names replacing the Hummer name. A few basic freight cars were issued including a gondola, box,

stock, and caboose. These continued in production until 1935 with a slot and tab coupler.

Flyer's rolling stock underwent the same type of evolution that the locomotives saw. Starting from the simple and unpretentious, the rolling stock became quite sophisticated in design. These pieces are highly collectible including the rather crude early pieces.

Passenger coaches were first seen about 1907 and are known as the "Chicago" coaches by collectors because of the Chicago imprint emblazoned above the windows. Lithographed on tin bodies, the majority rolled on two sets of two wheel axles. One 1910 set rolled on two sets of four wheel trucks. The bodies were squat and square and were joined by means of riveted or sliding hook and tab couplers. Later examples were printed with American Flyer or Pullman over the windows. This series was manufactured until 1913, and only a few cars carried numbers.

Freight cars first were released about 1910 and measured about 5 inches long. Though this set has not surfaced as of this date, Ward Kimball, in the *Greenberg's Guide to American Flyer Pre-War O Gauge* lists a wrecking car, log, box, coal, and tanker as units in the set. The 1914 catalog featured a series of 5½-inch long freights which included a log, tanker, coal, box, and caboose. Some of these pieces were manufactured by Karl Bub, Bing, and other German firms for Flyer until World War I. Many variations exist. The cars were basically four-wheel examples of lithographed tin, though the log car carried wooden stakes. A later series included a box, gondola, caboose, stock, and tanker in revised designs. This series was available through 1935, though not all of the pieces were produced during this time. These were much more diverse than the earlier freights and were somewhat longer.

The Chicago passenger coaches were replaced by the #1107, #1108, and #1120 Series in 1914. They bore these numbers on the lithographed bodies. All were four wheel examples. A baggage, coach, and observation were the basic cars, but this is too simplified. In actuality, a tremendous number of lithographed paint jobs were applied until the end of the series in 1934. Kimball states that at least 160 varieties exist. Several frame styles, roof treatments, and riveted or sliding tab and slot couplers were utilized. These combinations and interesting paint jobs make this series very collectible.

A series of 6½-inch long passenger cars was introduced in 1910. Four and eight wheel trucks were used and the bodies were manufactured in litho finishes with a few examples receiving enamel painted surfaces about 1935. Coupling consisted of a series of tab and slot mechanisms. Characteristically, most of the roofs featured simulated air ventilators. The first 6½-inch series was lithographed with "American Flyer" over the coach windows and "Chicago" below. The bodies were mounted on four-wheel trucks though four-wheelers were constructed for mail order company sets. Parlor and baggage cars carrying the #1106 and #1105 respectively were released in 1914, and one litho version

Fig. 7–11. This 6½-inch O Gauge passenger car is especially desirable because of its well-preserved lithography including the Union Pacific logo and the two sets of four-wheel trucks. Photo Courtesy of Joy Luke Auctions

carried the "Canadian National Railway" logos.

The following year an interesting design was added to the lithography. It was called the winged engine or loco logo. Wings protruded from each side of an oncoming locomotive. This logo was found on the side of the cars and helps date these examples. It was used on both four-wheel and eight-wheel examples by 1917. Two

Fig. 7–12. The winged locomotive herald on this c1920 passenger car is seen on many O Gauge pieces of Flyer rolling stock made during this period. The frame is an early type and shows itself as a separate unit from the coach shell. Photo from the Collection of John Ezzo

years later, the lightning bolt emblem was introduced. The lithographed bolts were placed at the top corners of the cars, in addition to the company logos, or in separate circular logos below the coach windows. They appear on the #1200 Series of baggage and passenger cars in eight-wheel and a few four-wheel models in a wide range of lithographed treatments.

A more rounded roof-body contour highlighted the 1925 examples of these cars, and a platform was added to the observation car. Lighted coaches were offered, and the #1205 Baggage Car with the automatic mail bag set was part of the series. The new lithographed designs instituted in 1923 continued to show a wide variety of choices.

Several sets were released in 1927 which featured unnumbered cars including the Oriental Limited, Bluebird, and Broadway Limited. Rolling on two sets of four-wheel trucks, the cars carried the set name or were painted in matching colors. Similar four-wheel unnumbered sets also were made available.

In order to meet their competition, Flyer introduced a more realistic line of

Fig. 7–13. This set of 1923 6½-inch passenger cars is lithographed in orange and maroon and is joined by means of a T-type slot and tab coupler. Photo from the Collection of John Ezzo

freight cars beginning in 1924 which measured 9½-inches long. The first series was called the #3000 Series (because of the numbers on the rolling stock) and consisted of a log, gondola, refrigerator, box, tanker, and crane in brightly lithographed finishes with painted frames and roofs. Some examples contained brake wheels, and all rolled on two sets of four-wheel trucks. Coupling was accomplished using manual tab and T-slot couplers. This series ran through 1927 and was replaced by the #3200 Series.

The #3200 Series was composed of a wrecker, dump car, log, searchlight, gondola, box, tanker, Borden's milk car, machinery (log car without the load), and caboose. What differentiates this 9½-inch series is that the parts were enameled as opposed to lithographed and had brass identification plates on the car sides. Roofs on the appropriate cars were ribbed. A great number of variations in colors and accessories such as brakewheels, ladders, steps, etc. existed. The series rolled on four different types of four-wheel trucks which were more prototypical than previous examples. Coupling was accomplished through a variety of methods. Plain slot and tab, sheet metal knuckle, a few link and pin, or link automatic couplers were used. The link was to be the standard coupling mechanism on Flyer's S Gauge examples. A special track segment was necessary to activate the uncoupling action.

This series ran through 1938 when it was replaced by the #400 series of 9½-inch pieces. Though the cars were essentially the same as the #3200 Series, except for paint treatments and decals, the major difference was that the #400s were fitted with the link couplers. The series lasted until 1940.

A new series of sleeker, lower profile passenger cars came off the drawing board in 1930 and was produced until 1939. It was known as the #3100 Series and contained a baggage, Pullman and observation. The #3100 Series was manufactured in 6½-inch long cars on four- and eight-wheel versions, and 8¼-inches long examples which rolled on eight wheels. The bodies were painted sheet metal with brass trim such as doors, window inserts, and steps. Decals, brass plates, and rubber-stamped logos and numbers were used from time to time. Both lighted and unlighted coaches were fabricated, and tab and slot couplers were riveted in place.

The #3180, #3280, and #3380 passengers were introduced in 1928. The main differentiation was in the car lengths. The #3180 measured 8½-inches, #3280 ran 9½-inches, and the #3380 a full 11-inches long. All featured enameled bodies with brass plates and trim, roller pickups for lighting, and slot and tab couplers. Each of the series was composed of a combine, Pullman and observation. The 9½-inch cars were enameled in blue-green and carried brass plates with the "JEFFERSONIAN" or "GOLDEN STATES" plate over the windows. Decals were used at later dates. The beautiful 11-inch cars were painted in dark red with darker red roofs. The plates had the "AMBASSADOR" name which was later replaced by decals. Since these later cars were so long, larger four-wheel trucks were placed on the undercarriages.

American Flyer's response to the streamlined era of the 1930s was the introduction of a cast aluminum Burlington Zephyr Set. Consisting of a #9910 Power Car, #9911 Combine, and #9912 Observation, it was designed to compete with Lionel's series of streamliners. The cast Zephyr appeared in 1934 and was in service until 1938. Though the power car simulated the prototype, the combine and observation differed from the originals. The cars had individual trucks and swiveling vestibules. Interiors were lighted, and electrical continuity was maintained through roller pickups. A coach was added to the set in 1935; the Silver Streak Zephyr featured a larger Power Car, #9914, to house a larger motor for the remote reversing sequence which also was born in that year. A whistle was added the following year which was activated by a fourth rail segment. Two coaches were added to the sets at later dates.

A less expensive lithographed version of the Zephyr was cataloged in 1935. The #562 Power Car could be purchased with an electric or clockwork motor which pulled a #564 Coach and Observation. This sheet metal set featured a manual reverse. Some of the units were lighted, while others were not. The power car moved on four-wheel drivers, and the observation car carried two sets of four-wheel trucks. The cars were articulated and connected by a locking pin device. Each car rested on the section behind it for support, and the observation car was needed to keep the pieces upright. The paint scheme was a distinctive silver with black trim.

The streamlined blue and silver Comet was issued in the same year and was similar to the lithographed Zephyr. The power car was set on two trucks, and each of the articulated pin locked cars was set on a single truck and rested on the car behind it.

The Union Pacific City of Denver was modeled by American Flyer from 1936 to 1939. Headed by the #1684 cast Power Car and featuring the same articulation as the Zephyr, it pulled two #1636 Coaches and a #1632 Observation fabricated from sheet metal. The unit carried a remote reverse and featured a whistle the first year of production, but this was later dropped. The power car rolled on forward power wheels and contained a four-wheel trailing truck, whereas the rolling stock was set on two sets of four-wheel trucks. This handsome set was painted in a striking yellow with brown roofs.

Flyer's version of the popular Hiawatha first appeared in 1936 and was a stunning set. The locomotive #1683 was a die cast piece and could be purchased with the tender separately or as part of a set. The loco moved on four-wheel pilot trucks, two of which were movable and a two-wheel, four-section false trailing truck. Painted in

orange and grey with a black roof, this engine headed the #1641 lighted Coach and #1642 Observation painted in orange and grey with maroon striping. The cars were articulated, and a whistle was mounted in the tender.

As with the Zephyr, a less expensive sheet metal version of the Hiawatha also was marketed by American Flyer. Both electric and clockwork motors were produced with the electrics modeled with several variations. The sheet metal rendition was smaller and could be purchased with a passenger or freight consist. A streamlined tender was mated for the less expensive version only. The locomotive was colored orange and black with red trim, whereas the passenger cars were orange and red with grey roofs and rolled on a single pair of wheels. Coupling was accomplished by means of a close fitting eyelet system.

The Champion Sets were cataloged in 1935. All were lithographed in dark orange and silver with American Flyer markings and were headed by 11-inch steamers. The New York Central was pulled by an electric locomotive and tender and consisted of a coach and observation, whereas the Streamline Set was clockwork powered

Fig. 7-14. Flyer's most impressive O Gauge streamliner was the #1683 Hiawatha which featured a die-cast locomotive and sheet metal tender. It made its debut in 1936. Photo from the collection of Don Speidel

Fig. 7-15. The Hiawatha observation car was painted in yellow-gold, maroon, and grey and terminated in a "beaver tail" shaped end. Photo from the Collection of Don Speidel

and pulled two coaches and an observation. An extra coach was added to the electrically operated Minne-Ha-Ha Set.

From 1936 through 1940, a series of beautifully crafted streamlined coaches and observations were manufactured for the Union Pacific and deluxe Hiawatha Sets. The sheet metal cars were lighted and rolled on either four- or six-wheel trucks. They mated well with the die-cast Hudson steam locomotive.

The second significant period in American Flyer's history was ushered in with the purchase of the company by A.C. Gilbert. Alfred Carlton Gilbert was a well-known name in the world of toys. He began manufacturing magic equipment as the Mystic Manufacturing Company. The success of the company led to the formation of the A.C. Gilbert Company in 1916. The invention of the Erector Set in 1912 propelled the Gilbert name into national prominence. The Erector Set became one of the most popular toys in the world. Marketing was Gilbert's strong suit. Gilbert purchased the American Flyer Company in 1938 and moved it to the company's headquarters in New Haven, Ct. Rather than reworking the existing American Flyer stock, which had stagnated, he introduced a completely new line of O Gauge based on $\frac{3}{16}$-inch scale dimensions. This changeover was the beginning of the Gilbert era at American Flyer.

Gilbert's successful marketing techniques included store displays and the Gilbert Hall of Science in strategic cities. It helped account for the success of the company under his hand. Even after the purchase of the company by Gilbert, Coleman maintained service shops for repair of Flyer trains for a period of time.

The $\frac{3}{16}$-inch scale O Gauge line was the forerunner of the post-war two-rail S

Fig. 7–16. The wheels on the freight and passenger cars are close to the center of each piece of rolling stock giving them a somewhat clumsy appearance. The middle shelf contains a streamline Minne-Ha-Ha Set dating about 1935. Photo Courtesy of Christie's

Gauge system. The locomotives were die-cast as well as some of the freight and passenger cars, though the majority of the pieces of rolling stock were fabricated from sheet metal. More attention to detail was the hallmark of this O Gauge line.

Locomotives were all of the steamer variety, and several models were issued in kit form. Finished kit locomotives tend to be less desirable to collectors as usually they lack the better finish associated with the factory models. Unassembled kits are very difficult to come by. Some of the steamers carried a choo-choo mechanism. Reversing was accomplished either sequentially with a steady current or remotely with a small spurt of direct current into the alternating current of the track for activation. Locomotives featured one or the other system at one time or another. The worm drive motor was the more desirable as it produced smoother operation, though some models used the conventional side spur gear mechanism. Coupling involved the link type automatic coupler manufactured in metal.

Major steamer styles included the cataloged #531 Hudson J3 4-6-4, #533 Northern 4-8-4, #545 Atlantic type with a K5 boiler 4-4-2, #559 Pacific K5 4-6-2, #565 Atlantic 4-4-2, #574 Switcher 0-8-0, #553 streamlined Atlantic 4-4-2, and the popular #556 streamlined Royal Blue 4-6-2. Variations occurred in these basic locomotive units. Tenders were both sheet metal and die-cast and rolled on a variety of trucks including both eight-and twelve-wheel arrangements.

Rolling stock was designed in 1938 to be released in 1939. These #500 Series cars were die-cast and included a gondola, box, hopper, stock, tanker, wrecker, caboose, passenger combines, and pullman cars. They were released in ready-to-run or kit form and were joined by the link coupler system. In 1940 and 41, the #400 Series sheet metal rolling stock was manufactured with the freight rolling on four-wheel trucks and passengers that carried four- or six-wheel trucks. The passenger examples included a baggage and coach for the Royal Blue as well as a coach, pullman, observa-

Fig. 7-17. A.C. Gilbert's acquisition of American Flyer brought new life to the company. This die-cast 1940s set was the forerunner of their post-war $\frac{3}{16}$-inch scale products. The scale-like detail is evident in comparison to Coleman's American Flyer products. Photo Courtesy of Christie's

Fig. 7-18. The link coupler was introduced prior to World War II and was the dominant coupling system on the post-war S Gauge trains until the introduction of the knuckle coupler.

tion, and baggage car (some of which featured the automatic mail pick-up accessory).

Sheet metal $\frac{3}{16}$-inch freights were released including a searchlight, hopper, flatcar with a girder, log, wrecker crane, tanker, box, gondola, caboose, and two automatic cars. The automatics were the coal dumper and the unloading platform car.

Wide Gauge

Flyer's step into the large Wide Gauge probably was due to Lionel's success in Standard Gauge as well as Ives and Dorfans release of Wide Gauge material. American Flyer Wide Gauge first appeared in 1925 and lasted until 1936. In its maiden year, the line was advertised heavily in the periodicals of the day with an emphasis on its size and heft. Compatible with Standard Gauge and other Wide Gauge train systems (except for couplers), Flyer devoted much of its attention during this period to producing some of the finest quality tinplate trains manufactured by American companies.

All of Flyer's locomotives were electrically powered and were either the electric profile types or steamers which appeared four years after the introduction of the first Wide Gauge train. The Electric profiles tended to fall into two basic outlines, the box shape (actually rectangular),

and the St. Paul profile which was like the O Gauge version. The box profiles were modeled after the New York Central prototypes, and a smaller version was modeled after the New Haven.

Fig. 7-19. A 1926 advertisement in the popular "Child's Life" magazine illustrates Flyer's first President's Special. Reprinted with the Permission of Lionel Trains, Inc.

96

The electric profiles were fabricated from sheet metal with painted enamel finishes. Brass trim was used fairly extensively including ladders, journal boxes, and window frames. All rolled on 0-4-0 configurations with the exception of three models which were top-of-the-line 4-4-4s. The electrics contained one or two nonoperating pantographs and one or two headlights, depending on the model. Several featured a ringing bell mechanism. Number plates of brass were used for identification and were located on the side of the body shell. In all, 21 electric profile models were produced.

Reversing was standard on these pieces. Manual reversing usually was found on lower priced pieces and was activated by means of a lever protruding through the body shell. Remote reversing and automatic track reversing were incorporated in the other models.

An inverted T-type semiautomatic coupler was located at each end of the locomotive. The female section of the coupler was a spring loaded scissors-type receptacle which received the male T. This type of coupling was unidirectional. The T could only mate with the scissors section, and each piece of rolling stock contained a male coupler at one end and a female at the other.

From this information, it can be seen that the Wide Gauge electric profiles were quite the engines. With their beautiful enameled finish, brass and nickel trim, and clean cut lines, they are very popular with collectors and when found in good condition, they tend to be quite expensive.

The first electric profile wore the #4000 plates. It was a New York Central prototype and pulled a series of lithographed 14-inch passenger cars consisting of a mail and baggage, and a pullman. The #4019 carried two headlights that reversed as the direction was reversed. This engine pulled the same passenger consist as the #4000 with the addition of an observation car.

The #4039 New York Central box type electric was introduced to the public in 1926 and headed the first of the President's Special Sets. Painted in a buff color, it pulled a series of lithographed 19-inch cars consisting of a #4080 Mail and Baggage, #4081 Pullman, and a #4082 Observation in a matching buff.

Three New York Central box profiles were produced with 4-4-4 configurations. The extra sets of pilot or pony wheels were located below the forward or aft platforms and were similar in arrangement to the O Gauge #3020. The first of the 4-4-4s was #4687 and appeared in 1927. This locomotive was the lead piece in the second President's Special. The rolling stock was again 19-inch lithographed cars in blue composed of the #4090 Mail and Baggage,

Fig. 7-20. The box cab #4019 was one of the earliest Wide Gauge locomotives offered by American Flyer. It appeared first in 1925 and was last cataloged in 1927. Photo Courtesy of "The Antique Trader Weekly"

Fig. 7-21. Flyer's first President's Special consisted of a #4039 locomotive and three brown litho-graphed cars that rolled on four-wheel trucks. Note the T-type coupling mechanism. Photo Courtesy of Christie's

#4091 Annapolis Pullman, and a #4092 West Point Observation. These cars rolled on six-wheel trucks.

The third President's Special featured one of the most beautiful Wide Gauge loco-motives ever produced. Carrying the #4689 plates and "Commander" plates (which this locomotive is commonly known as), it was loaded with brass trim including a modeled eagle standing on a globe on the forward platform. Painted in what is called "Rolls Royce" blue with a

darker blue roof and red sand barrels at each end of the platforms (a characteristic of Flyer electric profiles), it first appeared in 1928 and was cataloged until 1934. To complement this locomotive, the #4390 Series 19-inch passenger cars were re-leased. Featuring six-wheel trucks, brass trim, three-light interiors, and brass plates identifying the pieces as President's Spe-cial cars, they were truly magnificent ex-amples of tinplate trains. The observation carried platform lighting as well as interior

Fig. 7-22. The 1928 President's Special was painted in two-tone blue and traveled on six-wheel trucks. The electric profile locomotive carried pilot and trailing trucks. Photo Courtesy of Sotheby's

lighting. To see this set in motion was a sight that one would not soon forget.

A very rare chrome-plated President's Special was cataloged in 1928. It consisted of the same pieces that comprised the Special but was plated in chrome by special order. This set is very rare and subject to reproduction because of its rarity.

The smaller, less expensive New Haven profile was introduced in 1927. The New Havens were more basic and the brass trim, one of the hallmarks of the New York Centrals and St. Pauls, was reduced greatly. The electrics were sold in named sets, mostly passenger, but a few freights also were cataloged. Names such as Eagle, Commander, and Statesman were given to passenger sets that featured matching colored locomotives and 14-inch cars. The Trailblazer Freight Set appeared in 1928 and consisted of a #4017 Sand or Gondola, and a #4011 Caboose. An uncataloged freight set carrying the Nation Wide Lines plates was headed by a #4644 New Haven and pulled a sand, automobile car, and caboose. Several uncataloged sets exist, a common feature found in American Flyer trains.

During the Depression years, some of the brass plates were replaced with decals. This was part of Flyer's austerity program that was necessary for the company to be competitive. The last Wide Gauge New Haven was cataloged in 1933.

The St. Paul electric was the last of the Wide Gauge electrics to be issued. It appeared first in 1928 and was characterized by a heavy use of brass, a bell ringing device, and remote control reversing. It was a handsome locomotive. Both freight and passenger sets were released including a large freight set consisting of a #4010 Tanker, #4018 Automobile, #4022 Machinery, #4017 Sand Car, and #4021 Caboose. The sets were named like the other electric profile sets. Passenger sets were composed of 14-inch lithographed or enameled examples. An exception was the Legionnaire Set which consisted of 19-inch President's Special Cars which rolled on four-wheel trucks. The last St. Paul cataloged set appeared in 1934, the same year that saw the demise of the President's Special.

American Flyer's steam locomotives were comparable to anything that was produced by the other major companies. Steamers were first cataloged in 1929, about four years after the introduction of the electric profiles. The late start was partly due to Flyer's use of Ives' castings appropriated during the Lionel-Ives-American Flyer ownership. This was a method of saving on tooling for the new steamers. Most of the steamers were of the 4-4-2 configuration, but the two-wheel pilot also saw service. American Flyer cataloged their steamers as locomotive and tender combinations and numbered them as such even though the locomotive and tender were cataloged with their own individual numbers. Both coal and Vanderbilt oil eight-wheel tenders were joined to the locomotives. These locomotives usually were sold as parts of named passenger or freight sets but could be purchased individually. Most sets were cataloged, but several were not.

Fig. 7-23. Many of American Flyer's Wide Gauge sets were named. The Statesman Set on the top shelf was lithographed in orange and was pulled by a box cab loco. The Pocahontas set on the lower shelf was enameled in tan and green and carried brass plates. The set was headed by a #4637 St. Paul profile electric. Photo Courtesy of Christie's

Utilizing Ives locomotive castings, the #4692 was introduced. This piece came with two types of tender plates including a Golden State pair that help identify this piece. The #4692 was used with freight sets as well as passenger sets such as the Warrior which included enameled tan and green 14-inch cars. These beautiful pieces of rolling stock consisted of a #4340 Club, #4341 Pullman, #4343 Dining, and #4692 Observation, all of which carried Pocahontas plates above the windows. The #4692 was produced with two different types of valve gear arrangements. The #4664 steamer also utilized Ives castings, but featured a manual reversing unit, and was released in 1930.

In 1931, American Flyer developed steamers utilizing their own castings. One example was cast in iron while three were cast from zinc. The cast iron example was #4670 and was available for two years with both simple and complex valve gear ar-

rangements. Brass trim included handrails and lights. Bells were incorporated to add class to these pieces.

The first zinc cast example was released in 1931 and was designated #4692. It featured a single driving rod and lasted until 1932. Whereas the cast-iron shells featured piping as part of the casting, the zinc-cast pieces utilized separate copper air lines over the boiler. The #4692X zinc model carried a triangular valve gear as did the companion #4680. The top-of-the-line steamer also was cast in zinc and was known as the "brass piper." This #4695 featured a ringing bell, double driving rods with a complex valve gear arrangement, brass stack, sand dome, handrails, and headlight cover. It derived its nickname from the series of parallel brass pipes located above the driving wheels. This magnificent locomotive headed passenger and freight sets that often were quite large (up to six freight cars). American Flyer Wide

Fig. 7-24. The Wide Gauge #4695 is called the "brass piper" because of the series of fittings above the drive wheels. The #4693 Vanderbilt tender mates well with this locomotive. Photo Courtesy of Mike Hill's Hobby Shop

Fig. 7-25. Gondola, or sand cars, were popular pieces of freight rolling stock. This Wide Gauge example is especially desirable as it contains a center brass plate stating "Over 6 Million Happy Owners" have purchased Flyer trains. It helps date this car about 1928. Photo Courtesy of "The Antique Trader Weekly"

Gauge steam locomotives truly were impressive pieces and are very desirable collector's items.

The heart of any Wide Gauge system or any gauge, as a matter of fact, is its rolling stock. Flyer's freight cars were issued in 1926, a year after the passenger cars. The first series of freights was developed from a relationship with Flyer's rival, Lionel. The car bodies were manufactured by Lionel based on their #11-#17 Freight Car Series. These enameled bodies were fitted with Flyer trucks, names, and numbers which were stamped on the bottom. The #4008 Boxcar, #4005 Stock, #4007 Sand or Gondola, and #4011 Caboose made up this series. These pieces were sold individually, rather than in sets with locomotives.

In 1927, American Flyer offered their own designed freight cars. Brass journals and number plates were characteristic of this series. By 1928, cataloged freight sets were introduced which included new paint colors and renumbered cars. A lighted caboose was added as well as a machinery car

(a modified flat car), and a tanker. A good deal of brass trim and brass plates were part of the body shells. The cataloged sets were headed by electric profile locomotives. The first cataloged steamer set called Old Ironsides was released the following year, and in 1931, a #4006 Hopper Car was added to the inventory. Modifying the machinery car was the means of introducing the new Log Car #4023 in 1934. A scored load of lumber similar to the O Gauge example was used.

Characteristically, the early body shells were riveted to the frames, but later examples were spot welded, a method of determining early or late examples. Some of the trucks flexed below the frame, while others were fixed to the frame. The full range of Wide Gauge freights included a caboose, hopper, sand, box, tanker, stock, and a flat that was modified to a machinery, and again to a log car.

During the Lionel-Ives-American Flyer interaction, Flyer provided unpainted rolling stock parts for Ives in 1928 and 1929. Body shape was dramatically

Fig. 7-26. The ladders and brake wheels on these 1933 #4000 Series Wide Gauge freights are hardly to scale, but they served the purpose of adding detail without sacrificing strength. Photo Courtesy of Christie's

similar to American Flyer's #4000 Series freights, though they carried Ives plates.

Passenger units were manufactured in 14-inch and 19-inch sizes. These passenger cars represent some of Flyer's finest workmanship. The 14-inch cars rolled on four-wheel trucks, whereas the 19-inch examples traveled on four- and six-wheel trucks, depending on the model. The trucks were both flexed and fixed examples. Roller pickups provided the electric source for the lighted interiors. Some of the interiors were painted white to enhance the lighting effect.

The 14-inch cars were the first to appear, and they were cataloged in 1925. Four series were lithographed, and three were painted. Brass trim including window frames, spring-loaded doors, plates, and air tanks were used on the top-of-the-line pieces. Some less expensive lithographed cars were cataloged for the New Haven type electrics.

Generally roofs were removable to gain access to the lighting devices. These roofs first featured simulated ventilators, but later examples were without these markings and were smooth in profile. However, as the Wide Gauge line was phased out in the late 1930s, much mixing and matching occurred in order to use up the inventory of parts. Early body shells were riveted to the frames, but later examples were spot welded. Though the early shells

Fig. 7-27. American Flyer's #4042B Wide Gauge 14-inch Observation Car carries air tanks under the frame, brass railing on the observation deck, and reflector lights. Photo Courtesy of "The Antique Trader Weekly"

were lithographed, later ones were enameled. The enameling was of high quality and included much brass trim. However, less expensive painted versions were released about 1931. For instance, a set was made which consisted of a #4331 Pullman and a #4332 Observation which lacked much of the brass trim and plates associated with the better quality enameled versions.

The 19-inch cars were produced in lithographed and painted versions. They made their debut about two years after the introduction of the 14-inchers. The body shells were riveted to the frame, and some contained metal diaphragms that joined the cars to each other to produce a streamlined effect. On-off switches were located on the floor to control the lighting on these cars. These were some of the most beautifully crafted of Flyer's rolling stock.

Body shells were provided to Ives for their passenger cars in the same way that Flyer worked with Ives to supply pieces for their freight line. Ives used their own trucks, couplers, and plates for these unique pieces.

The approach of World War II called a halt to train production, but not to ideas. Many of the post-war designs were on the drawing board before the start of the conflict.

Priced Examples: Wide Gauge

Sets

Statesman–#4684 electric loco, two #4151 Pullman, #4152 Observation, lithographed, original boxes and set box	$1,200.00
Mayflower–#4689 electric loco, four passenger cars	A–$4,750.00
President's Special–#4689 electric loco, #4390 West Point Club Car, #4391 Academy Pullman, #4393 Annapolis Dining Car, #4392 Army-Navy Observation	A–$7,500.00
President's Special–#4039 electric loco, three tan lithographed passenger cars, c1926	$2,000.00
The Eagle–#4644 0-4-0 locomotive, #4644 Pullman, Observation, original boxes	$550.00
The Iron Monarch–#4692X 4-4-2 steam loco, #4693 tender, two #4331 Pullman, #4332 Observation	A–$1,150.00
Pocahontas–#4637 electric loco, #4340 Club, #4341 Pullman, #4342 Observation, #4343 Dining Car, original boxes	A–$2,000.00

Locomotives

#4683 0-4-0 electric, red	$400.00
#4692 4-4-2 steam, Vanderbilt tender, original box, c1930	$775.00

Adams 4-4-2 steam loco with red plate, #4694 Vanderbilt tender, original box $725.00

Rolling Stock

#4011 Caboose, red, flex trucks	$200.00
#4017 Sand Car, "8 Million" plate, rigid truck	$70.00
#4018 Boxcar, "8 Million" plate	$140.00
#4020 Stock, "6 Million" plate, flex truck	$225.00
#4023 Lumber Car	$75.00
#4380 Club, #4381 Pullman, #4382 Observation, tan and green Hancock	A–$1,200.00

Accessories

#2043 Train Controlling Semaphore, original box	$370.00
#97 lithographed Station	$65.00
#2116 Bell Signal, original box	$55.00

Priced Examples: O Gauge

Locomotives

#429 scale switcher, 0-6-0, 1937	$795.00
#447 scale Hudson	$850.00
#4621 switcher, 0-6-0 with tender, 1937, like new	$795.00
#4677 steam, 2-4-2 with tender, 1937	$350.00
#4680 Hudson, 2-6-2 with tender, 1937, restored	$650.00

Rolling Stock

#3018 Tank Car, 1937	$95.00
#3019 Dump Car, 1937	$95.00
#3207 Gondola, 1937	$75.00
#3208 Boxcar, 1936, very good	$75.00
#3211 Caboose, 1936, very good	$75.00

CHAPTER 8

American Flyer in the Post-War Years

Optimism was the key word at American Flyer with the cessation of hostilities following World War II. The factory geared up for post-war production with the introduction of the full line of $\frac{3}{16}$-inch scale-like S Gauge trains which were to travel on Flyer's two rail track system. A large format catalog was released to announce their new lines. The introduction of smoke in the steam locomotives was a carefully guarded secret during its development in order to keep the competition from gaining an edge.

Die-cast steam locomotives were assigned numbers that were descriptive. The first number indicated the piece was a locomotive, the second was the locomotive type, and third indicated the presence or absence of the smoking mechanism and the choo choo sound. Thus a #312 carried choo choo and smoke, while a #311 carried only the choo choo sound, and a #310 lacked both features. This numbering system was important for determining what accessories were found on the pieces. Both

choo choo and bellows smoke puffing units were housed in the tender. This was characteristic of locomotives of this early post-war period. Brass buttons were located on the bottom of the loco to trigger trackside accessories by means of a track trip mechanism.

Rolling stock was manufactured in precolored plastic. A few were mounted on metal frames when it was found that plastic frames tended to warp. The S Gauge tanker was introduced in 1946. It began on a plastic frame, but was changed to a metal

Fig. 8–1. Called the "Challenger" by American Flyer, this die cast 4–8–4 Northern was cataloged from 1946 to 1949. The Union Pacific shield is emblazoned on the tender. The #332 states that it contains smoke and choo choo units. Photo from the Collection of Don Speidel

frame. Coupling was accomplished by means of the plastic link automatic coupler which was quite fragile.

The #720 switches or turnouts were developed. They channeled electric power to the switched area and cut power to that area when the switches were realigned with the mainline. This allowed the running of two trains on the same layout with one train shifted to a passing track and power eliminated when the switches were returned to the straight position.

Locomotive tenders carried the roadname, but in the following years, the American Flyer name was incorporated. Several freight and passenger sets were issued including the #4622 Set which consisted of a #342 locomotive pulling a freight consist and a #332 locomotive heading a passenger group. The locomotives both featured choo choo sound and smoking units. In addition to the double trains, the set included passing siding switches, double train operation, and accessories.

Direct current power was introduced about 1948 as a method of smoothing out the operation of the AC motored locomotives. Alternating current resulted in jerky starts and delays in reversing directions, whereas DC current provided realistic movement. The introduction of the #14 electronic Rectifier converted AC house current to power DC motors in the locomotives. Gilbert-American Flyer coined the term "Electronic Propulsion" for those locos, and though the principle was interesting, they did not meet with a great deal of public acceptance. Plastic rolling stock

was painted in order to increase realism, but it tended to chip and peel.

The following year, American Flyer renamed its DC units "Directronic Propulsion" with power converted by the #15 Rectifier. The DC suffix was added to the locomotive numbers to indicate the type of motor incorporated. The smoke and choo choo units were standard in all locomotives and were moved from the tender to the locomotive section.

The handsome 4–6–2 Royal Blue streamliner in $\frac{3}{16}$-inch scale O Gauge was introduced in S Gauge heading a freight unit. The link couplers were stabilized with metal inserts which was one of the identifying features of locomotives and rolling stock for 1948. The use of this metal insert prevented inadvertent uncoupling. The popular #775 Talking Station also was marketed which stopped the train in front of the station, activated a record that called out stops, and restarted the loco.

Competition with Lionel during this period was very keen, and in order to meet or beat Lionel, Gilbert-American Flyer introduced such items as the #758 Sam the Semaphore Man which was similar to Li-

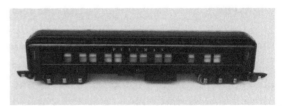

Fig. 8–2. The heavyweight coaches rolled on six-wheel trucks and were illuminated. The link couplers were the standard method of coupling, until the knuckle coupler was introduced. Photo from the Collection of Don Speidel

onel's Automatic Gateman. At the press of a button, the locomotive stopped, Sam exited from his shack, and the semaphore arm dropped. Releasing the button reversed the action and sent the engine on its way. A double tone #762 Billboard put additional realistic sound into the layout. A whistle was added to the popular Pennsylvania K–5 Pacific which was activated by a momentary flow of DC current into the track and into the whistle nestled in the tender. A new #290 Pacific 4–6–2 was introduced which included choo choo and smoke, though the numbering system did not reflect it. Cheaper freight cars also were added to the line.

To celebrate its 50th anniversary in 1950, American Flyer went all out with a variety of new and exciting products. Two handsome diesels came off the drawing board. The EMD GP–7 #370 was a workhorse. The beautiful Alco PA and PB units, #360 and #361 came to light. The Alcos were decorated in the Santa Fe red and silver Warbonnet pattern and a sleek chrome version. A realistic diesel horn was included to add to the desirability of this locomotive. Though the idea under various

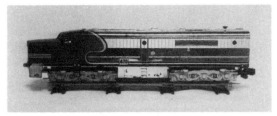

Fig. 8–3. The Alco PA was the workhorse for Flyer's post-war streamlined diesel fleet. This #470A unit carries the Santa Fe Warbonnet color scheme.

names was sound, the public reception was poor. Whistles were removed from the the standard steam locomotives and placed in the #557 Whistling Billboard. This was a sad loss. The anniversary year also saw the end of the DC rectifier after many years of coming and going. The popular Royal Blue was repainted a darker color and pulled a new series of freight cars. Automatic cars included a dump car and an operating boxcar, as well as a series of work train cars. An operating stock yard #771 was introduced.

One of the rarest Gilbert-American Flyer sets was marketed in this anniversary year. The Circus Set consisted of a red streamliner #353 which pulled two flat cars with cages and a circus Pullman-type car. Packed in the train box were cut outs of circus items including the tent and even entrance tickets. Very few of the accessories have survived, though they are being reproduced by Greenberg Publishing. A similar farm set was headed by a #300AC Atlantic with four freight cars and cutout farm pieces. These are also quite difficult to find.

Realistic locomotive sounds were important to the toy train manufacturers, and in order for Gilbert-American Flyer to compete, more accurate sounds were necessary. The electronic air chime whistle was introduced in 1951 and was added to the #295 Pacific, #325AC Hudson, and the Santa Fe diesels.

The automatic knuckle coupler was introduced the following year, but was limited to a few sets. The link coupler continued to be the most common method of

Fig. 8–4. This 1951 advertisement heralds Flyer's Union Pacific freight and its Santa Fe AB streamliner with two motors. In addition, a coupon at the bottom of the ad offers the latest catalog for only a dime. Reprinted with the Permission of Lionel Trains, Inc.

packaged with #660, #661, and #662 vacuum chrome-plated plastic passenger cars.

About this same time, the #17B and #19B transformers were cataloged. Featuring a ''dead man's'' throttle which automatically shut off the power when the operator's hand was removed, it simulated the controls found in the real locomotive cab. Concurrently, the company began experimenting with pressed wood frames for their

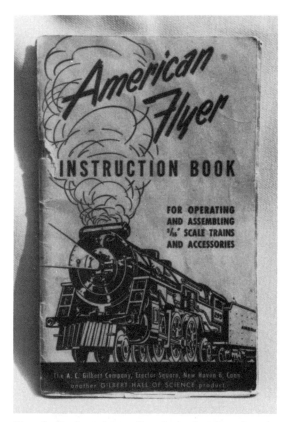

Fig. 8–5. American Flyer's instruction books were packaged with the train sets and contained such useful information as track patterns, operating tips, and maintenance techniques. Reprinted with the Permission of Lionel Trains, Inc.

coupling. The clear plastic stack placed on the #K325 was a most interesting piece of equipment. Utilizing the locomotive's headlight, the smoke was illuminated as it entered the smokestack. Plastic boilers and tender bodies began replacing the diecast pieces. Besides the lighter weight and reduced cost, Gilbert-American Flyer improved on the detail of the pieces. The #315K–5 locomotive was introduced in 1952 as well as the Silver Streak. This later locomotive was based on the Alco PA design of the earlier Santa Fe. The Streak sported the new air chime whistle and was rolling stock. These unusual bases sometimes cause confusion when they surface at train shows. The use of pressed wood in place of the metal frames was thought to be due to the shortage of materials resulting from the Korean conflict.

To answer Lionel's ''Magne-Traction,'' Gilbert-American Flyer added rubber tires to their locomotive drivers and christened it the ''Pull-Mor'' system. The rubber tires were supposed to increase traction and pulling power.

Several new diesels were introduced in 1953, the year of the diesel at Gilbert-American Flyer. The #466 blue and chrome Comet, #474-#475 green and chrome AB Rocket, and the brown and chrome #477-#478 AB Silver Flash were based on the Alco PA and PB units. A GP-7 with knuckle couplers also was introduced. The use of the air chime whistle on some locomotives resulted in a new numbering system where the final digit was changed to a ''6'' to indicate the inclusion of this sound effect.

The popularity of the Royal Blue was continued in the #356 streamlined Silver Bullet. This example featured one of the new plastic boilers and was covered in a silver finish. It was sold either with two #655 Silver Bullet passenger cars in chrome or silver, as the heading for a work train set, or to lead a freight set.

The days of the link couplers were numbered. In fact, 1954 was the last year that these popular linking devices were commercially manufactured at Gilbert-American Flyer. Locomotives that carried the knuckles received a new numbering system to indicate the presence of these units. The rolling stock was renumbered to reflect the emergence of the knuckle coupler as the dominant type of coupler. The chrome finish on the Alcos was replaced by a silver finish which was a step down in their appearance. Passenger cars received striping on the sides to match the Comet, Rocket, and Silver Flash. A two unit GP-7 was introduced which carried the Texas and Pacific herald. The power unit was #375, and the dummy which carried the diesel horn was #374. Though the power unit was introduced the previous year, the dummy combination came in 1954.

The catalog for 1955 illustrated several new and interesting pieces. True to life sound again was deemed important, and

Fig. 8-6. The complex valve gear adds to the interest on this 1953 Nickel Plate Road 0-8-0 switcher. Photo Courtesy of "The Antique Trader Weekly"

Fig. 8-7. Perishable goods were moved in the #947 Refrigerator Car. Note the knuckle couplers on this 1953 piece of rolling stock. Photo Courtesy of "The Antique Trader Weekly"

the "diesel roar" was mounted in the B units. This roar was variable and based on the amount of electricity that the unit received. A variable tone whistle was added to the #326 Hudson, #336 Northern, #346 Switcher, and the #296 New Haven Pacific, though this later engine was not cataloged officially. Another GP-7 appeared, but this example was painted in the Union Pacific colors. Variations of this diesel locomotive exist. The cataloged sets included Atlantic headed freights, Pacific freights and passenger combos, a U.P. diesel freight, Hudson freight, U.P. steam freight, and Alco passenger and freights— some with ABA units. A few passenger cars featured silhouettes in the windows; action cars included the #977 Caboose which contained a figure of a trainman who exited to the caboose platform when the train stopped and returned when the train began to roll.

In order to market rolling stock more effectively, car assortment packages were introduced. These packs contained several pieces of rolling stock in one handy package. One could select from several different packages and receive a wide variety of cars.

Automatic trackside accessories included an animated platform and passenger car that moved figures in and out of the car by means of a vibrating mechanism. The #787 Log Loader, #785 Coal Loader, and #779 Oil Drum Loader were the new "hot" pieces for the year. This last item dumped simulated oil drums by means of a cart into a waiting gondola. A most interesting set was the #784 Hump Set which simulated railroad yard work. The locomotive backs up the rolling stock, the coal car dumps its load, the hopper and action caboose are uncoupled with the hopper traveling through a switch to a siding, and the caboose continued in reverse down the mainline—a lot of action for the money.

One of the marketing techniques that A.C. Gilbert used for his products was the Gilbert Halls of Science. These buildings were located in Chicago, New York, Washington D.C., and Miami. They featured several floors of toys, science sets, and construction sets, as well as one floor usually devoted to the American Flyer line of trains. The Halls were used for displaying the new lines of trains for prospective store buyers. A trip to one of the Halls of Science was like a trip to fantasy land, not soon to be forgotten.

One of the company's most beautiful locomotives was introduced in 1956. The #499 Electric carrying the New Haven logo and colors featured pantographs that could bring electric power from a catenary system as well as receive power from the conventional track source. In the same year, the #355 Baldwin switching diesel was introduced. This piece saw service for the next five years. Several of the Alcos received new colors and logos, including the New Haven and Northern Pacific ABA units, as well as new markings for the Santa Fe ABA. A few steam locomotives included the #289 which carried the Chicago and North Western markings, and the #308 Reading which featured a 4-4-2 wheel configuration.

Rolling stock was reworked to produce such items as the #956 Piggyback Carrier that hauled truck beds, the operating #970 Walking Brakeman Car, and #973 illuminated and operating Milk Can Car. Several boxcars received new logos which included the State of Maine, Missouri Pacific Eagle, New Haven, and Central of Georgia examples. The huge set #5685Rh was issued which was comprised of Union Pacific ABA units and five passenger cars, two of which were the popular Vista Domes. A series of passenger cars #900, #901, #902, and #903 consisting of a combine, coach, Vista Dome, and observation were manufactured in Northern Pacific colors. These examples are fetching about $100 each in mint condition at train shows today.

The next two years saw a major change in the Gilbert-American Flyer numbering system. A new system was devised to maintain control of inventory and the placement of pieces. The three digit system was replaced by a five digit system with the first two numbers designating the item. A few examples include #20 for sets, #21 for locomotives, #23 for accessories, #24 for rolling stock, and #25 for operating rolling stock. An example can be seen in the rolling stock where #240 was used for boxcars and #243 for tankers. The last two digits determined the type of packaging. Though the system was instituted in 1957, the rolling stock, according to the *American Flyer Market Price Guide*, did not receive this new numbering system until the following year. Even then, some rolling stock was available with the old three digit numbers in place. This five digit system helps date

specific pieces as to pre-1957-58 or 1957-58 and later.

During this period, several new steam locomotives were introduced including the 0-6-0 Pennsylvania Yard Goat with a sloping tender, and the #21155 Docksider 0-6-0 that featured smoke, choo choo, and couplers on the front and back like the prototypes. New color schemes were added to the diesel fleet as well as new road logos and several pieces of rolling stock. A two position reversing unit was standard on most locomotives. The pride of the line was the Missouri Pacific Eagle passenger set with #21920 and #21920-1 AA units. The passenger coaches were colored in blue and silver with yellow stripes. The powered A unit featured double motors. A freight set was also available with this AA unit.

Another interesting set was the huge #20460 Yard King special freight set. This set included thirteen freight cars and a figure ''8'' track set. The set was so long that the locomotive barely cleared the caboose as it traversed the figure ''8'' layout.

Fig. 8-8. The body shell is formed from plastic on this #21813 Minneapolis and St. Louis-Peoria Gateway Baldwin diesel. Knuckle couplers are located on the front and rear. The five digit numbering system dates the loco about 1958. Photo from the Collection of Don Speidel

Nonoperating knuckle couplers were used on the new freight cars. These cars carried a "0" as the last digit to indicate this type of coupling mechanism. As an example, the #24610 Caboose carried the nonoperating knuckles. Along these lines, Flyer introduced the #969 Rocket Launching Car featuring a remote control launching unit. Bay window cabooses (models with windows extending from the sides rather than from the top cupola) also were part of this period.

The Station and Baggage Smasher #23789 was one of the interesting accessories that was marketed during this time as well as the #23796 Sawmill which simulated the action of cutting logs into wood boards and then dumping them into a waiting car. The sophisticated railroader would probably be amused by the #23791 Cow on the Track accessory. A model of a cow crossed to the track stopping the train. When the cow returned to the trackside, the locomotive continued its journey.

Another Golden Anniversary was celebrated in 1959. It was the 50th anniversary of the A.C. Gilbert Company. The anniversary year saw a decrease in the number of cataloged sets to nine. Heading the list was the #20550 Frontiersman Set consisting of an old time style Franklin 4–4–0 steamer, tender, and two passenger coaches painted in yellow with black roofs. An Overland Express Car was given as a bonus when the set was purchased. Variations occur in these passenger cars. The Pony Express Set was headed by a Union Pacific yellow and grey Alco AA unit with a double motor in the power unit and a bell in the dummy which pulled four matching streamlined coaches.

Another interesting set was called the Defender which consisted of a Chesapeake and Ohio GP-7 and pulled a Navy jeep transport, a new U.S. Marine Corp two car rocket launcher, and a new detonator box car. The last two were action cars. The New Haven electric was finally tied to a passenger set.

Anniversary rolling stock was highlighted by several interesting single domed tankers. Deep Rock, Baker's Chocolate, and Hooker Chemical were a few of the road logos and colors that were added to the lines. Watching a string of these colorful tankers moving around the layout was quite a sight.

The 1960s was a period of change and eventual decline at American Flyer. Strong competition from "cheaper" trains, slot racing sets, and a general interest in new lines of toys resulted in a deep decline in sales of such backbone items as the Gilbert Chemistry sets, Erector Sets, and of course toy trains. To meet this challenge, Gilbert-American Flyer began to substitute and, in effect, cheapen their lines. Generally, double motors were replaced with single motor units, plastic drivers with metal hubs replaced all metal drivers, and the number of cataloged sets declined. There was a decrease in the number of remote control action by demand accessories, and new track tripped action cars were introduced. The nonoperating plastic coupler was introduced in 1960. Locomotives and rolling stock were manufactured as single units, and much of the detail was curtailed. The "toy" train first appeared in 1961. Modeled after the GM F9, this AA unit was basically a plastic shell with the trucks attached to the shell rather than a separate chassis.

It was during this period that Gilbert-American Flyer manufactured sets for the discount stores. Some of these inexpensive sets are now quite valuable. An example is the set manufactured for the White's Stores. The Boxcar #C-1001 sells for several hundred dollars in good condition. Promotional items such as the #24067 Keystone Camera Boxcar and #24068 Planter's Peanuts Boxcar are highly sought after by collectors even though they were manufactured in 1960-61.

Pikemaster track made its first appearance in 1961. Though still S Gauge between the rails, it differed from the conventional track in that plastic, closely spaced ties were used in its construction in order to improve its appearance. The radius of the curve was decreased, and this made it difficult for early locomotives to navigate the tracks. Pikemaster became the standard track packed in sets from this time forward.

A few new locomotives were introduced during the 1960s including the Casey Jones type steamer which appeared in a deluxe model with smoke, choo choo, and conventional driving rods, and a plain version which lacked these features. Emphasis was placed on rolling stock which was a more expedient and inexpensive way of adding interest to each years' products.

By 1962, only six cataloged sets were available, though as was Gilbert-American Flyer's practice, uncataloged sets contin-

ued to be produced. The die-cast Hudson locomotive was reintroduced, but with modifications that tended to cheapen the piece. The following year, Gilbert-American Flyer marketed the #20768 Smokey Mountain Set and the Klondike Set which used the plastic GM F9's in the Great Northern motif. An interesting item was the Game Train Set #20800. Headed by a #L2001 locomotive and tender, it pulled a gondola and caboose. It included a gameboard with playing pieces.

The "All Aboard" series was the last major effort by Gilbert-American Flyer to keep its head above water. Three different sets were manufactured in 1965 with the major feature being the inclusion of panels that contained Pikemaster track and switches as well as scenery. An example was the Champion #800 Set which consisted of the Pennsylvania 4-4-2 locomotive, Hooker Chemical Tanker, Monon Gondola, Santa Fe Hopper, and a caboose.

Fig. 8-9. Many of Flyer's HO Gauge locomotives were not numbered. This 4-6-4 Hudson is an example of their post-war HO locomotives. Photo Courtesy of the "The Antique Trader Weekly"

These did not sell well, and in 1966 one new system was added. This was to be the last full year of production for the company. It folded the following year. After a few attempts at reorganization which also proved unsuccessful, the dies and inventory were sold to Lionel, Flyer's long time competitor, in 1967 under the Fundimensions branch of General Mills.

For collectors of American Flyer S Gauge, 1979 was a banner year. It was then that the first new S Gauge pieces were manufactured and marketed. They consisted of three freight cars with the same die-cast trucks, knuckle couplers, and paint jobs that collectors associate with the best of Gilbert-American Flyer. Since that date, several locomotives and rolling stock examples in freight and passenger models and sets have been issued.

In an interview with Richard A. Kughn, the new owner of Lionel Corporation, in a recent issue of *S Gaugian* magazine, Kughn felt that future releases of S Gauge Gilbert-American Flyer were dependent on how well Flyer carried its own weight in the Lionel-American Flyer production plans.

Very little attention has been paid to Gilbert-American Flyer HO Gauge examples. This facet has been overlooked but interest appears to be on the rise. Gilbert's introduction of this gauge occurred in 1938 with all metal examples called HO Tru Model. They were displayed prominently in the 1938 catalog, but the buying public's lack of interest resulted in their being placed in the back part of the 1939 catalog. They were to lay dormant until they resurfaced in 1947, but again they did not make much of an impression on the toy train enthusiast.

Following World War II, both metal and plastic examples were manufactured. Gilbert often used other toy manufacturers to produce trains and accessories that were overstamped with the Gilbert-American Flyer name. Ideal, Athearn, and Japanese manufacturers were involved with this HO line at one time or another. In order to compete in the discount store and catalog market, this practice of having other manufacturers produce items that were repackaged or overstamped was a fairly common practice. The last HO Gauge sets were cataloged in 1963. David Garrigues, noted authority on HO Gauge believes that these trains deserve further examination and consideration by the collector. A well researched book could influence the collectibilty of these examples. Perhaps one is on the horizon.

Priced Examples: S Gauge

Sets

#88 Franklin steam loco, tender, two #20 Passenger Coaches, #30
Baggage Car, #40 Observation $160.00

#21085 steam loco, 4–6–2, tender, #633 Boxcar, #24558 Flat Car, #925 Tanker, #24603 Caboose, c1960	A–$50.00
#307 steam loco, 4–4–2, tender, #24057 Boxcar, #921 Gondola, #625G Tanker, #24324 Tanker, #630 Caboose	A–$60.00
#301 steam loco, 4–4–2, tender, #632 Boxcar, #631 Gondola, #24310 Tanker, #42597 Log Car, #630 Caboose	$50.00
Diesel engine The Comet, #960 Columbus Pullman, #962 Hamilton Vista Dome, #963 Washington Observation	$250.00
#325AC steam loco, 4–6–4, tender, #637 Boxcar, #24103 Gondola, #629 Cattle Car, #638 Caboose	$130.00
#295 steam loco, tender, #637 Boxcar, #640 Hopper, #734 Boxcar, #910 Tanker, #638 Caboose	$440.00
#360 diesel A unit, #364 B unit, Santa Fe, #502 Vista Dome, #660 Baggage Car, #661 Pullman, #631 Observation	$575.00

Locomotives

#312 steam, 4–6–2 with tender	$80.00
#336 steam, 4–8–4 Union Pacific Northern with knuckle couplers, with tender	$350.00
#342 steam, 0–8–0 with tender	$25.00
#346 steam, 0–8–0 with tender	$28.00
#350 "The Royal Blue" with tender	$60.00
#370 diesel GP–7	A–$140.00
#21801 "Baldwin 400" diesel	$175.00

Rolling Stock

#228 Tanker	$10.00
#934 Floodlight Car	$10.00
#24569 Industrial Crane	$12.00
#311267 Hopper	$12.00

Accessories

#18B Transformer	$13.00
#561 Billboard with diesel horn	A–$20.00

CHAPTER 9

"Ives Toys Make Happy Boys"

Known as the "grandfather of the toy train industry," Edward R. Ives founded the Ives Company in 1868 in Plymouth, Connecticut to manufacture toys. After two years, the firm moved to Bridgeport and continued producing floor-running tin locomotives in brightly colored painted metal. By 1874, Ives was making his famous tin windup or clockwork trains plus a wide variety of other toys, mostly in cast iron. His firm changed names several times due to various partnerships. Edward Ives was a major supplier of mechanical toys and cast iron trains to the American market.

Clockwork mechanisms consisted of a combination of wheels, springs, gears, and other mechanical movements in a complex arrangement. This mechanism combined power with length of running time. Some clockwork or windup trains were able to run up to an hour on a single windup. Though Ives specialized in clockwork trains that ran on the floor, he also distrib-

uted toy trains made by Eugene Beggs of Paterson, New Jersey that were steam powered and ran on tracks. These were similar in power and mode of operation to real steam trains.

A major fire at the Ives factory in Bridgeport not only destroyed the facility, but virtually ended the mechanical toy industry in this country. The American market was swamped by German imports. With the insurance money, Ives and his son Harry decided to rebuild the factory and concentrate on manufacturing clockwork trains that ran on sectional tinplate tracks in O Gauge measurements. Ives made a commitment to develop a complete railroad operation called "The Ives Miniature Railway System." His catalogs illustrated engines, rolling stock, track configurations, and a wide variety of accessories. Catalogs were included in every set sold regardless of size. Ives was the first manufacturer in America to make clockwork trains to run on tracks. The Germans had been making them since the 1890s. Since clockwork was the method of operation that Ives understood best, he continued making some floor trains for another fifteen years.

During the period from 1900–1910, American toy and train makers saw ever increasing competition and large numbers of German toy products in the American marketplace. Actually this period was dominated by the European manufacturers since they had lower labor costs and were able to market their products to an eager American market at a lesser price. The U.S. makers were influenced by the European toy makers' designs. Ives was the most serious competition for the German manufacturers since he had the new, modern factory; a good method of distribution; and gave the customer good value for money spent. His company was always concerned with the quality of its products, excellent service, factory repairs which were usually free, and his refusal to compromise or short change his youthful customers on even the least expensive sets.

Ives made a high quality product in his clockwork trains. They were exceptionally popular because boys could enjoy them on the floor, on the carpet, and both indoors and out. Since electricity was not available readily at the beginning of the Twentieth Century and many people feared it, clockwork trains were a wonderful alternative that provided tremendous play value. All a boy had to do was wind up the engine, release the brake, and off it went.

The first Ives locomotives made at the new factory were made from thin tin-plated steel or cast iron, had a 2–2–0 wheel arrangement for the cast-iron wheels, and were hand painted in black with red and gold decorations. In 1904, Ives applied the process of lithography to decorate the locos. Locos were made in O Gauge and were produced in five different sizes. Until 1906, locos were made in both stamped steel and cast iron; after that only cast iron locos were made by Ives in O Gauge. He used the 2–2–0 wheel configuration until 1912, and then four drivers were utilized. Tenders were marked "F.E.No.1" (for Fast Express) on the sides.

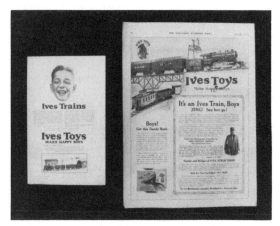

9–1. These two ads stress the "Ives Toys Make Happy Boys" theme. The emphasis is on "boys."

Fig. 9–2. Dating from 1901, the method of locomotion was by means of a clockwork motor. Photo from the Collection of John Ezzo

In O Gauge locomotives, the #17 clockwork loco and tender were used with both freight and passenger cars. This cast-iron loco had a black baked finish, red wheels, and was 7½-inches long. It was used to pull the #60 Series eight-wheel freight and passenger cars and the #500 Series four-wheel cars made before World War I. To increase the speed of the clockwork train, one could leave out a car to lessen the pulling load on the engine. The #17 was changed significantly in the 1920s. Size was reduced to 7-inches, and it was no longer used to pull the #60 Series eight-wheel cars. The cast-iron red drive wheels were replaced by die-cast metal ones that measured 1½-inch diameter with ten spokes each.

With the #25 eight-wheel clockwork power loco and tender in O Gauge (4–4–0), "Limited Vestibule Express" appeared on the side of the version made from 1903–1910. A unique feature of this loco was that the cow catcher and pilot trucks were made up as one unit and functioned as such. The loco was constructed of cast iron, brass, and steel, wheels were cast-iron machined with six spokes. In the later version made from 1910 until World War I, the cast-iron, machined drive wheels had ten spokes which were more realistic than the earlier ones. The tender had eight wheels, and the headlight and smokestack were modern. The cab of the engine was lower to give an illusion of greater length.

At first the only rolling stock was passenger cars. These were four-wheeled, hand-painted passenger coaches with cast-iron wheels that were essentially Marklin copies. Various changes in design included making the cars longer, changing the style of the windows, and using lithographed decoration to replace hand painting. Tin coaches said "Limited Vestibule Express" on the sides.

The #50 Series was the oldest Ives passenger cars and was made from 1901 until 1930 when the factory closed. The first cars were only 4-inches long and had flat-loop couplers. When the cars were made longer by ½-inch in 1903, vestibules were added to the ends. With the use of lithography in 1904–5, the cars had more detail than the hand-painted ones. They had simulated wood sides as did the actual cars. Additional changes were incorporated in to the #51 Series and #52 Series passenger cars, and in 1909 hook couplers were utilized. The #50 cars were lengthened to 5½-inches in 1910.

The #60 Series passenger cars including the #60 Baggage, #61 Passenger Car, and #62 Parlor Car also underwent a series of changes in size and design. By 1910, they had two four-wheel trucks that resembled an inverted T that were copied from Bing.

Fig. 9–3. Note the lithographed wood graining on this c1910 O Gauge #61 Limited Vestibule Car. Photo from the Collection of John Ezzo

These cars had hook and slot couplers. Two years later, automatic couplers were utilized and "The Ives Railway Lines" replaced "Limited Vestibule Express."

The #500 Series passenger cars made in 1913 were used in both clockwork and electric trains. They were 6⅜-inches long and had hook couplers. They underwent a series of changes all during the years they were made. In later years, Lionel was making longer passenger cars. Ives followed suit in order to stay in the market competitively.

After Ives introduced clockwork trains that ran on tracks in 1901, he concentrated on passenger cars and locos. The only freight car made from 1901–1907 was the #54 Gondola which used a #50 passenger car frame and was copied from a Marklin design. This gondola was hand painted in green with red stripes and had cast-iron wheels.

In response to growing competition, Ives added 4½-inch cars to the series with the #53 Merchandise Car and the #55

Fig. 9–4. These two examples of Ives products are typical of the pre-World War I designs. The #61 Chair Car could benefit from some careful restoration as could the #3220 electric profile which dates back to 1916. Photo Courtesy of Nelson's Auction

Stock Car during 1908–9. Several years later, the #50 Series increased in size to 5½-inches when the line was modernized. Additional cars included the #54 Gravel Car from 1905, the #56 Caboose, and #57 Lumber Car. These five car styles constituted the Ives freight line until it stopped production in 1930. There were many color changes and some modifications to the frames. Ives never installed working doors on his #50 Series freight cars as the other train makers did.

In the #60 Series freight cars, the first car made was the #63 Gravel with four wheels, 5-inches in length, and hand-painted. From 1901–1907 these cars utilized the flat loop coupler. 1904 was the year they switched to the hook coupler and that was used until 1930. That same year the cars were lithographed. In 1908, two four-wheel cars were added to the line, the #64 Merchandise, and #65 Stock Car. The #66 Tank Car, #67 Caboose, #68 Refrigerator Car, and #69 Lumber Car were added in 1910, and the earlier cars were also revised. In that same year, all the #60 Series cars had T-type trucks in a design that was copied from Bing. Automatic couplers that were stamped with the 1912 patent date replaced hook couplers in that year. The following year, Ives expanded his boxcar selections to include 14 different road names. Periodic changes were made in these freight cars all during the years they were made.

The #120 Series freight cars were eight-wheel versions that were 9-inches long. These were longer than the imported

German examples. Included in the series was the #125 Merchandise Car, #127 Stock Car, #128 Gravel Car, and the #126 Caboose which was only 6½-inches long and had four wheels. These cars had hook couplers and were lithographed in colorful tones. The pre-1910 examples had brake wheels.

Early series freight cars from Ives were not produced in great quantities. The #120 Series was revised in 1910, and a #123 Lumber Car was added. Eventually there were five versions made of these freight cars. Automatic couplers were used in 1912, and the #124 Refrigerator Car was added then too. The #560 Series four-wheel freight cars started with 550 numbers like the passenger cars in 1913, but were changed to 560 numbers in 1915 to avoid confusion.

Ives became an innovator in 1904 by being the only American manufacturer to produce European #1 Gauge trains. Ives offered a line in #1 Gauge for sixteen years. The #40 was a 4–4–0 steam type Gauge 1 loco that was 11½-inches long. It was cast in two pieces and had a separate heavy metal roof. Several different tenders were utilized with it. Changes were made in the #40 for several years of its use.

The S-class New York Central locomotive was utilized as a prototype for Gauge 1 electric models when Ives introduced electric trains to his line. In 1912 the #3240 was his version of the S-class.

Ives expanded the Gauge 1 line slowly. By 1906 there was a small series of lithographed freight cars. These were 11⅝-inches long and consisted of the #73 Merchandise Car, #74 Stock Car, #75 Caboose, #76 Gravel, and later the #77 Lumber Car. The trucks used were similar to early Marklin trucks, and the rolling stock had hook couplers. There were various changes over the years.

In 1915 Ives modernized the Gauge 1 freight cars and changed to numbers by adding additional digits, for example #73 became #7345 and #74 became #7446. This was a sturdier series than the original #70 cars. They were the last American prototype mass-produced freight cars made in Gauge 1 until the late 1970s when LGB offered American prototype cars.

Designed as competition for the German import models, the Ives Gauge 1 passenger cars were both large and expensive for their time. The #70 Series consisted of the #70 Baggage Car, #71 Combination St. Louis (Buffet Car), and #72 Parlor Car San Francisco. These handsome cars had lithographed simulated wood sides, came in three different colors, had hook couplers, and were quite realistic in copying real passenger cars of the period. When the series was modernized in 1910, "Twentieth Century Limited" was lettered over the windows which were celluloid for the first time. Hook couplers continued in use. The switch to automatic couplers was made in 1912. Several years later additional changes appeared. "New York Central Lines" was utilized over the windows, and a #73 Observation Car was included. The cars were cataloged last in 1920.

An additional series of passenger cars

Fig. 9-5. The 0-4-4-0 cast-iron electric profile (bottom) is listed as #3240 and is gauged #1. The "President Washington" (top) has been rewheeled to make it operational. An engineer is located in the cab. Photo Courtesy of Sotheby's

for Gauge 1 was the #180 which included the #181 Buffet, #182 Parlor Car, and #183 Observation with automatic couplers from 1912. This set also was large, expensive, and offered until 1920.

Though Ives was quite pleased with his Gauge 1 and clockwork trains, he realized finally the electric trains other compa-

nies were producing were not just a passing fancy. Ives could no longer ignore the popularity of electric trains if he were to stay competitive with Lionel, American Flyer, and the foreign imports. In one way, Ives had an advantage in starting later than the others to manufacture electric trains. He had the benefit of their errors and adapted only the successful ideas to his line of electrics in both O Gauge and Gauge 1. He also continued his clockwork O Gauge trains for those households still without electricity.

Ives's first line of O Gauge electrics sold quite well and were very popular with the train buying public. He also made a complete line of stations, tunnels, and other accessories to complement his train offerings. Ives products had excellent lithography and lots of detail work to them. The pieces were very durable because much attention was paid to construction details. Ives only made electric trains for twenty-three years.

During 1910, the first year that Ives started making electrics, he produced four steamers and one New York Central S-type electric loco. All had cast-iron bodies. The #1100 was made from 1910–1924. It was a nonreversing electrically powered steam loco with a 2-2-0 wheel arrangement. One wheel was geared, and there was a dummy headlight. Other steamers were the #1117 with a dummy headlight; the #1118 with a working headlight; and the largest of these steamers, the top-of-the-line #1125 with a working headlight and manual reverse.

The #3238 was the first of the New York Central 2-4-2 wheel arrangement electric locos. This was a top-of-the-line loco for Ives for many years of its production. Features included two working headlights, pantographs, a manual reverse

Fig. 9–6. Accessories were an important part of the Ives train system. This 1928 pair of lithographed Union Stations are separated by a #121 glass domed Passenger Platform. Photo Courtesy of Christie's

and a hook-slot coupler mechanism. The cast-iron body was made in two halves fastened together with two long, machined screws.

Many of Ives's earlier clockwork locos and boilers were utilized again when he started making electric locos. The number 11 was added to locos when they were changed to electric examples. The #25 clockwork became #1125 when it started its run as an electric loco. Though Ives was originally reluctant to make electric trains, his son Harry was quite enthusiastic about electrics. The Ives Company actually held many train patents for their inventions. Train buyers were impressed with the new line Ives produced.

Ives continued to expand the line in the years prior to World War I. There were numerous changes in his catalogs since he utilized these pages to explain electric train operation. Many steam engines had electric counterparts by 1911. Ives also made a Gauge 1 electric train, the #3240 that was patterned after a New Haven prototype. This model was 13½-inches long and utilized a combination of sheet metal and cast iron for its body construction.

Each year Ives expanded electric train production; its importance can be seen by ever increasing catalog space devoted to electrics. Changes continued to occur each year. In 1917–18, the complete line of Ives locos underwent streamlining. They had a sleeker, slimmer look, were longer, and had greater detail.

With the outbreak of World War I, the flood of German imports to the United States was halted, and American manufacturers filled in and expanded their markets. Ives and American Flyer took care of the lower end of the price spectrum, while Lionel had the upper end. Because of their location in Bridgeport, Ives did not get the lucrative government contracts that helped Lionel so much. Ives had difficulty getting materials shipped to him in New England. He also had trouble transporting his products to key markets during the war. The wartime situation weakened the Ives Corportation, and it fell behind the competition during the 1920s. They never recovered fully from their financial setbacks during the war period.

Ives continued to make changes such as adding brass name plates to New York Central engines in 1925 to replace rubber-stamped lettering. New electrics for 1926 included the #3257 and #3257R which were expensive locos, and the inexpensive #3258 based on a New Haven electric locomotive. On the #3258, imitation brass name plates were done by the lithographed process with details in gold brass color. Some of the details were eliminated such as handrails, engine bells, and overhead pantographs to keep the cost down on this lightweight tinplate loco. The underframe was stamped steel. This was the first time a steel frame was used. Ives normally used a cast-iron frame.

An O Gauge steamer introduced in 1929, the #1122, was one of the most sophisticated locos Ives made. This was a finely detailed die cast loco that was near to scale in size and was patterned after the Baltimore and Ohio's "President Washington" class of locos.

Ives stopped making Gauge 1 in 1921 and left that size for the European makers. Instead he started to produce trains in Lionel's Standard Gauge to compete with Lionel. Ives called his new line "Wide Gauge" since Lionel had a copyright on the name "Standard Gauge." Ives used a three-rail track that was 2¼-inches between the rails. He used similar construction techniques for his Wide Gauge equipment as compared to the smaller O Gauge examples.

Ives still used the New York Central S-class locomotives for prototypes for his electrics when he made the change to Wide Gauge in 1921. During the years these locos were made, there were differing versions of the locos. The least expensive was the #3241 with an 0-4-0 wheel arrangement, a cast-iron frame, and a minimum amount of trim. The #3242 had the same wheel configuration. It was the premium four-wheel Wide Gauge loco from 1921-25. This loco had a more elaborate frame, more trim, and two headlights. The top-of-the-line loco from 1921-28 was the #3243 with a 4-4-4 wheel configuration. This loco was a fine replica of its prototype and had two headlights, a cast-iron frame, and leading and trailing trucks.

In 1924, Ives #3235 was the biggest Wide Gauge seller. This New Haven box type electric loco had an 0-4-0 wheel configuration, was 11¼-inches long, and had a stamped steel body. Though this was the least expensive of the Ives locos, it was powered with the same motor as the larger, more expensive locos Ives made. There were two models. One had a manual reverse switch, and the other an automatic reverse with a remote control switch. "R" was used on the locos with the number to indicate the remote. In 1926 Ives offered the #3237 electric patterned after the Milwaukee Road St. Paul type loco that was used in large series passenger car sets.

Wide Gauge locos were heavier in construction, larger in size, made more noise, and emitted more and brighter electrical sparks. They required a large transformer because of the larger motors. One distinct feature on Ives Wide Gauge electric profile locos was octagonal brass headlights. Other features included oversized embossed rivet detail and wide louvre type ventilators that added interest to the plain sides of the body of the locos. Large rectangular windows helped to improve ventilation and kept the motor from overheating. Brass handrails were used on the roof, and the pantographs were undersized.

In steam, Ives made the #1132 with an 0-4-0 wheel arrangement to continue his tradition of steam engines in his offerings. Ives used the Brooks cab of the #1129 loco from Gauge 1 for this loco with a reversible unit and headlight. The steam loco was only used in two sets: a three-car freight set, and a three-car passenger set, the #705 with #184, #185, and #186 cars. Of the big three toy train manufacturers in 1924-28, Ives was the only one to offer a train set headed by a Wide Gauge steam engine.

A new steam loco, the #1134 in cast iron that was modeled after the Baltimore and Ohio President class loco was made in 1927. Each loco was named after an Ameri-

Fig. 9-7. It is difficult to find Ives electric steamers in good condition, especially in Gauge 1. This #1129 is missing its pilot and trailing trucks. The Brooks cab was used on the comparable Wide Gauge examples. Photo Courtesy of Sotheby's

can president. The Ives version, a 4-4-0, had "President Washington" under the cab and an engineer in the cab window.

It is important to take note of the differences in construction techniques utilized by Ives and Lionel during this period from 1921–1926 when they were quite competitive in Wide Gauge trains. Ives employed a heavily tinned, thin steel to make the cabs of the electric locos and bodies of both freight and passenger cars. This material was well suited for the soldered construction methods he used, but paint did not adhere well to this steel. Though a lot of expensive tool and die work was not required, Ives costs were high because he used so much handwork. Many small pieces had to be soldered together to produce his examples. This gave his trains a more realistic appearance than Lionel's, but required more labor, and thus addi-

tional expense. Eventually this led to Ives's downfall in the industry. It was difficult for Ives to compete with Lionel price wise when his manufacturing costs were higher. He actually had to sell many items below cost.

Ives best technical development was its automatic reversing unit that was a major innovation in toy train manufacture. This three position automatic-sequence-reverse was Ives's patent. Lionel was anxious to get this reversing unit for its own use.

When it came to producing freight cars for Wide Gauge, Ives simply renumbered Gauge 1 freight cars and added larger trucks to accommodate the wider track. These were the most significant changes since the "new" Wide Gauge cars still had black wheels, ratchet brake wheels, and automatic couplers without springs like

Gauge 1 rolling stock. These cars were painted, had painted or embossed rivet detail, had embossed ribs, and rubber-stamped lettering. The cars were 11½-inches long, the same length as Gauge 1 cars. The series made during the 1920s included the #190 Tank Car, #191 Coke Car, #192 Merchandise Car, #193 Stock Car, #194 Coal Car, #195 Caboose, #196 Flat Car, and #197 Lumber Car. The Flat Car was new in 1922 because it had not been made in the Gauge 1 series. The other freight cars underwent a series of changes during the years.

Wide Gauge passenger cars came in two sizes: 13¼-inches and 17-inches long. In 1921, Ives produced the #184 Buffet and #185 Parlor Car in the smaller size, and the #187 Buffet, #188 Parlor Car, and #189 Observation Car in the larger versions. Various changes were made in the window patterns of the cars during the 1920s. In 1922, interior lights were added to the larger cars. By 1925, the bigger cars were

made with six-wheel trucks and brass journals, and four-wheel trucks without journals. New cars included the #180 Buffet, #181 Parlor Car, and #182 Observation. The following year saw the addition of brass plates. Several sets in 1927 included the #706 Bankers' Special with the #3243 loco, #187 and #189 Passenger Cars, and the Set #707 President Washington with the #1134 loco, #180, #181, and #182 Passenger Cars.

Ives had a special arrangement with the John Wanamaker Department Store of Philadelphia to produce uncataloged specials for its retail stores and Christmas catalogs. The line that Ives made for them was quite extensive. All of the engines, passenger cars, and Wide Gauge freight cars were made in maroon for Wanamaker. They had the special store logo "Wanamaker Railway Lines" on the cars, and all the passenger cars said "Pullman" in addition. In Wide Gauge, all of Ives's electric locos were offered as Wanamaker specials along

Fig. 9-8. The #3239 electric profile was also used in department store special sets. Note the automatic couplers on this model. Photo Courtesy of Sotheby's

with the #1132 steamer in black with "Wanamaker" on the tender. The Wanamaker specials were duplicates of what Ives was offering in his catalog, but with different color and markings.

Despite the fact that Ives trains were well made and more realistic looking than what Lionel offered, they still had difficulties competing in the toy train market. Even with borrowed money infused into the company, and a well planned line, Ives was forced into bankruptcy in 1928.

Priced Examples: Wide Gauge

Sets

Black Diamond Express Senior set, #1134 locomotive and tender, #241, #242, #243 Passenger Cars, red and black, American Flyer-Ives	$5,000.00
Circus set, #1134 locomotive, wild animal car, equipment car, three flat cars, Pullman	A–$5,750.00
Transcontinental Limited set, #3273 green locomotive, #187, #188, #189 brass plate cars, original box	A–$3,000.00
White set, #3243 locomotive, #187-1, #188-1, #189-1 Passenger Cars	A–$5,100.00
#3242 locomotive, maroon, #187, #188, #189 Passenger Cars, original boxes	$275.00
#3243 locomotive, green, #187, #188, #189 Passenger Cars with 8 wheel trucks and rubber stamping	A–$900.00

Locomotives

#1131 cast iron with N.Y.C. & H.R. tender	$675.00
#1134 steam with tender, red, repainted	$600.00
#3237R, brass plates	$600.00
#3241, brass plates	$225.00
#3242 electric profile, brown, rubber stamping	$350.00
#3245R, blue-green	A–$1,025.00

Rolling Stock

#190 Tanker, Texas, orange	$300.00
#193 Stock Car, brass journals	$120.00
#194 Hopper Car, Pennsylvania R.R., brass journals	$130.00

#196 Flat Car $275.00

#197 Lumber Car, brass journals $280.00

Accessories

#89 Water Tower $250.00

#99-2-3 Bridge with original box   A–$675.00

2 light target Signal $150.00

double Union station with replaced dome   A–$750.00

CHAPTER 10

The Ives-Lionel Transition Period

The period of transition between the Ives family ownership of the company, joint ownership of Ives by American Flyer and Lionel, and finally complete sole ownership by Lionel is known as the Ives-Lionel transition period.

After Ives declared bankruptcy in 1928, Lionel and American Flyer assumed joint control of Ives. For the next two years, the Ives trains continued to be made in Bridgeport, but the line was a combination of Ives, Lionel, and American Flyer parts and car bodies in both O and Wide Gauges.

By the end of 1930, the Lionel Corporation had succeeded in becoming the single owner of Ives by buying out American Flyer interests. At this time they closed the Connecticut factory and moved the Ives operation to the Irvington, New Jersey plant. During the next two years, Lionel continued to publish the Ives catalog, but Ives trains were only partly Ives. In the following year, 1933, Lionel stopped print-

ing the Ives catalog, and no longer produced any separate line of Ives trains. The low end of their train production was called The Lionel-Ives Lines.

Lionel started to make the Winner Line in 1931, during the Depression. This line of inexpensive trains was geared "for little brother." They were the least expensive Lionel sets. Altogether there were seven train sets in the line. Three had electric style locos—while four were steamers made with converted Ives windup engines. The steam locos for this series had 1500

Fig. 10-1. The Winner Line of lithographed pieces was Lionel's answer to the lower scale market. Photo from the Collection of Don Speidel

numbers, including the #1501, #1503, and #1506. Some were red, others were black. Some had battery powered lights and bells. Tenders were #1502 or #1507.

A small series of lithographed freight cars with four wheels and hook couplers included the #1512 Gondola, #1514 Boxcar, #1515 Tank Car, and #1517 Caboose. These freight cars were used to replace the #50 Series Ives freight cars that were outdated. The line was continued in 1932, while the following year Lionel trains were intermingled with Ives trains to make the Lionel-Ives line. In 1934 Lionel-Ives was changed to Lionel Junior. This name was used until 1937 for the Lionel line of low-priced sets. Lionel Junior was renamed 027 in 1937 and was made until 1942.

After the Ives family lost control, and Lionel was making decisions about what

the Ives factory produced, there were many changes in the O Gauge line for locomotives, freight, and passenger cars. In New York Central type electrics, they still made the #3255 and #3255R, and the #3257 and #3257R St. Paul type electrics. The #3261 was made without a reverse. In steam, the #1125 was a new, inexpensive loco, while the #1122 in red or black was patterned after the B & O "President Washington Class" and was a top-of-the-line loco. The engine was offered with Ives automatic-sequence-reverse as an option, or with the less expensive manual reverse that was taken from Lionel. An inexpensive steamer, the #1125, did not resemble earlier locos using that number. The 7½-inch long #3258 was the least expensive loco made. All of the 1930 locos were quite colorful.

Significant changes continued with the locos made in 1931. The inexpensive #1810 with a hook coupler, and the #1651 with a Lionel coupler replaced the #3250 and #3260 Series locos. There were similar changes in steam locos. Only two models were made. The inexpensive #1815 with hook coupler, and the #257 and #258

Fig. 10-2. From 1931 to 1934, this transition set (top) was modeled in O27 Gauge. The clockwork loco pulled a #1507 tender, #1515 Tanker, #1514 Boxcar, #1512 Gondola, and #1517 Caboose. The locomotive (bottom) was cast-iron and the rolling stock lithographed tin. Photo from the Collection of Don Speidel

Fig. 10-3. One of the more common Lionel-Ives transition train sets was this 1934 lithographed passenger set in O27 Gauge. The lead piece was the #1810 electric profile locomotive. Photo from the Collection of Don Speidel

which were relabeled #258 Lionel steamers used Lionel couplers instead of Ives automatic couplers. The following year, Ives continued the #1651 New Haven box cab and the steam #258. Additional locos were the #1661 steam and a top-of-the-line engine, the #1694, that was quite elaborate. Lionel continued to lose money with these Ives examples, and finally discontinued the line totally by 1933.

We have already seen that the outdated #50 Series freights were replaced by the sturdy steel #1500 Series freights originally used by Lionel in the Winner Line and also used for the Ives-Lionel 1931–32 production. Changes in the outmoded #120 Series included the #121 Caboose which was a #3211 American Flyer caboose on Ives trucks. The #122 Tank Car was actually a #815 Lionel tank body and brake wheels. Brass nameplates were used on these cars with new Ives frames. When Lionel took sole control, the Ives #121 Caboose utilized a #817 Lionel Caboose for its parts. It is clear that the years 1929 and 1930 were strange because the Ives cars were being built with their own, plus Lionel and American Flyer parts. Although there was a need to revitalize the Ives line, there was no excess money to make new models. Rolling stock was pieced together with a variety of available parts.

With the #560 Series of freights, Lionel bodies also were used, so the #804 Lionel Tank became the #566 Ives Tank Car. The #1500 Series of lithographed freights also replaced the #550 Series. The #60 Series, another workhorse for Ives,

was replaced in 1931 with the #1677 Gondola, #1678 Cattle, #1679 Boxcar, #1680 Tank Car, and the #1682 Caboose. These were lithographed freight cars with two four-wheel trucks and Lionel automatic couplers.

In 1932, the #1700 Series of lithographed freight cars replaced Ives premium O Gauge #120 Series with 10-inch cars. Lithography replaced the brass nameplates; Lionel latch couplers that were not compatible with earlier Ives equipment were utilized on the #1707 Gondola, #1708 Cattle Car, #1709 Boxcar, and #1712 Caboose.

Even though Lionel broke up what remained of the Ives Corporation in 1933, they continued to produce this rolling stock in uncataloged sets through 1942, though the Ives cars were labeled Lionel after 1933.

As with the locos, the passenger cars of the transition period were more colorful. In 1929, the #50 Series cars had non-matching roof colors. In a #42 mechanical set with yellow lithographed cars, the #50 Baggage had a grey roof, the #51 Chair Car had a red roof, and the #52 Parlor Car had a green roof. In the same year, the #60 Series and #550 Series cars had blue-green lithography, brass trim, and outlined lettering. These two series were not offered after 1930. During 1931–32, the Ives #610 Series passenger cars were actually Lionel's #610 and #612 cars with new rubber-stamped lettering, new decals over the windows, and Lionel latch-type couplers.

When Lionel finally closed the Bridgeport manufactory and moved the works to

Irvington, they replaced the Ives designs with less expensive low-profile equipment. By forming the cars from one piece of metal without a separate roof piece, they could produce them at a lower cost. The #1690 Series had the new rounded roof profile. Only pullman and observation cars were made. With the #1695 Series, the enameled cars were 12 inches long, had the Lionel roof latch, decals with lettering on a gold background to imitate brass nameplates, and they had six-wheel trucks.

There were some important sets in O Gauge that came out of this transition period. Deserving special mention are the Yankee Clipper with a #3258 New Haven style engine and the #550 Baggage, #552 Parlor Car, and #558 Observation in yellow, light green, and dark green. The White Owl had the #3259 loco plus the #552 Parlor, #551 Chair Car, and #558 Observation in white, red, and black. The sleek Black Diamond consisted of the #1122 red loco, two #141 Pullmans, and #142 Observation. The

#1125 loco headed the Blue Vagabond with a #550 Baggage, a #551 Chair Car, and #558 Observation. All were very colorful sets produced in 1930.

During the transition period, starting in 1928 under Lionel and American Flyer joint management, Ives made a new die-cast #1134 steam engine and a matching die-cast #40 tender in Wide Gauge. The new design concealed the motor in the cab in such a way so that light was visible through the frame area as it was in an actual locomotive of the period. According to *Greenberg's Guide to Ives Trains 1901–1932*, Ives was the first American tinplate maker with an engine having this feature. This loco was a replica of the Baltimore and Ohio President Class Pacific 4–6–2, but was actually an Atlantic since it lacked one set of drive wheels, and the wheel arrangement was 4–4–2. Done in a matte black finish, this loco was put to good use. It headed six sets from this period. One famous set from 1929 was the copper

Fig. 10–4. Many of the Ives sets were named. The Black Diamond Set on the top shelf was actually painted red with black roofs on the coaches. The set on the lower shelf consists of #120 freights and a #67 Caboose. Both sets were released in O Gauge. Photo Courtesy of Christie's

Fig. 10–5. The Blue Vagabond Set on the lower shelf features a #1125 loco and #500 Series coaches. The passenger set on the top shelf consists of red and blue #1504 coaches. Both sets are clockwork powered. Photo Courtesy of Christie's

plated, nickel trimmed Prosperity Special with #241, #242, and #243 passenger cars along with the #1134 loco.

Other locos of the 1928 production included the #3236 with a stamped-steel frame that was used to head inexpensive trains, the #3243, a deluxe New York Central version with a 4–4–4 wheel arrangement that Ives modified so it could be used with the American Flyer passenger cars that were marketed under the Ives label, and the #3245 St. Paul.

Ives made some changes in the 1929 Wide Gauge electric locos. The #3245 had a die-cast frame that was based on a Milwaukee Road prototype. On the roof the pantographs were Lionel parts from their #408, #381, and #256 locomotives. This loco had nickel plated trim and was done in orange and black enamel colors. The

#3236 box cab electric had a Lionel #8 body on an Ives stamped-steel chassis. It was done in bright red or blue with Ives lettering.

In 1930, when Ives was owned solely by Lionel, once again there were changes in the loco lineup. The #1134 die-cast steamer was retooled with a new front design, and a red #1134 loco headed the National Limited Set with red and blue passenger cars. The retooled #1134R headed five different sets in 1930.

When both American Flyer and Lionel owned Ives jointly, they decided not to invest in new Ives designs, but to manufacture existing Ives models. They also infused the line with both American Flyer and Lionel substitutes in order to keep the Ives line in production. There was friction between Lionel and American Flyer under the joint arrangement, so American Flyer sold out to Lionel, leaving them in complete control over the Ives factory and product line. Additional changes were ordered, and Ives retooled to produce the #1764 loco in Wide Gauge and the #1694 loco in O Gauge.

The Bridgeport, Connecticut factory was closed by Lionel in 1931, and Ives operations were moved to Lionel's Irvington site. In that same year, the Ives line was a reflection of many obsolete pieces of Lionel stock that were reissued with Ives plates. The #1134 die-cast steamer was made again, but had a Lionel #390 tender, Lionel couplers, and was cataloged as #1760. Later this loco was replaced with a Lionel #384, but was listed as Ives #1760.

In 1932, the last of the new Ives models was produced by the Lionel factory in Irvington. A new version of the New Haven #1764E with a 4-4-4 wheel arrangement was made in maroon and terra cotta with brass nameplates. Featuring a low profile, this loco had matching passenger cars and utilized both Ives and Lionel parts.

Changes were also made in Ives freight cars when Lionel and American Flyer took over in 1928. Snake Track Pull couplers replaced the shorter automatic couplers. The Ives Railway Circus headed by the #1134 die-cast loco had the #192, #193, and #196 freight cars painted in yellow with green trim and red roofs. They were rubber-stamped "The Ives Railway Circus" and had a "C" added to their catalog numbers. Metal wagons came with the #196 Flat Car. Later that year, Ameri-

can Flyer supplied the unpainted parts for Ives's 14-inch freight cars. The American Flyer #4018 Automobile became Ives #20-192 Merchandise Car, #4020 Stock became #20-193 Stock, #4010 Tank became #20-190 Tank, #2021 Caboose became #20-195 Caboose, #4017 Sand became #20-194 Gravel (Hopper) or #20-198 Gravel (Gondola). Ives painted these American Flyer cars in their own colors, and added Ives couplers, trucks, numbers, and brass plates.

One unusual freight car from 1929 was an Ives #190 Tank Car that consisted of a Lionel #215 Tank Car mounted on a 14-inch American Flyer frame and was completed with Ives trucks, Snake Track Pull coupler, and an Ives #190 on its brass plate. This one freight car had parts from the three major train manufacturers.

Other cars from 1929 included the #199 Derrick Car that was 12½ inches long, had Lionel's #219 Crane, Lionel trucks, and a specially bent Ives coupler so it was compatible with other Ives rolling stock. This car was done in peacock blue with green trim.

During the 1930 manufacturing season, American Flyer freight bodies for Ives rolling stock were replaced by the Lionel #200 Series freights mounted on Ives trucks. Ives still used the #190 Series numbers for these cars, but without the "20" prefix of the previous year. The #191 Coke Car and #194 Coal Car continued to be produced along with the #199 Derrick, but they had Ives trucks and Snake Track Pull couplers. With the move to Irvington, the Lionel #200 Series bodies were replaced by Lionel's #500 Series which were smaller and given Ives #1700 Series designations. Continuing into 1931 and 32, Lionel decided to market Ives merchandise as a less expensive train line. They continued to make the #1700 Series freights. These were $11\frac{1}{2}$ inches long, were Lionel #500 Series bodies being sold under the Ives name, used Lionel colors and Lionel latch couplers which made them incompatible with older Ives rolling stock. In the series were the #1771 Lumber, #1772 Gondola, #1773 Stock, #1774 Box, #1775 Tank, #1776 Hopper, #1777 Caboose, and #1778 Refrigerator.

With Wide Gauge transition period passenger cars in the Lionel-American Flyer years, some Ives sets used 19-inch American Flyer passenger car bodies adapted to suit the Ives line. For the President's Special, the American Flyer car bodies had Ives six-wheel Pullman type trucks and Snake Track Pull couplers. There were three cars in this grouping: the #241 Club Car, #242 Parlor Car which used an American Flyer diner body, and the #243 Observation Car. "Made in The Ives Shop" was on brass plates beneath the windows, and "The Ives Railway Lines" appeared on brass plates above the windows. These passenger cars were made in several different colors in 1928 and 29. The most expensive set in the line, The Prosperity Special, used the die cast #1134 Atlantic loco with these three American Flyer passenger car bodies with Ives plates, couplers, copper finish, nickel roofs, truck sides, and trim.

When Lionel took complete control, American Flyer passenger car bodies were no longer purchased for use with Ives trains. To replace the American Flyer cars, Ives used Lionel's $18\frac{1}{4}$-inch #431 for its #246 Dining Car, #419 for its #247 Club Car, #418 for its #248 Chair Car, and #490 for its #249 Observation. These Lionel twelve-wheel car bodies were given six-wheel Ives trucks and Snake Track Pull couplers to create a new #240 Series of four cars that were finished in Ives colors. Lionel did not want the expense of making new dies for Ives passenger cars so they utilized their #400 Series cars which had been their most expensive passenger cars before the State Series was made in 1929. To cut costs, Ives used decals to imitate the brass nameplate. The series of four passenger cars was offered in three different color schemes for three sets. The National Limited had a blue body, red roof and trucks. The Chief had a black body, red roof and trucks. The Olympian had an orange body with black roof and trucks.

By 1931, the #400 Series of passenger cars no longer had Ives finishes, couplers, or trucks. Lionel's numbers, six-wheel trucks, latch couplers, and finishes replaced Ives parts. Some cars had Ives decal lettering and a white label on the car's bottom that said "Manufactured By The Ives Corporation/Irvington, N.J." These #400 cars were replaced in 1932 by 15-inch passenger cars. The #1766 Pullman, #1767 Baggage, and #1768 Observation had Lionel latch couplers, Lionel six-wheel trucks with copper journals, and "Ives Lines" in a diamond shaped "IL" herald in the center.

The #184 Buffet, #185 Parlor, and #186 Observation also underwent a series of changes with Snake Track Pull couplers with supporting brackets replacing automatic couplers in 1929 and 30. After that the cars themselves were replaced by Lionel's #332 Baggage, #339 Pullman, and #341 Observation in 1931 and 32. These cars were 12 inches long, were finished in Lionel colors, and had Ives decals covering the Lionel name.

Some accessories were renumbered when Lionel took charge and when the move to Irvington took place. Some accessories were the same for both Lionel and Ives, but with different numbers.

Priced Examples: Wide Gauge

Sets

#10 locomotive, peacock, #337 and #338 cars with "Ives Railway Lines" decals	$475.00
#1082 Interstate Limited Set, #3236 locomotive, #184, #185 #186 Passenger Cars, black and orange, original boxes and set box, 1929	$1,500.00
Prosperity Special Set, #1134R steam locomotive, #241, #242, #243 Passenger Cars, copper and brass	A–$12,000.00
#1764E locomotive, #1766, #1767, #1768 cars, terra cotta bodies with maroon roofs	A–$4,100.00
#1770E locomotive, #1760 tender, #1771 Lumber Car, #1772 Gondola, #1777 Caboose, c1931	A–$1,600.00

Locomotives

#1770E steam with tender	$800.00

Rolling Stock

#190 Tank Car	A–$400.00
#192 Boxcar	A–$425.00
#195 Caboose	$200.00
#198 Gondola	$200.00
#199 Crane Car	$350.00
#1770 Crane Car	$1,000.00
#20-192 Merchandise Car, American Flyer-Ives, 1928	$210.00
#20-198 Gondola Car, American Flyer-Ives, 1929	$210.00

CHAPTER 11

The Early Years of the Louis Marx Story

Louis Marx could easily claim the title as "America's Toy King". Nearly every child at one time or another has been touched by one of Marx's creations. Manufacturing toys that could be purchased from small budgets was the secret of his success. This was based on efficient low cost mass production methods which often utilized existing die models and reworked them to produce "new" toys. A good example is the Honeymoon Express. Basically consisting of a tiny keywind train that traveled around a circular channel which often had an airplane circling overhead, the Express was marketed in several variations such as the Mickey Mouse Express, the Subway Express, and various types of the Honeymoon Express.

Many of Marx's detractors and competitors labeled his toys "cheap," but in actuality, they were "inexpensive." There was nothing cheap about a Marx product. They were simple in design and execution, but were built to last through rough handling by a youngster. Marx's toys worked for many years. These same concepts of simple design and execution were used in his many toy train lines.

Louis Marx did not begin his career in the toy industry as a manufacturer, but as a salesman for the Strauss Toy Company of New York. This relationship was stormy, and in 1919, Marx established Louis Marx and Co., Inc. which marketed toys under the Marx logo but, in fact, was fabricated from a number of factories under contract to Marx. His strong suit was his ability to market his creations without investing the large sums associated with manufacturing. Catalog stores such as Sears, Roebuck & Co. and chain stores such as Woolworth's were vehicles through which Louis Marx brought his low cost toys to the marketplace. These mass markets provided exceptional exposure for his toys. This was another means of keeping costs under control.

Marx's entrance into the world of toy

trains began with his association with the Girard Model Works in Girard, Pennsylvania in 1928-29. Girard's Joy Line train was marketed under the Marx logo. The Joy Line became the standard train set in Marx's inventory for many years. He acquired the company in 1935.

The first Joy Line examples featured a keywind engine, and though the rolling stock remained essentially the same with changes in the lithography and colors, the engines underwent several minor changes, including electrification in 1930. All the engines bore some vague resemblance to steam locomotives. Picture if you will, large sheets of tin-plated steel receiving lithographed patterns which were then folded and assembled. This was the most common method of production at Marx for several years.

Joy Line engines featured four driving wheels and lacked pilot and trailing wheels, the 0-4-0 configuration. Marx believed that additional wheels such as pilots tended to cause derailments that could create problems in the hands of the young railroader. Pilots and trailers did appear later in the more prototype engines. The first Joy Line engine was born in 1927, and featured a clockwork mechanism. Several variations existed during their tenure until their demise in 1935. Both sheet metal and die casting were used for the body, and an electrified version appeared in 1930. This example lacked side rods. A battery was added in 1934-35 to activate the headlight on some models. A few of the Joy Line engines carried the "Joy Line" logo, but most did not.

Trailing behind these locomotives were a variety of rolling stock. In all, seven different freight or passenger cars were produced from 1926 to 1936, though several variations occurred in each car. All cars were lithographed, tin-plated steel rolling on closely spaced, somewhat clumsy looking double axles, each axle contained two-flanged wheels and was mounted on embossed tabs representing journal boxes and truck sides. The earliest frames were blue, and this helps date the

Fig. 11-2. One of the rarest of the Joy Line sets features an electric cast-iron locomotive, #357 Passenger Coach, and #458 lighted Observation. This set was released in 1931. Photo from the Collection of Don Speidel

Fig. 11-1. Many of the Joy Line locomotives were sheet metal. This example was covered in red paint and carried a clockwork motor. Photo from the Collection of Don Speidel

Joy Line rolling stock. Coupling was accomplished by a simple loop and tab arrangement that required manual uncoupling of the cars. The freight cars superceded the passenger cars with the Eagle Eye Caboose making its appearance in 1926. This was followed closely by the Everful Tank Car, Hobo Rest Boxcar, Contractor Dump Car, and the Venice Gondola Car. These cars saw service through 1934 when they were replaced by the 6-inch cars.

The Joy Line coaches appeared in 1931, as did the observation car, one example of which was electrified by means of a center trailing electric pickup. Each car carried the loop and tab coupler.

The last of the Joy Line series was the Bunny Express. Headed by a keywind figural rabbit, it pulled a series of gondola cars based on the Venice Gondola prototype, but featuring lithographed baby chicks on the sides. Originally issued to coincide with Easter in 1936, and launched with high hopes, the train was a financial disaster. Few still exist in reasonable condition, and these are highly sought after by collectors.

The Joy Line trains traveled on O

Fig. 11-4. The clockwork Joy Line passenger set dates about 1931 and consists of a cast-iron loco and three #357 lithographed coaches. Photo from the Collection of Don Speidel

Gauge track. Though most Marx trains utilized O27 or 27-inch radius track, the Joy Line examples were classified as O Gauge. The track was composed of three rails, similar to Lionel's popular trackage.

About 1934, the railroads of the United States captured the interest of the public with the introduction of the streamlined passenger trains. Such romantic names as the Twentieth Century Limited and the Milwaukee Road Hiawatha were examples of crack trains that raced across the country at breakneck speeds. Louis Marx introduced his version in 1934. Designated as the M-10000 and based on the Union Pacific M-10000 to the M-10006, it

Fig. 11-3. The Joy Line clockwork train was Marx's first venture into the toy train field. Examples are highly prized by collectors. Photo from the Collection of Don Speidel

Fig. 11–5. The Bunny Train is one of the rarest of all Marx trains. Issued for a short period of time, it proved to be a marketing disaster. The Vanderbilt headed passenger set (bottom) features red lithographed Bogota coaches. This set dates about 1935. Photo Courtesy of Christie's

bore little resemblance to an actual streamliner, though it carried the banner of the Union Pacific, the first of the superliners. The engine-mail car combination was called the power car. It led a series of articulated passenger cars that fit together snugly and were coupled by means of a metal tab and pin that extended through the roof of the car. The cars were set on a single, double wheel axle. The overall effect was that of a sleek, single unit. As with most Marx trains, they were sold in sets, and the number of cars varied with the set. Powered by a clockwork motor, this set was the forerunner of other streamliners that included an electrified example. The M–10005 appeared in 1936 and also featured a keywind motor. The M–10005 continued in production after World War II. A few of the models featured reversing switches that changed the direction of the train.

The M–10005 power car joined a series of freight cars and passenger cars which continued in production until 1954. Several variations existed in both the M–10000 and M–10005 since some of them carried a stop and go lever on the top of the power car. A complete set consisted of a power car, coach or coaches, and a coach buffet. Some of the cars were fitted with four wheels rather than the double-wheel configuration. The bodies were lithographed with embossed details such as

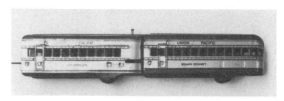

Fig. 11–6. The streamline M–10000 and M–10005 were linked by means of a vertical pin that dropped into a protruding tab located at the front of the car.

Fig. 11-7. Marx's M-10005 was a long train and the company's answer to Lionel's and American Flyer's well-modeled streamliners. It was more toy-like than the competition. Photo from the Collection of Don Speidel

rivets. Color combinations were consistent with the power car. The M-10003 was a one-piece clockwork train which featured a power-mail car, diner, and observation. It was first offered in 1936.

Before leaving the articulated streamliners, a few words must be said about the Mercury engine. Developed in 1938, this sleek looking locomotive with its streamlined tender also was used in conjunction with the articulated coaches to create new sets for marketing. This was another example of the Marx technique of getting the most mileage from a design.

In 1934, Marx introduced the Commodore Vanderbilt engine, and a new set of freight and passenger cars to mate with this powerhouse. Known to collectors as the six-inch cars because of the length of their frame, they were somewhat boxy in appearance and were set on four wheels mounted on two axles. The axles pierced the innermost journal boxes (represented as tab mounts extending from the frame), were embossed, and were outlined in silver. The couplers were fixed tab and slot couplers which rotated around a rivet. A sliding coupler which moved within a path in the frame also was used. These early six-inch examples were lithographed in very few colors (primarily red), and the rolling stock was limited in variety. They are easily distinguished from later six-inch cars by the short wheelbase and the position in the journal boxes.

Fig. 11-8. The M-10005 came complete with track and switches. Photo from the Collection of Don Speidel

Fig. 11-9. Three types of slot and tab couplers are found on Marx toy trains. The fixed example on the left is held in place by a rivet. The center example is limited by a dimple in the tail, while the coupler on the right moves within the limits of a twist in the tail.

Fig. 11-10. These late 6-inch cars are identified by the axle position through the center of the journal on the truck face.

By the end of 1936, the Girard Model Works became the Girard Manufacturing Company under Marx's control, and the six inch cars took on a sleeker, more realistic appearance. Variety was the key to this series. A single box car was printed in several colors with different roadnames to increase the sales potential without the need for retooling.

The later six-inch rolling stock centered the axles in a single journal box. The frames and bodies were lithographed and assembled using a foldover series of small metal tabs, similar to the early six-inch cars. This technique was the standby in Marx production techniques, was a method of controlling costs, and thus producing an inexpensive item. Several new cars were added to the inventory with such unusual pieces as log cars which carried loads, searchlight cars, and cabooses that featured lighted interiors.

A significant train that is highly prized by collectors was marketed about 1939.

Called the Army Supply Train, it consisted of a series of cars including an Ordinance Car, Radio Coach Car, Observation, Searchlight, Flat Car with various loads, Cannon and Machine Gun Cars. Several of these popular cars reappeared after World War II. Locomotives which accompanied these trains included lithographed steam models of the 0-4-0 or 2-4-2 wheel con-

Fig. 11-11. Complete army train sets including the original box are prized by collectors. Photo from the Collection of Don Speidel

figuration known as the #897 and #500 models based on the catalog number. An 0–4–0 Commodore Vanderbilt #597 also saw duty. All pieces, including a variety of tenders, were painted in olive drab. Many variations occurred including pieces that carried the "Army Supply Train" logo.

In order to capitalize on the Canadian market, the Canadian Pacific train set was introduced as part of the six-inch, four-wheel series. Each of the coaches carried the Canadian Pacific name as well as the name of a Canadian city such as Montreal or Toronto on sideboards. Later versions featured eight-wheel coaches with slot and tab couplers. Several different steam locomotives were used in these sets including 0–4–0 and 2–4–2 versions of #391, #494, and #495. Some of the sideboards carried a #3000 designation after the Canadian Pacific prototype. The engines first appeared in 1937 in conjunction with the coaches. Both clockwork and electric motors were used in the locomotives.

The Marx Corporation dominated the lower priced train market prior to the sec-

Fig. 11–13. The popular #495 Canadian Pacific profile with its #951A tender can usually be purchased for less then $20 at most shows. Photo Courtesy of "The Antique Trader Weekly"

ond world war. However, this fact did not prevent them from keeping an eye on their chief competitors, Lionel and American Flyer. Prototypical locomotives and rolling stock were the hallmark of these two manufacturers, and the designers at Marx stepped into this aspect of toy train development with two major changes in their products.

The first was the replacement of the double axle, two wheel trucks with four-wheel trucks that more closely simulated the true eight-wheel trucks found on American rolling stock. This occurred in 1938. The axles no longer were attached to tab extensions from the bases as in the Joy Line and earlier six inch cars, but rather true independent four-wheel trucks were attached to the underside of the frame, quite a difference from the older tab arrangement.

A new type of coupler was added to the eight wheel cars in 1938 which was called an "automatic" coupler. Based on a

Fig. 11–12. The Army train was one of Marx's most popular train sets. Painted in olive drab, this set is headed by the Commodore Vanderbilt locomotive. Photo from the Collection of Don Speidel

male–female post and slot configuration, each car carried one or the other fitting at each end. For mating, a male fitting on one car was attached to a female on another. This resulted in unidirectional rolling stock. A car could not be reversed in direction without changing the direction of all of the cars in the consist. Whereas Lionel's knuckle couplers could mate in either direction, Marx's could not. Though automatic coupling is found on most eight-wheel examples, the slot and tab coupler was still used on some of them.

The eight-wheel cars saw service until the war, but were not reissued after that, though four-wheel, six-inch cars were returned to the marketplace.

The locomotives that provided the pulling power for the Marx trains from this period showed quite a bit of variety. The Commodore Vanderbilt engine was inaugurated in 1934 and was designed in conjunction with the six-inch rolling stock. It was based on the Vanderbilt design used by the New York Central Railroad. Fabricated from sheet steel, it was the first production engine produced at Marx and saw service until 1952. Most models carried the Commodore Vanderbilt sideplates. The profile on the 0–4–0 engine was sleek and streamlined with a flat nose cowl. Both clockwork and electric motors were used for propulsion. Several colors were used during its life span, including olive drab for the Army set.

The Mercury came off of the drawing board in 1938, and was one of Marx's most successful engines. Marx was the only toy train manufacturer to market the Mercury

Fig. 11–14. Note the center pickup shoes made of copper on the electrically operated loco on the left. Compare it with the clockwork motor in the example on the right.

which was designed by Henry Dryfuss for the New York Central Railroad. It also was produced from sheet steel and featured an 0–4–0 configuration. The profile was similar to the Vanderbilt, but differed with its lack of steam domes on most models and its rounded nose cowl. Painted in a variety of colors, the Mercury was the mainstay of the company for many years. It was teamed with a streamlined tender and pulled a series of articulated coaches called the Mercury Sets. These sets were painted in a variety of colors. Marx's blue Mercury was an answer to Lionel's popular Blue Comet. Both clockwork and electric motors were used in the shell. The Mercury had a long and illustrious career that ended in 1952.

One of the most popular engines of the period was the #391. It appeared in 1937, and many variations occurred. The engine was used with the Canadian Pacific trains

Fig. 11–15. The curved cowling helps identify the Mercury locomotive. The top set is called the Grey Streamliner and carries Cleveland and Detroit coaches as well as a streamlined tender. The Blue Streamliner (bottom) consists of a conventional tender, Montclair coach and an observation. Both sets are keywind examples. Photo Courtesy of Christie's

as well as with many freight combinations. Styled more like a traditional steam engine, its chief characteristic was its large sideboards. The #396 and #397 were introduced in 1940–41 and were variations of the #391. Both 0–4–0 and 2–4–2 configurations were used. The #494 was a more streamlined version of the earlier #300 Series, and it carried the Canadian Pacific 3000 number on the sideboards. It appeared also in the early 1940s.

The lithographed body shell of the #897 was distinctive. Following the Marx tradition, the engine's details, such as piping and ladders, were printed on the shell. The 0–4–0 wheel configuration was powered by an electric and keywind motor.

A few words should be said about the Lumar Lines floor trains. These rather large pieces fashioned from sheet steel appeared in 1939 and lasted for only a few years. The engine was a streamlined-type, and the whole assembly ran on rather large wheels. Other floor trains were introduced first in the early 1930s in Standard Gauge. These models were designed to operate on Standard Gauge.

Priced Examples

Sets

#M–10005 Union Pacific clockwork, 2 Passenger Cars, Observation $40.00

Army train Set, #400 loco, tender, (2) #2246 Flat Cars with tank and truck, #2246 Flat Car with truck and searchlight, #234 Caboose $60.00

Joy Line clockwork locomotive, tender, (4) #357 Passenger Cars, #458 Observation A–$40.00

Locomotives

#M–10005 keywind $18.00

CHAPTER 12

The Post-War Years at Marx

Following World War II, the Marx Company turned its attention to marketing its scale rolling stock. Based roughly on the scale of $\frac{3}{16}$ of an inch to one prototype foot, the cars were patterned after rolling stock of the major United States railroads. Research and development on the $\frac{3}{16}$-inch scale designs began prior to the war, and a few were marketed just before Marx retooled for the war effort. The scale cars were an answer to Lionel's and American Flyer's domination of this aspect of the market. The major push came following the war when the company geared up for the peace-time market. As with other Marx trains, they were packaged as sets, and many were sold through the catalog houses and chain stores—a profitable method of marketing. Some of the sets were mixed, containing both freight and passenger cars.

In spite of the interest in the scale cars, the late 6-inch cars were the backbone of the company and were released in new road colors and heralds. These continued in service for many years.

The $\frac{3}{16}$-inch scale rolling stock was more realistic in appearance than any other rolling stock Louis Marx had produced. The body shell was lithographed steel with close attention paid to detail. This is the distinctive feature of these pieces. The freight cars were stamped with railroad names of the times and colors. N.Y.C. "Pacemaker", Union Pacific "Challenger", GAEX and others were emblazoned on the sides of cars in the appropriate colors. Each of the cars was placed on two sets of four-wheel trucks. The trucks were similar to the Bettendorf trucks found on rolling stock of the period. Much of the detail such as springs and journal boxes was embossed on the truck side.

A new automatic coupler was developed for these cars. It featured a scissoring type attachment that was multidirectional. Uncoupling was accomplished by a raised projection in the track which tilted the couplers and allowed for disengagement. The couplers were fabricated from metal or plastic. The plastic examples appeared in the early 1950s.

The basic inventory of freight rolling stock included boxcars, reefer-refrigerators, stock cars, hoppers, flats, tankers, gondolas with and without loads, and cabooses. To increase interest for the young railroader, each of the categories carried several roadnames and color combinations. Therefore, a boxcar could carry a N.Y.C., Penn R.R., or Union Pacific herald, and colors. Adding these cars to an existing consist changed the complexion of the train, and the play value of the set. The freight rolling stock was introduced about 1941 and continued in production to the mid-1950s.

Passenger coaches were added to the list of scale cars about 1950 and were available until the mid-1970s. The coaches, both domed and conventional, and the observation cars were manufactured from

steel with many of the features embossed into the body shell. Some included silhouettes of passengers in the windows, while others merely had frosted windows. Some carried metal couplers—others used plastic. Trucks were fabricated from metal, but later versions found on the passenger cars featured plastic mounts.

The $\frac{3}{16}$-inch scale rolling stock was packaged with the #999 steam engine and the #333 for the passenger sets. Featuring a die cast body, the #999 was a smart looking engine with a 2-4-2 wheel configuration and was released in both electric (early 1940s) and keywind (1949) versions. Variations occurred in the driving wheels on these pieces. The #333 was one of the most beautiful die-cast engines Marx produced. With extensive detail including piping and rivets, it rolled around the track on a 4-6-2 wheel arrangement. Primarily developed to compliment the $\frac{3}{16}$-inch scale passenger cars, it made its initial appearance in 1949 and was powered by electricity.

One other locomotive deserves consideration in this section. The Santa Fe diesel was issued in 1950 and consisted of two "A" units (one powered, the other unpowered or a dummy) that mated back-to-back. Painted in the Santa Fe colors of red and silver, this lithographed loco was intended for mating with the Santa Fe $\frac{3}{16}$-inch scale passenger cars though the engine was actually $\frac{1}{4}$-inch scale. The entire consist was a handsome combination. Marx #666, another impressive 2-4-2 die cast steamer, saw service with the scale cars. This ingenious electrically powered engine

Fig. 12-1. The knuckle coupler (left) was not operational, but the tilt couplers were. The center specimen was made of plastic, and the earlier example on the right was stamped from steel.

featured a smoke puffing device on some models that sent whiffs of a smoke-like substance from the stack as the engine chugged around the track.

Marx's sudden and somewhat unexpected introduction of the 7-inch freight cars in 1949 was thought to be related to the Unique Toy Company's presence in the train market. Quite similar in style to Marx's products, it brought an immediate response from Marx in the form of the 7-inch lithographed metal rolling stock. Though Unique dropped its train lines about 1952, Marx continued the 7-inch metal car line until 1958. Only one set of passenger cars was produced, and they were manufactured in one form or another until 1962.

The 7-inch car can be summarized as one group that had limited production. Freight examples were stamped for boxcars, gondolas, and cabooses. The cabooses had many variations, but the others were limited compared to Marx earlier series. Perhaps the company lost interest once Unique was no longer a factor. The cars were produced as both four- and eight-wheel examples. The four-wheel chassis were very similar to the wheel arrangement found on the 6-inch cars. The axle pierced the center of a tab projection representing a journal box. The four-wheel examples looked ungainly, probably because the long body was stretched over four wheels. The eight-wheel examples seem more at home on their wheelbase and were more realistic in appearance. The body rode on two pairs of swiveling four-wheel trucks with springs embossed on the sides.

Coupling devices included the old slot and tab, tilt, and plastic knuckle couplers. Some freight cars were found with slot and tab or plastic knuckles. The caboose, with its many variations, was found with all three types used at one time or another. The plastic knuckle probably was meant to mate with Lionel's knuckle coupler.

Two train sets that utilized 7-inch cars deserve special consideration. The Mickey Mouse Meteor Set was issued for the 1950–51 season and consisted of a steam locomotive and tender, boxcar, gondola, and caboose all brightly painted with random Disney characters. With its gay colors

Fig. 12–2. Marx's 7-inch freight cars were manufactured with two- and four-wheel trucks. The body was lithographed metal, and coupling was accomplished by means of metal tilt couplers. Photo Courtesy of "The Antique Trader Weekly"

and figures, it had the appearance of a circus train. The train was headed by an unusual steamer. Quite long as steam engines go, it was based on the #994 shell and featured four drivers, but the pilots and trailers were set into the shell above the track without making contact with the track. It gave the appearance of pilots and trailers without being functional. The engine was powered by a clockwork motor. The Mickey Mouse Set is one of the most sought after post-war Marx train sets and is considered the anchor of any Marx collection with the same appeal as the Bunny train. In good condition, this set can fetch from $600–$800.

The William Crooks train carried the only passenger cars in the 7-inch metal car series. Based on a Civil War period train complete with wide bellied smoke stack, the Crooks was modeled with a molded plastic engine shell and operated either with a clockwork or electric motor. The locomotives were designed in several different versions which included electric powered 4-4-0 and 0-4-0 configurations in 1959, and a clockwork motor driven piece in a 4-4-0 arrangement without siderods on the driving wheels in 1962. The passenger car styles consisted of a combine-mail car and a coach which were based on the St. Paul and Pacific railroad cars of the period. The cars were mounted on four-wheel or eight-wheel configurations. Slot and tab, automatic tilt and plastic knuckle couplers were incorporated at one time or another on these cars.

Many of the 7-inch car sets included the #994 steam engine, but several other sets were packaged with engines such as

Fig. 12–3. Marx's accessories were an important part of the Marx system, but were less dramatic than their competitors. The #418 Crossing Signal featured a bell that warned of an approaching train.

the #666, the #21 diesel units, and a variety of other diesel AA units. The long #994 seemed to fit the 7-inch cars in proper perspective.

During the 1950s, many important changes occurred at the Marx factory. Plastic, and plastic and metal combination rolling stock were introduced during this period. For convenience sake, these cars (of which there are numerous varieties) can be divided into two classes: lightweights and heavyweights.

The heavyweights contain ballast to improve the tracking of the cars, whereas the lightweights don't have the added weight. The heavyweights can be subdivided into $8\frac{1}{2}$-inch long cars (which were assembled from individual pieces and are quite detailed—some have moving parts such as sliding doors), and the shorter $6\frac{1}{2}$-inch cars which were molded as a single body unit and have details such as doors, ladders, and rivets cast into the body shell. Both heavyweight classes rode on two pairs of swiveling four-wheel trucks.

The lightweight cars were easily differentiated from the heavies. Not only was the weight different, but the wheel configuration was a dead giveaway. Whereas the heavies used the four-wheel independent trucks, the lights rolled on a pair of two-wheel axles attached to plastic trucks and projected from the sides of the shells. This scheme was reminiscent of the four-wheel 6-inch cars. The plastic body also was molded as a single unit with the appropriate details. The lightweights were used in conjunction with Marx's less expensive sets.

Examining the plastics in closer detail, we find that both heavies and lights were

represented as gondolas, tankers, hoppers, boxes, stocks, and cabooses. The plastic dumper was not made in the lightweight version. Combination plastic and metal cranes, and flatcars with loads were found in both the heavy and light versions. A plastic flat car for the 0-4-0 William Crooks Set also was part of the inventory. Slot and tab, tilt, and plastic knuckles joined the cars together. As one would expect with this number of freight cars, many varieties and coupler combinations, truck types, and finishes existed.

Somewhere in between these classes was a hybrid type. The middleweight class used the body shells of the lightweights but rolled on two sets of four-wheel trucks.

The 1950s saw the introduction of

Fig. 12-5. This well-designed heavyweight wrecker crane uses tilt couplers for joining. By turning the wheels located on the side of the housing, the boom and hook can be raised or lowered. Photo Courtesy of Joy Luke Auctions

Fig. 12-4. Mechanical sets geared for the youngster from ages three to six were a significant part of Marx's inventory of products. The rolling stock is the lightweight type plastic freights. Photo Courtesy of Nelson's Auction

Fig. 12-6. Dating about 1966, these medium-weight plastic freight cars are becoming very collectible.

many types of diesel engines. This was a period of diesel popularity with many diesels replacing steam locomotives. Marx, as well as the other toy train producers, was able to feel the country's pulse and joined the diesel revolution.

When one thinks of diesels, the image is that of Marx's #21 Santa Fe with its streamlined profile pulling a string of passenger cars. However, the diesel served many functions on the real railroad, and this was reflected in the Marx train sets. Not only did these diesels head passenger cars, they moved groups of freights from place to place. Based roughly on the E-7 and "F" diesel profile (Marx didn't concern itself with prototypes), the engines were either lithographed metal or molded plastic shells. The lithographed examples featured brightly painted color schemes, and details were printed or embossed on the shell. More detail and realism were found on the plastic molded shells. Both A powered and A dummy or unpowered units were fabricated along with B unpowered units.

Many of the lithographed A units were set on four-driver wheels, though some were equipped with additional four-wheel pilot trucks. The plastic shell diesels featured two sets of four-wheel trucks, similar to the prototypes. The B units were used with the litho and plastic shell locomotives. The wheel configuration matched those of the A units. Some of the larger sets included an A powered and B and A dummy units.

Another class of diesels that saw considerable duty was the road switchers.

Fig. 12-7. Relying heavily on lithography, Marx's diesels were manufactured in powered and dummy units. This 1950 #6000 Southern Pacific AA carried a single electric motor in the power unit that activated only the rear truck.

These little gems moved rolling stock around a yard in order to put combinations of trains together. Marx's rendition appeared in two versions. An eight-wheel model was quite similar to the prototype, whereas the four-wheel version was more of an industrial type switcher. All of the road diesels featured plastic shells. Some were incorporated in boxed sets. An example of this is the Lehigh Valley train set which was headed by a small plastic industrial switcher. Many of these sets were decorated in bright road colors.

In answer to Lionel's RDC (rail diesel car) or Budd car, Marx issued its example in 1956. It saw service for about four years, and only one version was manufactured. This diesel powered engine actually looked like a passenger car, but was somewhat boxy in appearance compared to Lionel's example. Silhouettes were installed in the windows which were accentuated by interior lighting. The Budd car carried the Boston and Maine herald on a grey body and was coupled by means of the old tab and slot couplers.

One final diesel which deserves consideration was a small battery powered engine—part of a set known as the Marx-Tronic set. The set consisted of a switching engine and a pair of high sided gondolas. The train traveled on two-rail plastic track.

Throughout the chapter on Marx trains, we have alluded to the fact that the trains frequently were marketed as sets, especially through the catalog and chain stores. This is by no means the only way the trains could be purchased. Individual pieces were sold across the counter and through catalog outlets. They were marketed in order to enhance any set, or a buyer could begin by assembling individual pieces. However, train sets were the heart and soul of the Marx marketing process, and we should examine a few of the sets, especially those sold through the catalog houses such as Sears, Roebuck. The Sears-Allstate association sold trains under their Happi-Times and Allstate names, as well as the Marx brand.

Most of the sets appeared in the Fall-Winter Editions of the catalogs. The 1935–36 Winter Sears Catalog featured a Marx Commodore Vanderbilt set with five passenger cars consisting of four coaches and an observation car with a red tail light. The cars were set on the early six inch frames and featured two- wheel sets at the innermost journal boxes. In addition, three 6-inch freight cars could be added to the set. These included a tanker, hopper, and caboose on the same frames. This provided versatility as both freight and passenger trains could be assembled. The basic set included track and a transformer.

On the same page were two examples

of Marx's Union Pacific M–10000. An electric version carried two coaches and an observation and was completed with track and transformer for $4.39. A clockwork example with one coach and observation, a battery for the headlight and a commemorative coin honoring the Union Pacific M–10000 was available for $1.59.

The 1937–38 book offered a clockwork Commodore Vanderbilt Set with a stop-start-reverse motor. The passenger cars were the "new embossed" models, the later 6-inch four-wheel cars.

Both electric and clockwork were offered in the 1948 catalog. The Red Flyer consisted of a keywind Mercury engine which sported a ringing bell and a sparkler device. It pulled a tender, coach, and observation car based on the later 6-inch four-wheel lithographed cars. A Marlines freight set was headed by a 0–4–0 Canadian Pacific steam engine and tender. The consist was a string of later 6-inch four-wheel stock, gondola, tanker, and caboose. It should be apparent by now that a good deal of mileage was obtained from the 6-inch lithographed cars.

The Happi-Times electric freight was the key set in the 1955 catalog. A plastic #400 engine and tender, lithographed later style 6-inch four-wheel stock, tanker, and caboose made up this set. The keywind train set for 1955 was known as the Seaboard set because of the lithographed Seaboard diesel AA units that were the power sources. A gondola, tanker, and caboose of the 6-inch four- wheel style made up the string.

When Marx launched the HO line,

Big $2.00 Value Last Year—Now Only $1.59
—27-Inch Train—Electric Headlight—Bell—Figure 8 track.
The streamlined engine with clockwork motor, brake and electric headlight and two cars are coupled together like real ones. Watch it speed around the track! They're metal, lithographed in Union Pacific colors. Headlight bulb, battery and Union Pacific Lucky coin included. 160 inches of track.

$1.59
49 K 5135—Shipping weight, 6 pounds..........

Your Choice 98c Each

Mickey Stokes His Own Freight Train
Brand New—Sold by Mail only by Sears
(A) The faster the train travels, the faster Mickey Mouse stokes the engine and the bell rings. It'll thrill the 'kiddies.' 7-in. locomotive with powerful clockwork motor and brake release. Entire train 30 in. long. Circular track about 80 in. around.
49 K 5104—Shpg. wt. 4 lbs........98c

Realistic Watch Sparks Fly
(B) Sparks fly out of smokestack. 29-in. train. Strong Marx clockwork motor. Engine is heavy steel with brake to stop or start. Tender and 3 cars lithographed metal in train colors. Oval track about 74 in. around, banked for speed. Extra flint included.
49 K 5133—Shpg. wt., 3 lbs. 13 oz.....98c

NEW MICKEY MOUSE CIRCUS TRAIN
With Mechanical Motor
$1.79

Lionel Product

SOLD BY MAIL ONLY BY SEARS

Mickey Stokes the New Commodore Vanderbilt Locomotive
30-Inch train, 84 inches of track—a whole circus. Gay 20x9x11 inch high cardboard circus tent, filling station and 5-inch composition Mickey figure. Strong clockwork motor hauls this big circus train with Mickey's kingdom of animals lithographed in beautiful colors on sides of cars. Headlight flashes, bell rings. Mickey stokes engine! 7-inch new Commodore Vanderbilt Streamlined engine with brake; tender, circus diner, animal car and hand car. Battery included. Shpg. wt. 6 lbs. 6 oz.
49 K 5103—Complete Outfit.................**$1.79**

SEARS GREATEST ELECTRIC TRAIN VALUES
Complete With Transformer
Nothing Else to Buy

$4.39

$8.79

New Marx Electric COMMODORE VANDERBILT TRAIN
● 41-inch, 5-car streamlined electric reversible passenger train or 3-car freight train, or combination of both... 8 beautifully lithographed metal cars in all, one tender and 12-pc. "O"-gauge oval track about 124 in. around... Transformer included.
Have a passenger train—a fast freight or a mixed accommodation! Latest type Commodore Vanderbilt locomotive. Transformer, which is included, changes its speed. Watch the train speed by with headlight piercing the darkness. Red tail light on observation car. For 110-volt 60-cycle A.C. current. Shpg. wt., 8 lbs. 12 oz.
49 K 5158—Complete Outfit.**$4.69**

$4.29 Without Freight Cars

Same Passenger train as above, but no freight cars. Shpg. wt., 7 lbs. 12 oz.
49 K 5157.....**$4.29**

Marx Streamlined UNION PACIFIC TRAIN
Save at Sears New Low Price
For This 35-Inch Electric Train
It's the 1935 flying streamline train that goes with a roar over this 124-inch oval track, with headlight streaming ahead. Pull the lever on transformer to change speed or stop it. Wheels mounted to take train at record speed around curves without jumping off track. Four cars in the Union Pacific colors, coupled together. For 110-volt 60-cycle A.C. current. Complete train with 12 pieces "O"-gauge 3-rail track. Transformer included. Shipping weight, 8 lbs. 4 oz.
49 K 5156 ....**$4.39**

Distant Control LIONEL ELECTRIC TRAIN
Sold by Mail Only by Sears
$15.00 Value Last Year
40-inch electric steel train. 9½-inch reversible steel engine; concealed electric headlight; 2 colored pilot lights. Distant controlled so train can be stopped, started or reversed at any point. 6½-inch coal tender. Two 7½-inch pullman cars, and one observation car; all base double trucks. 10-piece "O"-gauge oval track about 114 inches around. For 110-volt 60-cycle A.C. current. Transformer included. Shipping weight, 11 pounds 13 ounces.
49 K 5155 ....**$8.79**

Electric Train Tracks
"O" Gauge Lionel Track
For trains 49 K 5155. Shpg. wt. 10 oz.
Curved Track — 49K5235 — 2 pcs. for 37c
Straight Track — 49K5236 — 2 pcs. for 37c

"O" Gauge Marx Track
For trains 49 K 5156 and 49 K 5157 and 49 K 5158. Shpg. wt. 11 oz.
Curved — 49K5217 — 4 pcs. for 39c
Straight — 49K5216 — 4 pcs. for 39c

Lionel Switches with lamps for "O"-gauge trains. Shpg. wt. 2 lbs. 14 oz. 49 K 5215 Pair **$5.29**
Lionel Crossover for "O"-gauge trains. Shpg. wt. 15 oz. 49 K 5210 **$1.45**
MARX Crossover for Trains 49 K 5156, 49 K 5157 and 49 K 5158. 49 K 5238—Shpg. wt. 1 lb....59c

Mechanical Train Tracks
Curved Track For trains 49 K 5103 and 49 K 5104. Shpg. 49K5207 4 pcs. for 19c
Straight Track For trains 49 K 5103 and 49 K 5104. Shpg. 49K5206 4 pcs. for 19c
For trains 49 K 5133 and 49 K 5135. Shpg. wt. 14 oz. 49K5213 4 pcs. for 19c
49 K 5133 and 49 K 5135. 49K5212 4 pcs. for 19c

For All Mechanical Trains
Switches 49 K 5203 Pair 39c
Crossover For making figure eight track. Shpg. 49 K 5205 19c

Jefferson Transformer For "O" gauge trains. 75 watts, unbroken voltage control 8½ to 22½ volts. 110-volt 60-cycle A.C. Shpg. wt. 3 lbs. 49 K 5277...**$2.79**

Low Priced Transformer For "O" gauge trains. 110-volt 60-cycle A.C. Shpg. wt. 3 lbs. 1 oz. 49 K 5288...**$1.19**

WILL HOLD 200 LBS

$1.29

Ride and Steer This Locomotive
23 inches long. A child can ride on it. Will hold 200 lbs. Heavy 20-gauge steel, 9½ in. high. Steering bar on top of boiler. Bright baked-on enamel finish. Steel wheels. Shpg. wt. ... 79 K 5024...**$1.29**

The larger the order the less your postage per pound

743

Sears sold the Allstate Freight Set which consisted of a plastic A unit and a Lehigh hopper, Boston and Maine box, gondola, and a bay window caboose. Additional individual rolling stock included a searchlight car and a flat car with a lumber load. A small industrial diesel switcher was offered as an accessory piece.

The smaller HO scale model railroad boom took hold after World War II, and the Louis Marx Corporation added a line of HO scale and semi-scale trains to their other lines. By 1957, the company had geared up for production and issued a handsome plastic smoke puffing 4-6-4 Hudson style engine and an eight-wheel tender. The freight cars consisted of a plastic molded box, gondola, hopper, tanker, caboose categories, and a die-cast flat car. The cars rolled on a pair of scale four-wheel trucks. The coupling mechanism was a device called a horn-hook coupler which was the standard in the model railroading world. This allowed Marx rolling stock to mate with scale model rolling stock and thus increase sales potential. The rolling stock was designed to keep up with the times. Rocket, military, and atomic cars were issued to keep interest alive.

A series of diesels based on the GP-7 and F-7 profiles and an industrial switcher appeared in the following year along with additional freights and a series of illuminated passenger cars. In addition, a small steam switcher was added a few years

Fig. 12-9. The HO Gauge rolling stock included a variety of up-to-date pieces, such as this Rocket Fuel car. Photo From the Collection of Don Speidel

later. The semi or non-scale pieces were pulled by a battery operated engine.

HO Gauge was not as popular as the manufacturers thought, and like their competitors, Marx began phasing out the line. By the mid-1960s, marketing of the line had ceased to be active, though pieces were available until the mid-1970s. Because of the small size of the gauge, accessories were manufactured to compliment the trains.

With the unsuccessful HO venture and the failure of the company to compete effectively with the slot racing and electronic game boom, Louis Marx and Company was sold to the Quaker Oats Company in 1972. At this juncture, Quaker renamed the toy branch, calling it Marx Toys. Marketing of the products was poor, and the train line came to an end in 1976. Quaker Oats sold Marx Toys to the British firm of Dundee-Combex-Marx in the same year. By 1980, D-C-M filed for bankruptcy, thus ending Marx long history.

Fig. 12-8. Sears 1935-36 Fall-Winter Catalog offered electric and keywind versions of the M-10000 and the Commodore Vanderbilt passenger set. The Lionel Mickey Mouse Circus set is featured in the upper right corner. Photo Reprinted with the Permission of Sears, Roebuck & Co.

Priced Examples

Sets

#490 steam loco, 0–4–0, plastic, three freight cars, track	$75.00
#6000 diesel powered, #6000 diesel dummy AA units, #80982 Wabash Hopper, #37956 Pennsylvania Boxcar, #1235 Caboose, track, transformer and accessories	$60.00
#999 steam loco, tender, #6424 Auto Transporter with two autos, #3461 Pipe Car, #6519 Allis Chalmers Car	$40.00
Mickey Mouse Meteor train, locomotive with three cars, 1950, mint	$825.00

Locomotives

#901 diesel AA, Western Pacific, plastic shells	$20.00
#1666 steam, tender	$30.00
#1998 switcher	$15.00
#4000 diesel AA, New York Central, plastic shells	$20.00

CHAPTER 13

The Lesser-Known Train Manufacturers

To the collector, Lionel, Ives, and American Flyer are considered the big three, and the later arriving Marx firm also has its legion of followers. As a result, most of the material in this book deals with these four giants. However, it would be remiss to overlook the contributions of the lesser known American toy train manufacturers. Most were dominant in the early part of the Twentieth Century; some lasted a short time, while others showed some staying power.

For the most part, these manufacturers produced and marketed toys. A line of trains was secondary. Each of the companies made significant contributions or unique items that were important in the evolution of the toy train business. All are very collectible, and in many cases, demand top dollar at toy and train shows. Others are scarce, but do not garner much interest from collectors.

An example of one of these early manufacturers that produced some credible pieces was the Knapp Electric and Novelty Company located in New York City. Started in 1890 by David Knapp, the company's knowledge in the electric toy and game field made it a natural for their introduction of a line of electric toy trains in 1906. Consisting of 2-inch gauge cast-iron steam profile locomotives, passenger coaches, and traction pieces, the cost of tooling up and competing resulted in the closing of the line in 1913. During this eight-year period, the cast-iron, wood, and later all metal locomotives rolled on sectional track which included mechanically operated switches and crossings. Knapp examples appear occasionally in auctions and train shows and are very collectible.

One of the true pioneers in American miniature railroading was a firm located in Cincinnati, Ohio. The Carlisle and Finch Company was founded in 1893 by Morton Carlisle and Robert Finch, and one year after their founding, they entered the competitive train market with well-made electric examples. Their wheels were set at a 2-inch gauge, and the track consisted of ribbons of steel set into precut wooden ties in order to maintain gauge width. They were later to introduce sectional or piece track. Trolleys with trailers, streetcars, and interurbans were their earliest attempts at cracking the tough train market. These early traction vehicles were manufactured from sheet metal with wooden floors to reduce weight. Carlisle and Finch's electric powered trains were the first to be produced in this country. The Company was a true American pioneer.

The mining train appeared in 1897 and was one of the trains associated most frequently with Carlisle and Finch. A cut cornered rectangular engine pulled a series of ore cars. The first model was propelled by a belt drive which was later replaced by gears, and simple ore cars were replaced by dumpers.

The first true road locomotive appeared in 1899 and was #4 in the company catalog. It carried an 0–4–0 configuration and featured a reversing unit in the cab. Passenger cars #13 and #13B, coaches and baggage examples, mated with this locomotive. The following year saw the intro-

duction of the first freight cars. An electric working derrick car was part of the line in 1905, and the top-of-the-line nickel-plated #45 locomotive was previewed in 1903. This 4–4–2 Atlantic type loco carried a pin and lock type coupler. In 1914, both freights and passengers were issued for this locomotive. A larger series of passengers was to follow.

Because many homes did not have electric current, Carlisle and Finch provided several alternative electrical sources for their trains. Many of the sets were packaged with dry-cell batteries or wet cells. Water driven dynamos also were part of their catalog inventory. Due to the constant electric current, train speed could be regulated without a rheostat. For those houses with current, Carlisle and Finch manufactured a transformer to reduce the current and a light bulb type current controller.

Mail order was Carlisle and Finch's major method of marketing. Since electric miniature railroads were relatively new and at times difficult to construct, they published a fifty-eight page book entitled *Miniature Electric Railway Construction* that was listed for fifty cents in their 1911

Fig. 13-1. Carlisle and Finch is most often identified with its simplistic mining train. However, they manufactured some splendid steam locomotives, such as this white metal example with its accompanying brass passenger coach. Photo Courtesy of Sotheby's

catalog. However, competition from such companies as Lionel, Ives, Knapp, and American Flyer resulted in the company dropping its train lines in 1915 and concentrating on the production of other electric devices, especially marine lighting. During the 1930s, the company again toyed with the idea of entering the lucrative toy train market, but none of the ideas were put into production. Putting together a working Carlisle and Finch railroad layout can be a challenge.

A most interesting toy train company was founded in 1909 by two ex-Ives employees. The American Miniature Railway Company, located in Bridgeport, Connecticut manufactured toy trains that resembled closely the Ives cast-iron and tin pieces. Modeling in O and #1 Gauge, their products often were confused with Ives trains, but the numbers found on American Miniature Railway Company examples never were used on comparable Ives pieces. Cast iron and tin clockwork locomotives pulled lithographed passengers and freights that rolled on four- and eight-wheel sets. The use of brake shoes on some of the examples also was an identifying feature of the American Miniature Railway cars. Eight-inch O Gauge passengers and freights, and 12-inch #1 Gauge cars were produced to travel on two rail track that was packaged with the train sets. Freight cars included gravel, gondola, box, stock, and caboose examples in well printed lithographed tin. In spite of the good quality of the products, the company folded after just four years of operation in 1912.

The Dorfan Company had its roots extending back to Germany. Following World War I, the Forcheimer brothers started the company in 1924 in a factory located in Newark, New Jersey. Dorfan was innovative in many aspects of toy train manufacturing. Once a strong contender with Ives, Lionel, and American Flyer, the company produced both Wide and O Gauge examples in its productive years.

In order to be competitive, the company realized they had to develop new manufacturing techniques. The Forcheimer brothers introduced the zinc-copper cast body shell that became the backbone of their line. This unbreakable shell locked the wheels and motor in place without the need for a frame. In addition, the shell was cast in two sections and could be dismantled by removing two posts, thus gaining easy access to the motor for service. Called the "Loco Builder," it was a successful marketing technique. The heavy weight of the shell resulted in positive traction, but warping and cracking were constant production problems. Ball bearings were employed in the top-of-the-line locomotives such as the Wide Gauge 4-4-4 electric profile #3930 for smoother operation. The earliest cast shells were all electric profile locomotives in both Wide and O Gauge. Clockwork and electric O Gauge examples competed with the Wide Gauge electrics. O Gauge 0-4-0 steam profile locomotives in electric and clockwork also were manufactured. Quality control was a major problem in this innovative casting technique, and it led eventually to the downfall of the company. It is also a problem for collectors as the die-

Fig. 13-2. Dorfan's Wide Gauge #3930 loco is pictured in its 1928 advertisement. The strong points such as ball bearings, and the Take-Apart shell are emphasized.

cast shells tend to disintegrate over time, and good examples are extremely difficult to find.

Lithographed rolling stock was exceptionally well done both in Wide and O Gauge. Dorfan's freights and passengers rolled on the first die-cast trucks and wheels in the industry. Some people consider these trucks the best that were manufactured. Stamped trucks also were incorporated. Dorfan's use of decals in place of rubber stamping was a strong selling point. The decals were bright and colorful. Silhouettes frequently were employed in the passenger cars. Both freights and passenger cars were stamped from heavy gauge steel and have stood the test of time better than the locomotives. Tab and slot coupling was standard.

The Dorfan Wide Gauge coaches rolled on two sets of four-wheel trucks, and a few of the O Gauge pieces rolled on these trucks too, though many of the simple O Gauge passengers traveled on four wheels. Passenger coaches often were illuminated,

Fig. 13-3. The rolling stock manufactured by Dorfan mirrored the freight cars of the day. This series includes a wood-sided boxcar, caboose, hopper, gondola, and tank car. Photo Courtesy of Sotheby's

and three-rail track was standard for both gauges.

Distribution of their products was through a dealer network, and mass consumer publicity was not in the company's thinking. However, some beautiful catalogs were issued that included a wide variety of accessories, such as lithographed tunnels, stations, and signals. The Dorfan automatic circuit breaker was another innovative device that was a Dorfan original. When wired to the layout, it would turn off the current if a short circuit developed. This prevented damage to the equipment as well as providing protection for the young engineer.

Like many other toy manufacturers, Dorfan did not survive the Depression of the 1930s. It was able to hold out until 1938 when it closed down production.

William Hafner was no stranger to the manufacture of toys. Using pressed steel as the basic building block, Hafner formed the Toy Auto Company in 1900, and by 1904 the W.F. Hafner Company was well on its way to producing steel cars, trucks, and other vehicles. After Hafner's experience

Fig. 13-4. The Chicago and Northwestern herald on this Hafner coach makes it an especially desirable piece. Photo Courtesy of "The Antique Trader Weekly"

with toy trains at American Flyer, he formed his own company in Chicago in 1914. The Hafner Manufacturing Company produced toys, hardware, and a line of toy trains. Early train pieces were imported from German manufacturers prior to World War I, and these carried the Hafner logos. Its most popular line was the Overland Flyer. It lasted for many years.

Modeling in O Gauge, Hafner's toy trains all were clockwork powered, and the early cast-iron locomotives bore a striking resemblance to Flyer's steam profiles. The trains were designed to sell for a low price compared to their competition. Rolling stock was lithographed and rolled on two double-wheel axles on two rail track. Freights and passenger cars were coupled by a simple non-automatic tab and slot mechanism. Switches, crossings, and accessories were part of the Hafner system.

Lithographed designs changed with the times. These included more streamlined locomotives and rolling stock, but the clockwork mechanism still was the only method of power. In 1950, the company was sold to All Metal Products, maker of the famous Wyandotte toys, who continued the line. However, in 1955 Marx purchased the Hafner dies and production ceased.

Some truly fine trains were manufactured by the Voltamp Electric Manufacturing Company of Baltimore. Quality was the key word for Manes Fuld's trains. Fuld founded the company in 1903, and electric examples were a natural extension of the company's line. Its pieces rolled on 2-inch gauge and Wide Gauge track. All Voltamp pieces were painted, and early examples

Fig. 13-5. Modern day Hafner trains were brightly painted and bore little resemblance to any prototype. They were very toy-like in appearance. Note the vertical tab coupler on the tender. Photo Courtesy of Joy Luke Auctions

Fig. 13-6. Voltamp Electric manufactured toy trains like these for a relatively short period of time. Its well executed examples are great collectors items. Photo Courtesy of Christie's

Fig. 13-7. The Voltamp name is embossed on the driving wheels of the company's #2100 steam locomotive. Note the detail on the tender trucks. Photo Courtesy of Sotheby's

featured operating sprung trucks. Voltamp marked all of its locomotives, some with rubber stamping and others with embossing on the wheels. Rolling stock was "automatically" coupled, but manual un-coupling was required to separate the pieces. A wide range of locomotives was offered to the public ranging from simple mining locomotives to attractive steamers. Trolleys also were an important part of the

Fig. 13-8. Voltamp modeled in Gauge #2 and Wide Gauge. The electric profile loco on the left is the larger Gauge #2, and the interurban trolley on the right rolls on Wide Gauge track. Photo Courtesy of Sotheby's

production line. Many of the accessories were imported from Germany. Voltamp was the first company to power its electric locomotives by means of the electric light socket. This top train line had stiff competition from several of the other American stalwarts. As a result, it was sold to the H.E. Boucher Manufacturing Company in 1923.

Boucher is best known for its Blue Comet which was modeled after the New York to New Jersey passenger train by that name. Boucher also imported steam powered locomotives from European toy train manufacturers. Boucher became insolvent in 1934.

Another Newark, New Jersey company was the Unique Art Manufacturing Company. It was founded in 1916 but did not enter the toy train market until 1948. Their electric and keywind trains were not very dramatic, though they were a strong competitor of Marx in the lower priced market with their tinplate lithographed trains. All of the locomotives were simple, lithographed pieces with the detail incorporated into the printing. Rolling stock all featured two sets of double wheel axles that were mounted close to the middle of the car. Lithography was colorful with the Jewel T Circus cars being the most sought after. These cars showed circus animals

Fig. 13-9. The c1930 Blue Comet was Boucher's most popular train set. It was headed by this 4-6-2 locomotive. The sleek appearance of the profile accounts for its popularity. The loco and tender measure 21-inches long. Photo Courtesy of Sotheby's

behind cages. Both closed and open top circus cars were stamped. The "Benny the Brakeman" caboose featured a swing-out character on the rear platform of the caboose. Coupling was accomplished by a vertical hook and tab system.

The pressures of material shortages resulting from the Korean War caused Unique to reassess its position in the train market. Much to the delight and relief of Marx, Unique abandoned the market in 1952. Though much of the material from this company is quite scarce, there is not much collector interest in their products. Possibly this is due to the lack of creativity in their designs which some collectors consider ugly.

Located in the heartland of America, the Buddy "L" Company flourished for many years with some innovative train sets coming from this company. Founded by Fred Lundahl in 1910 as the Moline Press Steel Company in East Moline, Illinois, the factory produced a wide range of truck and farm equipment parts for actual pieces. By 1913, the company changed its name to the Moline Pressed Steel Company. Lundahl prepared a few toys for his son Buddy, and the success of these pieces resulted in the establishment of a toy division at the company in 1920. Doll furniture and toy vehicles were the initial offerings.

The Buddy "L" line (named after his son) was introduced in 1921 and such outlets as F.A.O. Schwartz and Marshall Field and Company guaranteed the success of Lundahl's products. Buddy "L" toys were characteristically large pieces constructed from strong pressed steel and painted with baked enamels. The stength and finish were strong selling points. These pieces were made to last.

Buddy "L" entered into the toy train field in a dramatic manner. Its first train set was designed for outdoor use and featured a push-pull or riding 4-6-2 locomotive. It was strong enough to support a child's weight. No mechanical or electrical mechanism was used. All of the pieces were spot welded for solid construction, and the finish was baked enamel. Rolling stock was linked by an automatic coupling system. The loco and tender measured 44-inches long, with each of the cars reaching 20 to 22-inches in length. The dimensions were scale, but the gauge was not. The locomotive rolled on sprung trucks. Curved and straight track segments were fabricated from stamped steel. The entire output included a hopper, boxcar, side dump car, tanker, flat, stock, gondola, and caboose. There were also specialized cars, including a locomotive steam shovel, pile driver, clamshell dredge, and wrecking crane. These pieces were produced until 1931 when the line was discontinued.

A new type of rolled steel track manufactured by Bethlehem Steel debuted in 1927. Switches and crossings added to the variety of the layout design. Moline Steel continued to mount the rail on its own ties.

The second train set to be released by Buddy "L" was another push-pull type that was known as the Industrial Set. Also manufactured from pressed steel and enameled like the outdoor set, the Industrial rolled on 2-inch gauge stamped-steel track and was primarily an indoor set. The

Fig. 13–10. Called the outdoor train, this Buddy "L" example was strong enough to carry the weight of a youngster while still maintaining the look of a prototype train. Photo Courtesy of Christie's

Fig. 13–11. Buddy "L" trains were constructed of heavy gauge steel and finished in enamel. Most stood the test of time quite well. The Industrial Train is one of the company's few attempts at manufacturing toy trains. Photo Courtesy of Leslie Hindman Auctions

locomotive and rolling stock carried two axles each. The locomotive measured 10-inches long, and each of the cars measured 8-inches long. The set consisted of a gondola, rock car, ballast car, stake, and rocker dump car. Accessories included a one stall and three stall roundhouse as well as a turntable. Examples from the set occasionally are available at shows and auctions.

The Depression years were hard on Moline Pressed Steel and the Buddy "L" line. The company was purchased by J.W. Bettendorf in 1930 and called Buddy "L" Manufacturing Company. The Buddy "L" version of the Burlington Zephyr was released in 1935 and again was a push-pull or steered system. Measuring 66-inches long, the articulated unit was not meant to roll on track but to travel on rubber tires. A manually operated battery light was located on the lead car. In addition to the basic three unit train, single and double units were cataloged. The last example was available in 1940. Examples of this train are difficult to find.

A wooden train called the "Chuckling Choo Choo" appeared in 1946 and was an example of the wooden toys that replaced steel ones because of the shortage of steel during World War II. The limited number of trains produced by Buddy "L" are very collectible. There are many enthusiasts who covet them.

Priced Examples: Dorfan Wide Gauge

Sets

Grey locomotive with two grey cars marked "Chicago," set box	A–$600.00
Green locomotive, two #789 Mountain Brook Pullman, #790 Pleasant View Observation, maroon, set box	A–$700.00
Locomotive with #770 Baggage, #772 Washington Pullman, #773 Observation, set box	$725.00
#3930 locomotive, five freight cars, set box	A–$1,000.00

Locomotives

Orange electric profile	$500.00

Rolling Stock

Boxcar, A.T. & S.F	$110.00
Hopper car, Pennsylvania R.R.	$275.00
Tank car, Union	$260.00
#789 Pullman with green window frames	$85.00

Priced Examples: O Gauge

Sets

#53 electric locomotive, two passenger cars, baggage car, track, original box	A–$425.00

Rolling Stock

Dorfan Lines Passenger Coach	$20.00

#493 Seattle Passenger Car $20.00

#496 Boston Passenger Car $20.00

#492 Railway Express $22.00

Accessories

Cast block signal   A–$140.00

Cast circuit breaker $55.00

Bridge $85.00

Priced Example: Unique

Jewel Circus set, steam locomotive, tender, two circus cars, caboose $190.00

CHAPTER 14

The Toy Train Industry in Europe

Though the focus of this book deals with American toy trains, it is important to look across the ocean to examine what the European toy manufacturers were making and see what impact they had on the American industry. Many of these companies geared their production for export, and the United States was one of those lucrative markets at which they aimed. The British market also was a favorite target for the Continental makers. Toy train production was active in Germany, France, Belgium, Switzerland, as well as the British Isles, and was in direct competition with a young but vigorous American toy industry. The competition at times was fierce as a statement in the 1911 catalog of Carlisle and Finch states: "Beware of foreign made railways. They are made in a flimsy manner." In some cases this was true but, for the most part, European toy trains were well designed and constructed.

During the 1800s, the European firms paralleled American ones with push-pull floor trains being the most common product. By the late 1800s, the live steam locomotive was the dominant type. Steamers were produced well into the 1930s. The early ones were powered by a single set of drivers, but later several drivers were involved. Early examples moved internally, but, by the turn of the century, power was transmitted to the exterior by means of valve gears and the driving rods. A few had reversing mechanisms. The early steamers were floor runners but were eventually brought onto tracks. Some really fine examples were produced in live steam that were never quite matched by the American toy manufacturers. Prior to the tracked versions, some companies had adjustable pilot wheels that prescribed the course of the engine. Companies such as Karl Bub, George Carette, and Schoenner were active in steamer production.

Characteristically, toy trains of the 1800s bore little resemblance to the real thing. Emphasis was placed on motion rather than appearance. By the turn of the century, more attention was given to modeling the prototypes. Many were based on existing railroads, and such names as "The Black Prince," "Flying Scotsman," and the "Cock of the North" were examples of the European manufacturers switch to the prototypical during this period. Profiles of European locomotives were quite different from American engines. Splash plates over the drivers and shields on the sides of the boilers, as well as the use of buffers (a system designed to cushion the coupling process), were hardly ever found on the American counterparts. European locomotives were quite low slung with long boilers.

As discussed in the chapter on gauges, the larger gauges were more popular in Europe. The larger size gauges #2 through #4 rarely were seen in American examples. Gauge #1 however was the most popular prior to the first world war. Since these larger gauges required a considerable amount of space to operate, the smaller gauges began to gain favor. Gauge O became the most popular between the wars as a challenge to the popularity of this gauge in the United States. Gauges often were arbitrary. One company's gauge #4 was equivalent to another's gauge #3.

During the 1800s period, construction often was hand done. Pieces were assembled by using solder or by lapping the body joints. Painting also was applied by hand and was quite good. Colors frequently followed those of existing railroads. Though not prototypical, attention to detail was usually the order of the day. Passenger coaches were more popular than freight cars or "goods wagons." Coaches often had operating doors, and it was not unusual to find figures representing passengers incorporated into the coaches. Often manufacturers produced short, medium, and long versions of the same coach. Some were mounted on single axle trucks, while the longer versions were placed on double axle trucks. In addition, the same coach frequently was made in a less expensive, nonoperating version.

Lithography was used extensively on rolling stock after the turn of the century, but locomotives, for the most part, continued to be hand painted. Lithography helped reduce the cost of production and thus the selling price. Some wonderful examples of the lithographic technique were found on European trains including some that simulated wood bodies.

European toy companies produced clockworks and electrics in addition to the popular live steam. Clockworks frequently featured slow and fast speed controls as well as forward and reverse mechanisms. Electrics were manufactured in high and low voltage models depending on the energy source. Some companies produced the same locomotive in all three types of power sources, while some utilized the same basic body style, but in high and low voltage versions. Frequently one locomotive type was reworked to produce a different version. Parts often were interchanged. For instance, a Gauge #1 body was found mounted on Gauge O trucks. In this manner, a good deal of mileage was obtained from a few basic parts.

Fig. 14-1. Forward and reverse levers protrude from the rear of the cab of this Bing clockwork locomotive. Photo Courtesy of Joy Luke Auctions

Fig. 14-2. This Bing O Gauge electric locomotive features an internal forward and reversing mechanism.

The English and American markets were important to the Continental toy train manufacturers. British railroads were imitated to appeal to this market and were more faithful to the prototypes. Americanized European trains often were basic European designs with a cowcatcher added to the pilot as well as a headlight—an American fancy. Buffers were removed from rolling stock, and American logos and road colors were added to these pieces. Some were well done and are extremely scarce. An example of this is Bing's Chicago and Northwestern passenger set. America's fascination with cast iron was reflected in the fact that European tinplate examples were cast in iron for the American market.

Collectors consider the period from 1900 to the beginning of World War I as the "Golden Age" of European toy train production. Emphasis was placed on prototype styling, and some outstanding examples were manufactured during this period. Companies both on the Continent and in England cooperated by using their strong suits to design, manufacture, and market their products. This type of relationship was unique to the period. Engines and rolling stock usually were compatible from one manufacturer to another. However, the difference in wheel flanges and track style caused derailment of these units. Goods wagons included action pieces such as dump cars, searchlights, and cranes.

The onset of World War I was disastrous for the European manufacturers, especially those on the Continent. Gearing up for the war effort, the Continental companies greatly curtailed toy production, though some examples of fairly crude war train sets still were being marketed. More important, the strong relationship between the English and Continental manufacturers all but disappeared. In England, emphasis was placed on "British made" products. The near collapse of the European interests was one of the major factors in the rise of the toy train manufacturers in the United States.

Accessories were another strong point regarding the European train manufacturers. Many had considerable experience in the toy field, and the manufacturing of accessories was a natural for them. Several included their accessories as part of the whole train package or set. Lithography was used extensively on items such as stations, whereas cast metal and painted pieces also found form as accessories. One characteristic of the European manufacturers was their attention to detail. Ticket offices with real paper tickets, departure schedules, and destination markers patterned after the real thing were not found in

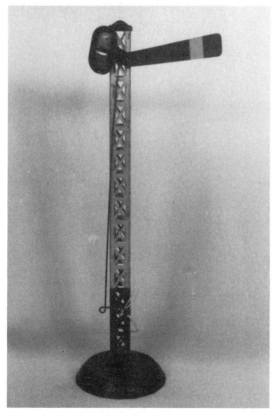

Fig. 14-3. European accessories are very collectible and quite elusive. They fit well in most American layouts. This hand-operated semaphore is a Bing product.

the American manufacturers' inventory. But these truly superb accessories were produced across the ocean.

Germany, whose toy capital was Nuremberg, was a major center for toy production on the Continent. Nuremberg became the toy train capital as well. Several noted companies manufactured excellent toy trains there dating back to the early 1800s. Mathew Hess was one of the first of these manufacturers. The company began in 1826. Along with a general line of toys, Hess introduced a line of painted steel floor trains with a decided European flavor. He later utilized examples using clockwork mechanisms.

Live steam locomotives were the specialty of the Doll Company. Their early examples bore little resemblance to any prototype on the rails. Because of the high pressure built up by the steam, many of Doll's locomotives were quite heavy looking. Doll manufactured toy trains from about 1918 to 1938, mostly in O Gauge. The electrics also were fairly simple in design and were brightly painted. Doll was incorporated into the Fleischmann organization, another Nuremberg company that dated back to 1887. In 1938, the incorporation was complete. Fleischmann began actively producing toy trains following World War II. The company is still in existence producing the smaller HO Gauge trains.

The Frenchman George Carette founded a tinplate toy factory in Nuremberg in 1886 and produced a line of floor runners as well as solid metal steamers. Carette was one of the first to introduce electrics in Europe about 1897. Noted for his excellent lithography, Carette worked in conjunction with the British firm of Bassett-Lowke for sales in England, and with the German company of Karl Bub. Some considered his lithography the best in the field. Gauges were as large as #3 and ran the gamut to the European O. Carette's company was one of the casualities of World War I and closed in 1917.

Steamers were one of the earliest products of the tinplate factory of Karl Bub which was founded in 1851. Trains were modeled in O and #1 Gauges, and Bub was one of the earlier innovators in OO Gauge. The specialty of this company was its fairly extensive line of tracked clockwork trains

introduced about 1905. They became the mainstay of the company even after the introduction of a line of electrics prior to World War I. Bub maintained an English factory as an outlet for his products in that country. Many of Bub's trains were marked with the KBN company logo.

The factory of Ernst Plank was founded in 1886 at Nuremberg. It worked in many of the larger gauges as well as O Gauge. The company's first electrics were introduced in 1882, but steam locomotives were its best sellers. By the 1890s, the steamers were a dominant part of its production in the larger gauges. Accessories were another of Plank's specialties. Production decreased dramatically following

Fig. 14–4. Karl Bub was a major manufacturer of toy trains as well as a supplier for American firms. The upper level train represents Bub's 1920 clockwork style. Boucher produced trains in the United States as well as importing examples from Europe. The lower train is a Boucher piece. Photo Courtesy of Christie's

World War I. Though this company's products have not gained the notoriety of the larger European manufacturers, collectors are beginning to take a second look at these rather scarce examples in good condition, and clean pieces are rising in price quite dramatically.

One of the leading toy manufacturers located in the Nuremberg region was founded by the Bing brothers. Established in 1865 as a toy factory, the Bings produced some remarkable tinplate toys, especially the sailing vessels which are bringing big prices at auction houses. The company was best known for its excellent use of the lithographic technique. It entered the toy train field in 1882 with both floor and tracked examples. The steamers were fashioned from sheet steel and ran on cast wheels. Workmanship for the most part

was good. The lithographic technique was added about 1898 and used extensively on their train accessories. The brothers manufactured four- and eight-wheel coaches with the four wheelers lasting the entire life of the company. These four wheelers were often less expensive versions of the eight wheelers. To capitalize on the American market, they exported "Americanized" trains in the proper road colors and heralds. The electric tunnel train was their most popular design.

About 1900, the Bings formed an important working relationship with the British toy firm of Bassett-Lowke. Utilizing the designs and engineering skills of Bassett-Lowke, the Bing brothers manufactured toy train sets under that banner for sale through the Bassett-Lowke outlets. This combination of expert design and

Fig. 14–5. These three Bing Gauge #1 locomotives illustrate the range of the company's designs. The top steamer is a conventional outline, the loco on the bottom left is an English outline, and the electric profile (bottom right) follows the American outline. These examples range from 1914 to 1920. Photo Courtesy of Christie's

manufacturing technique as well as marketing ability utilized the strong points of both companies.

Bing trains were executed in gauges ranging from the large #4 down to the smaller O Gauge. The smaller gauges were added as the size of the train layouts was uniformly brought under control by most of the train manufacturers. About 1920, the smaller OO Gauge was used by the Bing

Fig. 14–6. Fabricated from cast iron, these three clockwork Bing steamers all have the Bing name under the cab window.

brothers, mainly for sets marketed through English department stores. Following World War I, Bing reissued some of its earlier designs for Bassett-Lowke, especially the steamers in Gauge 1. The great Depression signaled the end of this giant. Bing toy trains are among the most frequently sought after foreign made trains by collectors. Prices are climbing steadily for good examples.

One of the most dominant forces on the Continent was also located near Nuremberg. Marklin Toy Company was founded by Theodore Marklin in the early 1800s, but with the acquisition of the company in 1888 by his two sons, the firm stepped forward as one of the leading toymakers in Europe, known as the Marklin Brothers. Marklin was the first European company to produce clockwork locomotives that were true to scale. Its first clockwork examples, produced about 1891 were fabricated in Gauge #2. The early clockworks had internal drives without external driving rods. Marklin produced a large line of steamers in a variety of gauges, though the company worked in Gauges O, 1, 2, and 4. It was the first company to assign a numbering system to its gauges and to produce commercial electrics in large numbers. Their steamers were not based on prototypes. Several other firsts can be attributed to this successful company including the introduction of sectional or piece track in 1891, followed the next year with the first tinplate switches and crossings. The use of the crossing was an immediate success, since until that time trackage was limited to circular and oval configurations. The crossing allowed for a figure "8" configuration.

Many of Marklin's early trains were hand painted, including its floor runners, and the use of solid colors with contrasting accent colors based on existing railways (especially the English lines) was quite dramatic. The addition of brass trim, especially on the steamers, added to the effect. Workmanship was at times uneven but, for the most part, was quite good. The first rolling stock was placed on single axle trucks, but as the coaches increased in length by the early 1900s, double axle trucks were incorporated.

Trains made for the English market were never cataloged in Germany. During the 1930s, Marklin produced a line of American trains in O and #1 Gauges. The last clockworks were manufactured in 1953 when Marklin turned its attention to the popular HO Gauge. Following World War II, die cast and plastic replaced tin examples. The company continues to produce a full line of locomotives and rolling stock in HO Gauge, and recently has begun to market #1 Gauge examples. Marklin, like several other European companies, dabbled in OO Gauge in the 1930s. Many American train shows and swap meets feature dealers who specialize in this company's toy trains.

During the 1870s, the French toy train manufacturers were active with rather deli-

Fig. 14-7. The two Gauge #1 Marklins in this photo date from about 1925. The lower example is an English outline steamer manufactured for that market. Photo Courtesy of Christie's

178

cately constructed and finely painted examples. Such companies as Rossignol issued large clockwork floor trains that were basic or even primitive in design when compared to their German counterparts. During the 1920s and 30s, some truly fine scale toy trains quite accurate in detail were marketed by French companies, but they never were significant competitors to those produced by the German and English toy train industry.

Across the Channel, the British toymakers were actively competing with their European counterparts, and in some cases in conjunction with them, for the English and American markets. The English manufacturers produced their share of floor runners, clockworks, electrics, and live steam toy trains. The latter were first manufactured in brass and were simple in design, but the workmanship was commendable. Train sets were fabricated after existing British railroads and painted and decorated in the railroads colors and heralds. Often the name of the train was emblazoned on the engine, especially on the splashplate over the drivers.

Wenmann Bassett-Lowke was one of England's most successful toy entrepreneurs. Beginning in 1899 at Northhampton, Bassett-Lowke was more of a distributor than a manufacturer, since the company utilized the toys and trains of other companies which it sold through an extensive catalog and mail order business and Gamage's, one of England's largest department stores. Trains manufactured by Bing, Carette, Marklin, Schoenner, and Issmayer were all listed under the Bassett-Lowke banner at one time or another. It was Bing's finely crafted trains that resulted in the success of Bassett-Lowke in the early 1900s.

Locomotives were sold in construction sets as well as the usual completed pieces. Clockworks in O and #1 Gauges were introduced in 1904, and rolling stock was supplied by Carette in all gauges, especially the popular #1 Gauge. Carette's lithographed rolling stock was some of the finest of the times. In conjunction with Bing's scale locomotives, it accounted for the success of the company until the beginning of World War I. Bassett-Lowke also marketed a full line of steamers including its beautifully modeled "Black Prince" which appeared in 1910.

By the 1920s, Bassett-Lowke began to fall from favor with the public. Products from the period often were reworked older

Fig. 14-8. The English firm of Bassett-Lowke issued complete train sets as well as construction sets. This 1949 kit produced an O Gauge Mogul locomotive when assembled properly. Photo Courtesy of Joy Luke Auctions

dies and styles from Carette, Bing, and Marklin. The British firm of Winteringham became the major supplier of pieces when the German manufacturers declined as a result of the war and the Depression.

During the 1930s, there was a renewed interest in O Gauge, and Bassett-Lowke again marketed products, especially steamers from Winteringham and Marklin. Steamers were sold in the United States through the American firm called Boucher. Bassett-Lowke's "Flying Scotsman", a 4-6-2 lithographed O Gauge locomotive was issued in 1932, and was one of the company's most popular designs. Powered by steam, clockwork, and electric, this beautiful piece was a standby until 1950. In 1937, streamliners were introduced, and these are among the most sought after Bassett-Lowke examples.

In the late 1930s, Bassett-Lowke stepped into the OO Gauge field by handling the Trix line from Bing. With the demise of Winteringham in the 1950s and the failure of the OO or tabletop trains to become as popular as first thought, Bassett-Lowke closed its doors in 1953.

Several other British firms were active during the late 1800s and early 1900s including the Stephens Model Dockyard and Newton who specialized in primitive brass steamers. The British Modeling Company, which was active after the 1880s, produced a variety of locomotives, and James Beeson who specialized in finely detailed O Gauge trains, marketed his trains through other firms such as Bassett-Lowke. The Bateman Company was actively into live steam locomotives in the 1880s.

No discussion of the British toy manufacturers would be complete without mention of the Hornby Company. Founded by Frank Hornby, the company introduced its famous Meccano (Mechanics Made Easy) Construction Set in 1901. It was the backbone of this company. Toy trains were added in 1920, and these first examples were quite simple in design and construction. Actually they were based on the Meccano principle and could be taken apart and reassembled with a few tools. Modeled in O Gauge, these first examples were activated by clockwork motors. In fact, Hornby worked mainly in O Gauge. Realizing the importance of reaching the youth market, Hornby issued yearly colored catalogs, the *Meccano Magazine* and the *Hornby Train Book*, all of which were geared to capture the attention and imagination of the young railroader. These were wonderful and powerful marketing tools.

During the 1920s, more detailed and scale-like trains were introduced based on the tab and slot construction technique. They were painted in bright colors. The trains were carefully packaged in attractive, eye-catching boxes. Many accessories also were issued to develop a complete railroad system. Electrics in high and low voltage examples were introduced in the 1920s.

Aside from the English market, Hornby concentrated his efforts on the French marketplace rather than the overcrowded American market. Following World War I, Hornby established a factory in France and began producing a line of French inspired trains in earnest. This

Fig. 14-9. Hornby was one of England's premier toy train manufacturers. This pair of clockwork locomotives is typical of its products. The stop-start mechanism on the top locomotive is below the driving rods, and it protrudes over the walkway on the lower example. Photo Courtesy of Christie's

proved to be quite successful. Gauge O continued to be the dominant gauge until 1937. The huge Princess Elizabeth was one of the last in this gauge. This piece, though a delight to see, was a real boondoggle for the company. Because of the locomotive's length, trackage and coaches were not available, and it was in constant need of service.

The interest in tabletop railroads resulted in Hornby's introduction of its OO line, called Dublo, in 1938. This gauge re-placed O Gauge and kept Hornby active in the field until their HO line replaced OO Gauge. The Hornby company is still in business and has survived by being able to read what the public is interested in and packaging and marketing its products to meet these needs.

Dating of European trains is based on coupler types, wheel types, and company markings. In addition, old catalogs are a wonderful source for finding and dating both locomotives and complete train sets.

Priced Examples

Sets

Bassett-Lowke/Bing, clockwork, O Gauge steamer George The Fifth, 4-4-0,
6 wheel tender, two passenger carriages, one guards van "LMS", c1920. $1,800.00

Bing, clockwork, Gauge #1 steamer, 0–4–0, 4 wheel tender, two passenger carriages, c1906–1912 $525.00

Bing, electric, cast iron locomotive, 0–4–0, 4 wheel tender "N.Y.C. & H.R.", 1 passenger coach, 1 mail car, c1906–1912 $250.00

Bub/Bing, clockwork, O Gauge steamer, 0–4–0, tender, goods van, cattle van, c1930s, spring broken $390.00

Hess, penny toy litho train, combo engine tender, one coach, new wheels, original box, c1900–1910 $230.00

Marklin, electric, O Gauge steamer, 4–4–0, 6 wheel tender, seven passenger carriages, postal van, c1930 $2,290.00

Marklin, clockwork, O Gauge steamer, 0–2–2, 4 wheel tender, two coal cars, petrol wagon, luggage van, c1895–1915 $2,490.00

Locomotives

Carette, electric, O Gauge trolley $295.00

CHAPTER 15

Collecting Toy Train Accessories

Watching a train travel around an oval track pattern may sustain interest for awhile, but the luster is quickly worn away after the 20th or 30th time around. The toy train manufacturers were aware of this problem and were quick to accessorize a layout. Once the accessories were available to the public, a train functioned as it was supposed to, by moving passengers or freight from one point to the next with stops at intermediary points. Without accessories, all freight and passenger trains were "highballers," whereas the same train became a local carrier when stops were introduced. Nothing enhances a layout more than a few well-placed static and action accessories.

Some toy train accessories are collected in their own right, but most are collected in conjunction with specific manufacturers. Lionel enthusiasts collect Lionel accessories as they mate well with their Lionel trains. For convenience sake, accessories can be divided into "static"

and "action" categories. The first are those that are "on-line" (in the layout) but do not have any major moving parts, though some may have electric units. Early examples of these included lithographed stations, tunnels, bridges, signs, and telegraph poles. Some of these were manufactured to correspond to gauges used by the manufacturers, such as Ives' papier mâché tunnel which was produced in O Gauge in 1910 and in their Wide Gauge in 1929. Others were interchangeable, and many Lionel Standard Gauge pieces were used effectively with their O Gauge trains.

Static accessories often were quite simple, and detail was accomplished by the lithography process. A tunnel, basically an arched piece that fit over the track, was painted or printed with trees, bushes, and buildings. Bumps were molded into the piece to simulate rocky terrain. Conversely, simple bridges such as girders featured simulated rivets, steel members, and often carried railroad heralds. Truss bridges were more dramatic in design, and the effect of a train passing over a truss bridge could be breathtaking. Usually the bridges were modeled after prototypes.

Every working railroad had a station either at its terminus or somewhere on the line to pick up and deposit passengers and freight. The station frequently was the focal point of the layout. Early examples were fabricated from wood and metal, but the most common method of production was lithographed tinplate. Doors, windows, surface texture, roofing, and even people, were printed in two dimensions on a three-dimensional piece. This gave the illusion of depth to the surface. Stations often were modeled and named after prototypes, and carried such romantic names as "Union," "Glendale," and "Grand Central." The lithographed stations saw many years of service, and as a result, many versions and variations exist; all are collect-

ible. American Flyer's #96 and #104 are found with different wall and roof treatments as variations of the original designs. Some stations featured a projected area over which the track was placed, thus tying the train to the depot. This type of arrangement was fairly common in Marx's lithographed stations.

One of the most beautiful station combinations was issued by Ives in 1901. It consisted of two lithographed #116 Stations that were joined by a center passenger waiting platform which incorporated glass skylight segments over the base. This three piece combination recently sold at auction for over $1,700.

Other less glamorous static accessories, but still vital to a train's operation, included such items as railroad warning signs, telegraph poles, and billboards. Frequently issued in sets, they added that special touch to a layout that changed it to a

Fig. 15-1. The Hellgate Bridge was modeled after the prototype that spanned the East River in New York. Lionel produced it in two different color schemes. This is an excellent example of a static accessory. Photo Courtesy of Sotheby's

Fig. 15-2. One of the most common accessories manufactured by American Flyer was the passenger station. Many versions exist of these lithographed pieces including this #102 example. It was available from 1928 to 1939. Photo Courtesy of "The Antique Trader Weekly"

Fig. 15-3. Lionel's #256 Illuminated Freight Station also was the basic frame for the #356 Operating Freight Station. The action model included a baggage carrier and figure that moved around the platform. This #256 included adhesive posters for customizing the station. Photo from the Collection of Joel Kaufmann

more realistic version. Finding complete sets can be a challenge for the collector. Figures of passengers, train personnel, and combinations of these, also were sold to give a human touch. Lionel's #550 consists of a set of six railroad figures. These accessories seem to be less popular with collectors than the major accessories, but they do serve an important function in filling out the layout.

Some accessories received electric input or had major moving parts, but were basically static pieces. These examples included stations with illuminated interiors or exteriors, and often included moving or sliding doors. Basically painted or lithographed tinplate, they are placed in this category because the illumination was an adjunct rather than a major feature. When the lighting was disconnected, the piece became a static accessory. Dorfan's #427 lithographed Passenger Depot possessed an interior light, and American Flyer's #237 was not only illuminated, but fea-

tured a manually operated semaphore attached to the base. Many of the statics were available for many years and were reissued frequently. Many variations occurred, all of which are collectible.

Lighted bridges, street lamps, and illuminated trackside structures also fit neatly into this category. Lionel's 1928 Lionelville illuminated set with #186 metal Bungalows and #192 Villas featured removable roofs for gaining access to the light fixtures. The entire set comprised a miniature village. American Flyer manufactured their own version of a train village. These sets are quite popular.

Such items as water towers with manually activated spouts and illuminated light towers, such as Lionel's #92, increased the play value of a setup. By dimming the room lights, dramatic effects were produced from the engine light, towers, street lamps, and on-line buildings.

Pleasing forms and shapes had strong eye appeal. Some simple pieces were very popular because of their crisp lines and

Fig. 15-4. Lionel's #438 Signal Tower is a fine example of a static accessory that adds significantly to the interest of any layout. Photo Courtesy of "The Antique Trader Weekly"

Fig. 15-5. This massive Power Station is one of the featured accessories in the 1928 Lionel catalog. The schematic drawing at the top left shows the positioning of the transformers. Reprinted with the Permission of Lionel Trains, Inc.

attractive paint schemes. Lionel's #438 Signal Tower and #126 Lionelville Station were good examples of this type of accessory.

One extraordinary piece deserves a closer look. The Lionel #840 Power Station was one of the most imposing pieces ever manufactured. Consisting of several levels and many small accessories, it housed transformers and switches that sent electric power to trains on the layout. However, operable or not, it was often the centerpiece of many a layout. It is highly prized by collectors.

Though not as spectacular as the action accessories, the statics often were less expensive, and when mixed with a few action pieces, a real working layout was the end result. Static bridges, tunnels, and stations blended well with such action accessories as crossing gates and train activated warning lights, much like the real railroad.

The second group of accessories are those that excite the imagination. They are the "bells and whistles" of the accessory field. The action accessories moved mechanically or electrically to produce dramatic effects. Movement was effected by

Fig. 15-6. Quite different from the detailed Hellgate, this truss bridge was much less expensive and served as a functional accessory in many a layout. Photo from the Collection of Joel Kaufmann

the passage of a train over a mechanical or electric triggering device, or from a distance by means of a box called a controller. The controller provided action on demand, whereas the tripping device was activated everytime the train passed over it. Most warning devices were train activated. Crossing gates, ringing bells, and flashing warning signals indicated a train was passing a crossing section. Block signals and semaphores directed traffic on the line. They notified the engineer if a segment of track was occupied, recently vacated, or totally free of traffic.

Non-electric action accessories included such pieces as Marx's #412 Derrick which required hands-on activation to rotate the derrick on its base and to raise or lower the hook. The movable crane or derrick was one of the most popular accessories, and several of the major companies produced their own versions. Mechanical crossing gates, some of which had colored glass panels to simulate flashing lights, were lowered or raised by hand. Marx's #317 and Ives' #216 Crossing Gates were excellent examples of this type of accessory. Moving trains from track to track was accomplished by using Ives's #145 manual Turntable.

The advantage of mechanically activated accessories was that they could be placed anywhere on the layout without regard for electrical contacts. However, they had to be placed within reach of the operator. Often crossing gates remained down or up as a train passed by because of the operator's inattention to these pieces. Their main appeal was their initial low cost.

The physical weight of the train also activated some mechanical accessories. Most notable were crossing gates that dropped and raised as the train passed over a trip lever in the track. Some were independent, such as Marx's #0217, while others were part of a larger piece, such as Marx's #1600 Glendale Freight Depot which featured a crossing gate in front of the lithographed station. Since the weight of the train was the crucial factor, often lighter rolling stock caused the crossing gates to bob up and down as the train passed.

Clockwork mechanisms were used occasionally in early accessories, but as with keywind pieces, the action depended on the unwinding of a spring, and was thus limited in endurance. It also required frequent rewinding. Companies such as Ives produced some interesting clockwork accessories. The c1910, Ives #140 Crossing Gate was a good example.

Free-standing action accessories occasionally used batteries as the source for electric imput. The Marx #404 three light Block Signal was activated by an off/on switch. The #2900 Glendale Station featured a battery illuminated crossing signal and lamp, and a crossing gate that was tripped by the weight of the train. Battery operated accessories were initially inexpensive, but relatively few in number compared to those which received power from the layout.

When one thinks of "action" accessories, the Lionel name is synonymous with the best. Some very dramatic effects were developed at Lionel, and they were publicized heavily each year in the company's catalog. Picture if you will a train approaching a bridge; the train stops, the bridge raises and lowers, and the train proceeds, all at the touch of a controller. This was how the 1940 Lionel #313 Bascule Bridge operated. Long a favorite with collectors, it was one of Lionel's most dramatic accessories. The #116 Station manufactured by Lionel was issued in two color combinations. The early version was cream with green trim, and the later version featured maroon trim. The piece sported lovely detail, was based on the New York Grand Central Depot, and it also contained a unique feature. As the train approached the station, it stopped and remained stopped for a period of time before it resumed its journey. This stopping mechanism was based on a heat activated bimetal strip located in the track. The station was a favorite from 1935 to 1942. As a companion piece, Lionel issued the #129 Terrace with lighted globes on the railing. The Union Station fit into a section of the terrace, and the entire complex was breathtaking. These pieces are being reproduced in their original colors by T-Reproductions of Johnson City, Tennessee.

Though some action accessories were activated from a distance by a controller, others were sent into motion by contact of the train wheels with an electrical contact. Railroad crossing signals, gates, semaphores, and block signals usually were activated in this manner. One of Lionel's most popular accessories was set into motion by this method. The #45 Gateman popped out of his trackside shed waving a lantern when the train passed. After activation, he returned to his shed. This popular accessory appeared with many variations and is presently being reissued. American Flyer's answer was Sam the Semaphore Man.

Some action accessories, such as Lionel's #116, utilized heat to set them in motion. Stopping sections of track relied on the expansion and contraction of bimetal strips to carry out the function. Heat from bulbs also played a part in motion. Marx's #0446 revolving Beacon Tower used the heat generated from a bulb to set the beacon revolving, and the #465 Water Tower featured a rod of illuminated bubbles that began the motion once certain temperatures were reached from a bulb. Lionel utilized this principle in its #455 Oil Derrick.

Fig. 15-7. One of the most popular action accessories is Lionel's Automatic Gateman. Many variations exist including this 1949 example which is dated by the center position of the crossbuck on the pole. Photo Courtesy of Nelson's Auction

Fig. 15-8. The heat activated rotary beacon frequently is missing the colored lens at the top. This is one part that is presently being reproduced. Photo Courtesy of Nelson's Auction

Fig. 15-9. The Gilbert-American Flyer Billboard carried a diesel horn sound. Other versions were manufactured with whistles. Photo from the Collection of Joel Kaufmann

Many of the train manufacturers incorporated train whistles and horns in their engines. American Flyer produced a series of billboards which simulated train whistles or diesel horns from a controller. The billboards were covered with advertising similar to the prototypes. Many of the placards are difficult to find and are a challenge for the collector.

The quintessence of action accessories were those that usually required an action piece of rolling stock to complete the scene. Coal towers or coaling stations drew

imitation granules of coal up to an exit shoot by means of a knob on the controller. A press of the second button on the controller activated an electromagnet that opened a chute which allowed the coal to be dumped into a waiting car. The car was then brought to the receiving end of the coaling station, and on a special piece of track, dumped the coal back into the catcher to start the whole cycle again.

This basic load and dump principle was found on other action accessories, such as log and barrel loaders which were manufactured by the major toy train producers. Most worked on a conveyor belt or continuous chain principle, while others required a vibrating mechanism to move pieces along the accessory. Lionel released a pair of accessories that complemented each other. The #342 Culvert Loader appeared in 1956, and a year later, an unloader was introduced to complete the cycle. The #464 Saw Mill gave the illusion that raw logs were cut into boards. One of the most popular action accessories

Fig. 15-10. Lionel's #97 Coal Elevator was introduced in 1938. It is one of the company's most recognizable accessories. Photo Courtesy of Nelson's Auction

Fig. 15-11. The Icing Station is an action accessory that frequently is found at train shows and auctions. The action consists of a figure sweeping ice blocks into a waiting refrigerator car. Photo Courtesy of Nelson's Auction

was the magnetic crane. Utilizing an electromagnet, it lifted and loaded bits of scrap metal and discharged them when the electric current was disengaged.

Talking stations incorporated phonograph records which called out stops and schedules when activated. These records frequently are missing or badly scratched, but replacements are now available. Nearly every type of trackside industry was represented by static and action accessories.

When companies such as Marx, Lionel, and American Flyer introduced their HO Gauges, it was necessary to also manufacture scale size accessories to mate with these trains. Both static and action accessories were made. Due to the short life span of HO, few accessories were produced compared to the other more popular gauges.

CHAPTER 16

Collecting American Tinplate

The toy train collector approaches his field of collecting with the same passion that one finds with a collector of porcelain, glass, or silver. The hunt and subsequent location of a set or key piece will often bring joy that can only be understood by a fellow collector. The division between a collector and an accumulator is quite sharp. The accumulator collects pieces without regard for display, study, or operation, much as a stamp accumulator tosses stamps into a drawer. The collector takes pride in each piece added to his collection. Rather than keep them boxed without regard to viewing, the collector takes his field of interest very seriously. One merely has to spend a short time at a train show to see the flurry of activity associated with the buying, selling, and swapping of tinplate material. The serious collector knows what he or she wants, and often spends a good deal of energy and time to find the right example.

Wants vary from collector to collector. Each of the major toy manufacturers has its own legion of followers. This also holds true for some of the minor producers, but the majority of collectors congregate around the big four: Lionel, Ives, Marx, and American Flyer. The devotion to a specific train maker often brings friendly rivalry regarding such factors as which company produced the more realistic or scale-like pieces, which paint jobs were better, two-rail versus three-rail operation, and who had the better smoking or choo choo device. This competition adds to the fun of collecting.

Collectors tend to have favorite periods or gauges within their areas of interest. It is highly unlikely that a collector will desire all Lionel pieces from its inception. Collectors tend to specialize within a period such as prewar or post-war Lionel O Gauge. Prewar Lionel Standard Gauge, trolleys, American Flyer prior to Gilbert's acquisition, Gilbert-American Flyer, Flyer

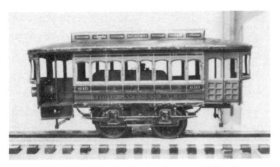

Fig. 16-1. Trolleys have a charm of their own. This Bing example was made for the American market. Photo Courtesy of the Children's Museum of Indianapolis

O Gauge, or Flyer S Gauge, are just a few of the many areas that are in favor with the toy train collecting world.

Companies such as Ives have followers that covet all of this company's products, whereas others limit their interest to specific gauges, methods of locomotion (whether electric or keywind), and even pieces fabricated during the transition period. O Gauge is the most popular gauge among collectors. This may be due to its availability, but new collectors entering the field tend to favor this gauge. It is also popular because most major companies worked in this gauge, and so operation of a layout utilizing several companies' products is possible. Flyer's S Gauge is gaining interest, partly due to Lionel's reissue of some pieces. It is no longer a "dead" gauge. Standard or Wide Gauge continues to be popular, but pricey.

Within a specific time frame, collecting also can be specialized, and many a superb collection revolves around such pieces as Fundimension examples or Marx army train sets. Categories are subdivided further to include locomotives or rolling stock, and even finer divisions to include diesels as opposed to steamers. Electric profile locomotives also have their following, and splendid examples by American Flyer, Ives, Dorfan, and Lionel are sought after in all gauges. Variations in diesels, steamers, and rolling stock increase the possibilities.

Fig. 16-2. Wide Gauge tends to be quite pricey, especially classic pieces such as these "State" cars. Photo Courtesy of Christie's

Fig. 16-3. The long and short stripe are two versions of the Lionel #746 Norfolk and Western tenders. Both are sought by collectors. Photo from the Collection of John Ezzo

Collecting variations can be as basic as gathering all of the road names and colors for a specific locomotive such as Lionel's O Gauge FM Trainmaster which was issued in Lackawana, Virginian, and Jersey Central logos. The first two examples are more readily available than the Jersey Central one which was issued for only one year and is quite difficult to locate in prime condition. Within this series, there are color variations that are very collectible, and these variations exist in nearly every piece offered by each company.

In addition, many pieces were manufactured with more subtle variations. Examples can be found listed in such books as *Greenberg's Guide to American Flyer S Gauge* by James Patterson and Bruce Greenberg. The #963 Washington passenger car, which was produced from 1953 to 1958, exists with ten different variations.

These include differences in finishes, striping, and type of identification. All are highly collectible. Some are easily obtained; others are very scarce and can provide a major challenge. However, the hunt is half of the fun. One can assemble an impressive collection of American Flyer S Gauge passenger cars, O Gauge cabooses, or Marx $\frac{3}{16}$-inch scale-like freight cars.

Variations also occur in couplers, trucks, and types of lettering, especially on rolling stock. Brass plates versus rubber stamping, and the presence or absence of nickel trim is also part of the collecting mystique. This is especially true if the piece was produced for a long period of time. Examples may exist with several types of couplers as well as two-wheel ex-

Fig. 16-5. The Army train set is popular with Marx enthusiasts. This series of tank carrying flat cars illustrate the change in loads that add interest and variety to any collection. Photo from the Collection of Don Speidel

Fig. 16-4. These two FM Trainmasters are decorated in Lackawana and Virginian colors. Photo from the Collection of John Ezzo

amples, four-wheel trucks, and variations in the truck frame which holds the wheels. Window treatments on coaches can vary considerably. Some examples are lighted while others are not.

Collecting can be for display, study, operation or a combination of these approaches. A few collectors assemble collections merely for the satisfaction of owning and displaying their treasures without concern for operation. Those who collect for display may settle for examples that are not in running order, but usually this is not the case. Even though they may never feel the rails beneath their wheels, the ardent collector still strives for the best possible

Fig. 16-6. Train pieces with original boxes are a perfect way of storing the treasures. Photo Courtesy of Nelson's Auction

Fig. 16-7. Clean, well-preserved examples are highly desirable and are priced accordingly. Photo Courtesy of "The Antique Trader Weekly"

examples available. Some sacrifice may be made if a coach contains a lighting unit which is not operational, but locomotives that are not functional and, for the most part, are not able to be fixed, usually are avoided.

Some collectors are partial to passenger consists, while others tend to find freight cars more to their liking. However, most collectors mix their collections with examples of both, while staying within the same gauge. Often, collectors will begin general collections, but, as they become more knowledgeable, they tend to have favorites; thus specialized collections are born. The unwanted material becomes available for swapping. This specialization usually leads to study which is an important part of collecting. Vital new information may be added to the area through research by the devoted collector since there are missing links in all of the companies' chains. Certain examples are known to exist but may not have surfaced.

The next logical step is the operation of the collection. Though some collectors maintain a nonoperating collection, more often than not, an operating layout is constructed to put the collection in motion. Watching a prized Blue Comet or President's Special go through its paces can be an exciting experience. The operating layout also affords the opportunity to change the locomotive and rolling stock so that much of the collection sees action from time to time.

Layouts take many forms. A layout can consist of a simple circle, or several ovals can be used side-by-side to operate multiple train sets at one time. This creates the feeling of activity. More often, the inclusion of switches, crossings, and elevated sections is the rule rather than the exception.

Original track is fairly inexpensive and reproduced track is readily available for a nominal cost. Some collectors lay their own track, while others use a realistic three-rail Gargraves modern substitute. The profile of the rails and closeness of the ties make Gargraves most appealing to collectors who utilize two or three rail operation. Switches are a little more difficult to find in operating order, but many can be brought back to life with a little work. These tend to be fairly expensive when found in sets which consist of a right and left example.

Few layouts consist of mixed gauges. The norm is for an operating layout to be constructed in Standard, O, O27, or S Gauge. It is not uncommon for collectors to operate several different manufacturers' trains on the layout. American Flyer, Ives, and Lionel Wide Gauge examples work quite well together on a track setup and add interest to a layout. Mixing gauges such as S Gauge with O Gauge is not done as frequently. The proportions are not as pleasing as a unified gauge layout.

Some operational layouts can provide a major challenge, especially if the collector attempts to use only original equipment. Some of the early examples such as Dorfan, Hafner, and Carlisle and Finch pieces, can be a real challenge for the collector to obtain. Sometimes substitute pieces may be necessary as the search goes on for the originals. Attempting to locate original ribbon track, ties, switches, and crossings for a Carlisle and Finch layout can be difficult. The sectional track pieces are also hard to find.

Accessories for the layout can be collected in their own right, but most often they are used in conjunction with the layout. Mixing manufacturers is acceptable if the gauges are in the right proportions. European accessories fit well into American layouts and are fun to collect. Some accessories work well with both Wide and O Gauge layouts. Bridges, stations, and other static accessories are somewhat easier to find than action accessories. Action pieces may need the skill and patience of a seasoned collector or mechanic to bring them back to working order. Static accessories usually need just a touchup here and there to bring out their original beauty.

Collecting accessories that fit the pe-

Fig. 16–8. Gargraves track is more prototypical than the usual tinplate variety. The top example carries a center rail, and the middle piece is used for O scale layouts where power comes from the outer rails. Compare them with the tinplate example at the bottom.

Fig. 16-9. Gilbert-American Flyer S Gauge accessories work best with their mating operating cars. Finding an accessory in the original box is an added bonus.

riod of the layout is also an important factor. A 1920s O Gauge signal works much better with a layout than a 1950s example. However, the 1950s piece may be a stopgap until the earlier example is located. Collectors tend to wait for the right piece rather than substitute an incorrect era example. Some collectors delight in mixing tinplate and scale trains in their layout. O scale and O tinplate often work well together.

Finding power units such as transformers can be another major undertaking. Early transformers often need considerable rehabilitation just to make them safe,

Fig. 16-10. Modern O scale works well with O Gauge tinplate. This Williams #4811 GG-1 is an example of the type of material available. Some run on two rails, while others are designed for three-rail operation.

let alone operational. As an alternative, collectors are turning their attention to modern power units that handle tinplate quite well. The modern units can be hidden from sight and operated through a series of knife switches and rheostats that are compatible with the unit.

Not only is the home a good place to operate the trains, but collectors enjoy showing their prize examples on layouts at local or national club meets. Clubs often maintain layouts built and stocked by club members, and during get-togethers, when knowledge is exchanged and points argued, time is allocated for operation. The movement of the trains is not a random race around the tracks, but follows prescribed timetables, loads, and destinations. This also holds true for the operation of the home layout, but often the club layouts are larger and many more trains may be moving along the mainlines and sidelines at one time. The club layout is a perfect place to show off one's recently acquired or restored jewel.

Pieces are acquired for a collection by purchase, trade, or a combination of both. Many a collector will "trade up" to get what he or she desires by trading for the pieces or adding a dollar amount along with the trade if the step up is a giant one. Some collectors set up booths at local train shows with the idea of swapping what they have for what they want. Trading is an acceptable method of eliminating surplus material or material that no longer holds any interest for the collector. A good swap can result in the exchange of desired material and also develop friendships along the way.

American toy trains tend to hold their value. The collector, as opposed to the speculator, enters the field because of his love of the pieces. It is an added bonus that these pieces may become solid investments. Some of this is due to the constant influx of new collectors who have the money to spend. But speculation in the toy train market can be iffy. Those who were fortunate enough to have assembled a collection in the 1950s and 60s when prices were low, can realize a substantial profit if they decide to market their collection. More often than not, trains are passed down to family members. If profit is the motivating force in entering the market, a great gulf separates the speculator and collector. The latter collects for the pure joy of ownership. Appreciation in value is secondary.

CHAPTER 17

Condition, Missing Parts, Repair and Restoration

Toy trains, as the name implies, are first and foremost toys and were manufactured to be handled in the rough and tumble world by the young engineer. Pieces such as ladders, headlights, and brakewheels were attached to stay in place, and often were out of scale due to a need for strength rather than realism. When looking at a true scale model with its accurately proportioned piping, ladders, and brakewheels, it is apparent that these delicate pieces would not last long in the hands of a child.

Even though the toy train was designed and executed in a rugged fashion, the very nature of the world that it existed in resulted in heavy use and handling without regard to surface beauty. With this in mind, it is apparent that perfect condition examples are few and far between, and when found, can bring significantly higher prices than everyday examples that show considerable wear and tear.

For those that buy, sell, or trade in the train market, a standardized grading system is imperative. Remembering that "beauty is in the eye of the beholder," a slightly worn example may be considered near mint by one person and somewhat less by another collector. The Train Collectors Association has developed a grading scale that is published with permission from this excellent organization in order to help the novice collector understand what each grade should be. This is especially helpful when dealing with mail order houses where the item cannot be seen. The standardized grading system helps bring everything to a common ground. The following is the TCA's grading system and is placed here for reference.

Mint—brand new and completely original and unused

Like New—free of blemishes, scratches, dents, or rust

Excellent—minute scratches, but no dents or rust

Very Good—few scratches, but very clean and without dents or rust

Good—scratches, small dents and dirty
Fair—well-scratched, chipped, dented, rusted, or warped
Poor—junk condition, for parts only

The techniques of repair and maintenance are beyond the scope of this book. However, there are some facts that the collector should be aware of, and that is the purpose of this chapter. For those who wish to recondition a locomotive, rolling stock, or accessories, a series of excellent references are listed at the end of the book (p. 225). In addition, factory manuals, usually available at train shows, can provide helpful maintenance and restoration tips.

The test track is one of the collectors' best friends. Usually available at train shows and hobby shops, it affords the opportunity of determining if a locomotive runs or not. This convenience is not available at auctions, though some collectors bring their own testing devices. A working locomotive that is balky or slow often can be brought up to snuff with a little tender loving care. Locomotives that have stood on shelves or have stayed hidden away in boxes for long periods of time may simply need to be cleaned and relubricated. The removal of old lubricants that tend to solidify, the relubrication using the proper amount of grease and oil (never over oil or grease), and the cleaning of the wheels and electric contacts often do wonders for a herky-jerky locomotive.

A locomotive that merely sits on a live track without signs of receiving current to the motor may be missing some key parts. One of the most obvious is the electric pickups. One should check to see that the shoes or rollers are present and making contact with the hot rail. If missing, usually they are not difficult to replace. Some locomotives receive electrical pickup from the tender, and if the tender is missing, the locomotive will be dead on its tracks. In addition, if the tender is present, faulty wiring to the locomotive from the tender may be a problem that can be rectified. Frayed or broken wires or poor connections can cause a break in the electrical continuity, but often can be repaired.

The books listed at the end of this chapter feature schematic drawings and repair techniques that can help the collector disassemble, clean, repair, and reassemble a locomotive with the minimum of effort. Without knowledge of what lies behind a screw, one can uncover serious problems. Flying springs and rolling bearings can result from removing a key screw without understanding what is behind it or what it is supposed to hold.

Most parts for restoring a locomotive

Fig. 17-1. Replacement doors in every color for the Lionel #6400 Series box cars can be found at most toy train shows. Photo Courtesy of David Pushis

to working order can be purchased from dealers who specialize in original and reproduction parts. Some dealers purchase large inventories of used pieces, and from these, they frequently obtain a supply of replacement parts. As an example, roller and shoe pickups can be purchased both as originals and reproduction parts for many locomotives. A clockwork locomotive with a broken spring or missing key can be restored to working order in most cases since some dealers specialize in parts for vintage trains. However, major parts for these older pieces are more difficult to find. One attempting to rebuild a Voltamp or Carlisle and Finch piece may find it quite a challenge.

The body shell of the locomotive as well as the rolling stock presents a different set of problems. Lithographed bodies that are badly dented, rusted, or scratched may only be useful for parts such as trucks, couplers, or even screws. Minor scratching can be touched up if the work is done carefully. Those proficient with an airbrush often can make scratches disappear. Some collectors believe that minor scratching should not be tampered with, whereas others feel that this retouching only adds to the beauty of the piece.

Missing parts from the body shell such as headlight lenses, bells, bulbs, and smoking units usually are available from suppliers. Wheels, frames, tender shells, reversing units, and armatures are advertised in model train magazines specifically for this type of repair. Most train shows feature dealers who provide these replacement parts, and frequently a collector will find a box of "junk" cars that may provide a missing coupler or truck. Some of the reproduction bells, ladders, etc. are faithful recreations of the originals and are totally acceptable in restorations.

Major missing pieces are another story. A die-cast locomotive that has a large crack as a result of being dropped or is missing steps, or a portion of the cab, as a result of mishandling may be beyond the realm of satisfactory restoration. Rolling stock with missing sides, roofs, or frames may be useful for parts, but unless one has

Fig. 17-2. Complete couplers and coupler parts make restoration of these pieces relatively simple, especially when working with the common types. Photo Courtesy of David Pushis

Fig. 17-3. Trucks, frames, tracks, and wheelsets make up an important part of the inventory for replacement and rehabilitation.

Fig. 17-5. Delicate pieces such as Lionel's hobo and cop, or the horse from the General Set, are being reproduced in large numbers for replacements. Figures such as the horse for the Lionel Corral Car are easily lost and just as easily replaced. Photo Courtesy of David Pushis

experience in sheet metal work, restoration may be impossible. Smaller missing segments such as doors, ladders, or brakewheels are found more easily, and the restoration can be completed. However, it may require some diligent searching. Most post-war trains are easier to restore, as there seems to be a sufficient amount of material available for these projects.

Operating rolling stock and accessories also can be brought back to life by following repair procedures outlined in the factory manuals or instruction sheets originally packaged with the pieces. Such fre-

quently missing pieces as milk cans and cattle figures for Lionel's operating cars are replaced easily from specialized dealers. Some of the most frequently lost or damaged parts have been reproduced in large numbers, such as the delicate rotating lens atop Lionel's rotating beacon light accessory.

Scarce examples can provide a real

Fig. 17-4. This Lionel Standard Gauge gondola is missing a pair of wheels. Photo Courtesy of Joy Luke Auctions

challenge to the restorer, and custom made replacement parts may be necessary to complete the restoration. In some cases, it may be more expedient to replace a segment of a train with a reproduced piece.

When to repaint or not to repaint is a most perplexing question, and one that generates a good deal of controversy in the collecting community. We recently came across an Ives Wide Gauge locomotive and three freight car set at an antiques market. Though the rolling stock was in decent condition, the locomotive, though working, was without paint on 80–90% of the body shell. From the remaining bits of paint on the body and under the brass plates, we identified its original color. By comparing the model to one found in Greenberg's or McComas' books, we determined trim and roof colors.

A locomotive such as this certainly would benefit from a fresh paint job. Preparation should include removing the motor

Fig. 17–6. Rolling stock with missing doors such as this #1108 American Flyer Baggage are more easily restored because so many pieces were manufactured. But it may be more expedient to find a complete example as they are priced competitively. Photo from the Collection of John Ezzo

unit, frame, shell, and trim pieces. While the motor is accessible, it is a good time to clean, tune, and relubricate this unit. Preparation for the shell and frame painting should begin with the removal of all of the old paint down to the bare metal and cleaning the surface with a mild soap solution. Two thin coats of primer are necessary and should be sprayed on either from a spray can or airbrush. Masking out the trim portions such as the window frames and roof will make the finishing easier. Next, two coats of the appropriate color should be applied. When the trim is finished, the final coats should be allowed to dry thoroughly before replacing the accessories such as ladders, plates, and bells. Missing parts often can be purchased from dealers handling replacement or reproduction parts. The end result should be quite dramatic and can be the pride of any layout.

While discussing repainting with collectors, several "does" and "don'ts" have surfaced. Repainting a common piece in a different color scheme from the original factory colors is acceptable if the piece is marked as such. Rare and unusual pieces always should be restored in the original colors, and any repainting should be noted. Occasionally a novice collector will discover a rare piece in its appropriate color scheme, only to find out later that the piece had been repainted to simulate the rare color pattern. By looking inside the body shell, one can find traces of the original colors in the form of overspraying. This is a good method of determining the original shell color.

Several companies offer paints that

match factory colors for the major toy train producers. A good peacock or mojave will match the original colors quite well. These are available in brush or spray form. The brush type can be adapted for use with an airbrush. Learning to use an airbrush is not difficult, and the end result is often steps ahead of the brush painted example.

As in any field of collecting, the collector should be aware of dicey pieces that are purposely altered to imitate rare or unused examples. The Lionel FM Trainmaster in the Jersey Central markings is difficult to find compared to the Virginian or Lackawana examples. Virginian or Lackawana body shells painted to match the Jersey Central colors and lettering occasionally surface and cause confusion. Careful study of the original may prevent these pitfalls. Much of this knowledge comes from handling the originals enough to be comfortable with them, as well as studying the texts and articles on these pieces. With a little knowledge, it becomes apparent when a piece has been altered, though at first glance it may cause the heart to skip a beat or two. In order to be safe, the collector should check on the documentation of the piece, such as who owned it prior to its sale, the provenance.

Reproductions do exist, but are marked clearly, or should be. However, it behooves the collector to know exactly what constitutes an original as to lettering and numbering, heat stamped, or decalled, etc. Mistakes will not be made often if people use their heads rather than their hearts!

Repairs on pieces could have been performed by the original owner, repair shop, factory, or at the factory prior to its ever being shipped to the retail outlet. Using original parts is paramount right down to the last screw. The home repairer may substitute a handy screw rather than the appropriate factory screw. Though this seems a small item, to the purist it is something that would need correcting.

The TCA requires that all repairs and repaints must be identified on its members' pieces. Examples cannot be graded above EXCELLENT grade if they have been refinished. The TCA provides pressure sensitive labels to its members that should be placed on those pieces that have been rehabbed. This is a solid method of maintaining integrity and uniformity in the field. However, the final judgment concerning the merits of a piece belongs to the collector.

Reproductions abound in the world of toy trains. These are not manufactured with the purpose of deceiving the unwary buyer. They are a substitute for some rather pricey or rare train sets. To the experienced eye, there is little confusion between repros and the original article. Most repros are marked as such, though occasionally they may be passed off as the genuine article.

Locomotives, rolling stock, trolleys, and accessories are being reproduced by both large and small companies. The demand for this type of material is such that a continuous supply is being presented to the marketplace. Wide or Standard, O, and S Gauges are the most popular gauges for reproduction. In most cases, the repros meet the standards of the originals in quality of construction and faithfulness to the prototype.

Heading the list of reproductions is a line manufactured by Lionel called the "Classics." Such favorites as the #384E and #90E steam locomotives are being reproduced for a hungry market. The #384E is teamed with a tender, searchlight car, gondola, stock, and caboose in Standard Gauge. The popular #300 Series passenger cars also are rolling off the assembly line in Mt. Clemens, Michigan. The superb Hiawatha streamliner set in O Gauge also is making a comeback, and is a faithful reproduction of the original. These repros are somewhat costly, but are below comparable originals. Prices on these repros are competitive, but a review of toy train magazines, or a visit to a local train show will reveal that prices do vary. Lionel's #440N Signal Bridge, #126 Lionelville Station, and #1115 Station are being reproduced as accessories for new or existing layouts.

For those who do not want to invest in the originals or cannot find these pieces in acceptable condition, reproductions are good alternatives.

The popularity of Lionel's O and Standard Gauge pieces has resulted in the reproduction of key pieces by companies other than Lionel. Some excellent examples of Lionel's Blue Comet, Flying Yankee, FM Trainmaster, and #263E are just a few of the examples presently being manufactured and marketed by train shops and smaller manufacturing companies under their own banner. Most are offered in two- or three-rail versions. They are advertised heavily, reviewed in toy train magazines, and displayed at specialty train shows. They pop up at toy train auctions from time to time.

Flyer's S Gauge releases have brought new life to the S Gaugian. These pieces are compatible with existing Flyer S Gauge equipment, and are a delight to the growing

Fig. 17–7. Lionel has reissued some of its classic trains and accessories. The Lionel City Station is one of the company's most popular accessories and features entrance lamps and a stop/start mechanism.

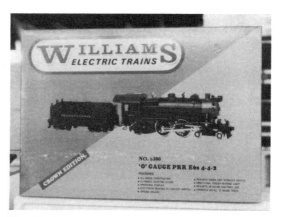

Fig. 17–8. Williams is typical of the many companies that manufacture modern day O Gauge three rail locomotives that are compatible with vintage tinplate.

legion of S Gauge enthusiasts. In addition, S Gauge scale locomotives and rolling stock are being manufactured for operation on existing S Gauge layouts.

To augment an existing layout or step further into the world of scale, several manufacturers, including Weaver, Williams, and K-Line, produce O and O 27 compatible equipment. Though not usually considered reproductions of vintage equipment, it falls within this category when it works well or complements existing equipment.

CHAPTER 18

Collaterals that Add Zest to a Collection

The collecting of collateral material as it relates to American toy trains is a wonderful offshoot of the main field. It offers insight into what was available at specific times, and what marketing techniques were employed to promote each company's products. Most of the collateral material on the market is promotional in nature and is printed on paper or paper products. Because of this, often they have suffered the ravages of time, but they are sought after eagerly by the serious toy train collector. With some items that are in great demand, reproductions have been issued that copy the originals, but are available at considerably lower cost.

Even though Lionel coined the phrase "wish book," the toy train catalogs from all of the train manufacturers were in fact wish books. These slick pieces of literature heralded the arrival of that year's trains and accessories. Children anxiously awaited these booklets. Early examples is-

Fig. 18–1. Business stationery such as the Hafner sheet are highly collectible. This particular sheet illustrates the company's rolling stock in full color. Photo Courtesy of Tony Hay

sued by some of the smaller manufacturers frequently consisted of a single sheet which displayed their products in simple line drawings, though the text was quite descriptive if not bordering on the flamboyant. Original catalogs from companies such as Carlisle and Finch, Dorfan, and American Flyer are quite difficult to find in decent condition since the nature of the product often resulted in tears, stains, and general disintegration. Colors usually were lacking in these examples though the drawings often were quite well done.

During the 1920s and 1930s, Lionel catalogs evolved into their modern format with illustrations designed to capture the imagination of the young engineer. Colors were incorporated to show the pieces at their best, and often the schematic drawings showed the trains whizzing around the tracks with a gleeful young boy at the controls. Color covers were designed to catch the attention and draw the train customer inside. Some were so full of action that it was difficult to determine which examples the manufacturer was highlighting.

Some of the train sets carried exotic names such as "The Mercury," "Blue Comet," "President's Special," and "Hiawatha," but most carried a number designation. The 1927 Lionel catalog offered individual locomotives, rolling stock, and accessories in O Gauge and Standard Gauge as well as complete sets. The top of the line #409E Standard Gauge set consisted of a #408E locomotive, #418, #419, #490, and #431 passenger cars, track, rheostat, and "Lockon" for the astronomical

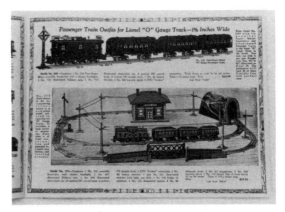

Fig. 18–2. The layout on the lower half of the page helped promote Lionel's products, including their accessories. Reprinted with the Permission of Lionel Trains, Inc.

price of $82.50. This set was coded the "ETTA" set.

Conversely, the Elecktoy 1911 catalog was a single sheet which offered a variety of numbered sets ranging from $6.00 to about $15.00. The price included track and wiring equipment. Though this simple page was not as glamorous as later catalogs, it is an important piece of material for the collector who is attempting to put together original factory train sets. The early catalogs also are fascinating reading as many describe the techniques of construction characteristic of the company, as well as the advantages of one company's products compared to the others.

Not all trains which appear in catalogs were made available to the public. The catalogs often were published in advance of distribution, and modifications in train sets frequently were made after the catalog was released. A tender that appeared in a catalog might have a substitute in the actual train set. This holds true for other parts of the consist.

Following World War II, most toy train manufacturers geared up for the postwar period and its anticipated desire for products. Because of the existing paper shortage, Lionel issued its general catalog as part of the advertising in *Liberty* magazine for 1946. This most interesting item is a solid collector piece. At times, several catalogs were issued in the same year. The "Golden Jubilee" year at Lionel was 1950, and several pieces of literature were issued. All are collectible. Gold colored Executive Advance catalogs and Regular Advance catalogs, which carried changes from the Executive catalog; a third Advance catalog with new art work; a general color catalog; and a substitute Advance catalog, which supplemented the general catalog when the supplies ran short, all

Fig. 18-3. Original catalogs such as this 50th Anniversary Lionel example extols the virtues of the company's Magne-Traction. All of the company's catalogs are collectible, but anniversary pieces are especially desirable. Reprinted with the Permission of Lionel Trains, Ltd.

appeared in this banner year. Celebrities also were found on these catalogs. In 1948, Superman was featured on a pocket-sized catalog from Gilbert-American Flyer. The cover showed the "Man of Steel" flying toward the Gilbert Halls of Science.

Early catalogs, especially those in near mint condition, can be quite costly, sometimes reaching three figures. This is especially true with early examples from Ives and American Flyer. Lionel catalogs from the teens and early 1920s can reach $50–75 in fine condition, falling to about $30–$50 for examples from the 1940s and 50s, and dropping again to $15–$20 for those from the 1960s. The same pricing structure applies to American Flyer examples. After the acquisition of American Flyer by A. C. Gilbert in 1937, catalog prices tend to decline and fall into Lionel's pricing pattern. Again, condition is all important with near mint examples bringing top prices. Catalogs with missing pages have significantly less value. The Greenberg Publishing Company has reproduced Lionel catalogs from 1923 to 1942 in a two volume set. This particular set also is becoming a collector's item.

For those who want the text and drawings found in the originals, but object to the fairly stiff cost, reproductions of many of the classics are available for a few dollars. Some are reproduced in authentic colors, but most are printed in black and white. These pieces are marked as reproductions and are rarely confused with the genuine articles. Some companies such as Lionel, Marx, and American Flyer manufactured

Fig. 18-4. Reproduction catalogs including this 1927 Lionel and 1911 Carlisle and Finch usually are printed in black and white and sell for a fraction of the cost of the originals. Most contain notices on the front cover that they are in fact reproductions. Reprinted with the Permission of Lionel Trains, Inc. and Carlisle and Finch.

train sets for sale exclusively through department stores. These sets never were found in the company's general catalogs. They were detailed in the Fall-Winter issues of catalogs from Sears Roebuck, Montgomery Wards, and J. C. Penney. They were printed in single colors, but some were reproduced in colors. The catalogs are very collectible, especially those from the 1920s to the early 1940s. The Allstate Sets found in the Sears catalogs

were made exclusively for this company and were not found in any of the manufacturers' general catalogs. Condition also plays an important part in these items. Examples with full binding and contents are definitely more appealing to the collector.

Less well known, but highly prized are the company promotional sheets sent to store buyers listing the manufacturer's products and prices for the upcoming year. As with the general catalogs, not all of the items that were found on these promo sheets ever saw the light of day. Some promotional sheets were simple typewritten lists, while others featured schematic drawings designed to tantalize the store buyer. Since these were not generally available to the public, they are found infrequently at flea markets and train shows.

Most train sets were packaged with instruction sheets. They were single page affairs that illustrated and described some of the basics, such as wiring, track layouts, and attaching the wiring to the power source. Accessories and specialized pieces of equipment also came packaged with set-up procedures for the item, as well as wiring, operating, and general maintenance hints. Generalized train set instruction sheets are difficult to locate and are seen less frequently than those packed with accessories.

Operating manuals were packed with train sets, especially during the 1940s and 50s. Often they were general rather than referring to the specific train set with which they were packed. Some contained track plans, troubleshooting, and general information such as the care and use of the smoking mechanism found in locomotives of the period. An example is the 1951 American Flyer Model Railroad Handbook which is filled with useful information and insights into the trains of that particular year. These interesting pieces usually can be purchased for a few dollars, though earlier specimens can be quite costly.

In order to promote their products to the general public, toy train manufacturers spent large sums advertising new lines. Magazines were a favorite format for this promotion, especially children's magazines. Highly stylized examples of the family actively engaged in running the train and its accessories delighted the young reader. These advertising pages promoted the special features such as "realistic two-rail operation" and "it puffs smoke like the real locomotives do." In order to establish realism, the advertisers were not above show-

ing a small boy holding a toy train locomotive with the prototype in the background.

These ads also appeared in magazines published for the adult reader. *National Geographic, Liberty*, and *Saturday Evening Post* magazines featured full page ads illustrating the family side of toy train operation. The ads showed a father and son sharing the joy of miniature railroading. New operating accessories usually were prominently incorporated into the ad, such as Lionel's rocket launching car where the rocket came bursting out of the top of the carrier into the air.

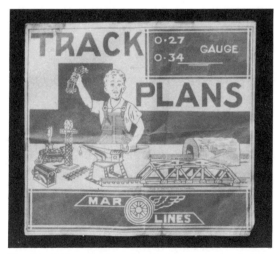

Fig. 18-5. Track planning books are available for a few dollars. The 1941 Marx example contains track plans and illustrations of the company's accessories.

Fig. 18-6. Pages from weekly or monthly magazines were geared to capture the attention of the young reader. Many were printed in multicolors and showed the company's hottest items.

Newspapers also were used to promote the products. Some of the ads offered the opportunity of obtaining the company's catalog, usually for a dime. Other promotional pieces were available through this format. They were located in the comics section.

Soft drinks, breakfast foods, and the like occasionally featured toy trains in their ads. At times, celebrities such as sports heroes were included in the ad to increase interest in the product. However, the toy train manufacturers' products were well integrated into the ads. These magazine ads and covers are very collectible and can be found as single sheets, removed from the magazine. Copies of the intact magazine tend to bring higher prices.

What the train sets came packaged in also is of interest to the collector. Pieces such as rolling stock and accessories with their original boxes command premium prices. The boxes alone are collectible since many carry the name of the item and catalog number on the flap. The familiar orange and blue Lionel product box always

stirs the blood of the dedicated collector. Boxes vary in size, and some Lionel boxes are larger than others. A few boxes were lined with corrugated binders to protect delicate plastic rolling stock, whereas metal cars often fit snuggly into their boxes. Many of these boxes are being reproduced and can be purchased for a few dollars. Interest also extends to boxes that held accessories and transformers.

Many train sets were packaged in very attractive set boxes, especially those from the early part of the Twentieth Century. Some boxes carried colored lithographs on the face depicting the enclosed train set, though at times the set itself was quite different from the one shown on the cover. Some boxes had simulated leather textures, and some were trimmed in gold which was quite attractive. More often than not, these boxes were just simple affairs with the company's name and set number on the surface. A few of the set boxes were printed to become part of the train set, such as the station boxes produced by Louis Marx. When the train set was removed, the box was converted into a trackside structure with the appropriate features printed on the surface, a good selling feature. These boxes are very difficult to find in reasonable shape. Many were discarded or the cover section misplaced after years of use.

Another effective method of keeping a company's name at the forefront was the use of specialized items printed with the young engineer in mind. Lionel released a 78 RPM plastic record with diesel and steam sounds and color pictures of its

Fig. 18-7. Train boxes come in a variety of sizes and styles depending on the year of production and what the box was intended to hold. Photo Courtesy of Beute and Son

trains in the plastic body. Magazines such as those published by Lionel and Hornby's *Meccano Magazine*, kept the young reader up to date on what was happening at these companies. Track planning manuals and layout design books also promoted a company's products.

In addition to these examples, Lionel kept the train enthusiast on edge with a series of trading cards that pictured their locomotives. The Gilbert-American Flyer Company published a series of action comic books that kept the company's name on the reader's mind. Stories revolved around the American Flyer trains, and a coupon was furnished on the back cover for receiving additional paper goods. These little comic books were packed in boxes of cereal. They occasionally pop up at flea markets and are very desirable collectibles. During the 1950s, Lionel cutouts were printed on boxes of breakfast cereals. This technique was especially fruitful as the child had the most contact with these products. After all, it was the era of the cereal premium, and boxes of cereal were consumed in great numbers to collect boxtops or to catch the latest prize.

Quite difficult to find are items that were used for the instore displays. Some were elaborate and included display stands, plaques, and large multi-colored cardboard signs. One striking example of this type of material was a twenty-foot-wide American Flyer display piece which featured a lighted locomotive headlight, flashing signal lights, and a large crossing gate that rose and fell periodically. Obviously, pieces like this are quite rare,

Fig. 18-8. Plan books such as this 1946 example feature tempting photographs of the company's accessories in action. Reprinted with the Permission of Lionel Trains, Ltd.

Fig. 18-9. Dealers' advance catalogs may contain pictures of trains that were never manufactured or sets that were changed before reaching the public. Photo from the Collection of John Ezzo

Fig. 18-10. Classic enameled toy train signs have become quite pricey. Reproductions in the companies' colors are presently being reissued for Lionel, Ives, and American Flyer.

and when available, they may require significant restoration to bring them back to life. Advanced promotional flyers heralding new trains and accessories are of interest to the collector because many are illustrated dramatically.

Businesses that sold and serviced toy trains often displayed signs that indicated the product was available. Many collectors are familiar with the orange and blue Lionel signs, as well as those from American Flyer and Ives. While the originals are expensive and difficult to find, many are being reproduced in brightly painted metal examples in the appropriate color schemes. Distinguishing the originals from the present day repros is not a difficult task, and the modern reproductions serve a function of bridging the gap until one is fortunate enough to find an original.

Old stock certificates relating to common stock offered by the train companies are part of many good collateral material collections. Shares of Lionel and American Flyer common stock were executed beautifully and occasionally appear in bundles of old certificates.

Collecting collateral material is both entertaining and informative as much knowledge regarding the history and the products can be gathered from this type of material. It also makes a wonderful display to complement a collection. The opportunity always exists of finding something that has not been recorded previously.

Priced Examples

American Flyer 1929 catalog $95.00

American Flyer 1935 catalog $95.00

Carlisle and Finch 1911 general catalog, reproduction $10.00

Gilbert-American Flyer catalog, 1952 $40.00

Ives 1924 catalog $50.00

Ives 1927 catalog, colored covers   A–$50.00

Ives 1930 catalog $40.00

Lionel 1930 catalog $150.00

Lionel 1933 catalog $125.00

Lionel 1953 catalog $15.00

Lionel sound effects record, $5\frac{1}{4}$-inches d, 1951 $25.00

CHAPTER 19

Shopping in the Tinplate Marketplace

Armed with the information provided in the previous chapters, any collector, whether beginner, intermediate, or advanced, can find a place to purchase pieces. The train marketplace takes many forms, some of which are more accessible than others, depending on the location of the collector. Certainly, being located in a major metropolitan area has its benefits. There are more outlets. But the rural dweller may have access to pieces that never reach major population centers.

For the beginning collector, the task is easy. Any piece added to the collection probably would enhance it. An intermediate or advanced collector may spend a considerable amount of time looking for a specific piece, but the hunt can be almost as exciting as finding the piece. However, no matter what category the collector falls into, there are many outlets for obtaining what he needs.

Train shows take on many faces. Though originally billed as shows for the scale modeler, nearly half of the exhibit tables are filled with vintage tinplate pieces, as well as tinplate reproductions. Most of the shows feature working tinplate layouts as well as sophisticated model railroad layouts. The train show is a variety of things all wrapped up in one package. It is a place to browse and examine early toy trains and accessories, a place to purchase or swap examples, and a forum for learning. Most dealers specialize in one manufacturer and are willing to pass their expertise on to the neophyte collector. It can be a place to locate the rare and unusual. Part of the entertainment is being able to negotiate a price on a prized piece for one's collection. Some dealers hold the line on price, while others openly state "make me an offer I can't refuse."

Whatever is purchased at the train show, the buyer is responsible for knowing what he is buying. It would behoove the collector to carefully examine each piece before purchasing it to guarantee the piece

Fig. 19-1. Vintage and modern trains are put through their paces at the tinplate layout found at most train shows. Future collectors watch every move of these classic trains.

Fig. 19-2. Many toy train dealers set up shop at local train shows. Though billed as model railroad shows, more and more booths are being occupied by dealers offering toy train pieces like these.

has all the original and correct parts intact. Most train shows maintain a test track that enables the purchaser to "test run" a locomotive to determine its electrical status. Rolling stock also should be tested to examine the wheels, axles, and coupler position.

When one attends his first train show, it can be an overwhelming experience, especially for the neophyte. Most shows are

quite large and occupy several buildings. Each vendor's table is crammed with goodies. Crowds can be intimidating, especially just before Christmas when many children attend in hopes of persuading their parents to purchase their first toy train set. When attending a show, a sufficient amount of time should be allocated so that items can be examined carefully. If a specific piece is not readily available, sometimes if you discuss your "wants" with a dealer, the dealer will place your name on a list. If the piece surfaces in the condition you require, the dealer will contact you. It also pays to be a competitive shopper as several dealers

Fig. 19-3. Attendance is especially strong during the Christmas season.

Fig. 19-4. A variety of accessories in all degrees of condition offer the collector something to fit every pocketbook.

may have the same piece, but in varying conditions. The rule of thumb that applies to all antiques and collectibles certainly applies in the toy train market—"Always buy the best example that you can afford." A good, clean, well-running locomotive is certainly a better investment than one that requires a major overhaul and new paint job. Those who are skilled in engine maintenance may enjoy the challenge, but a beginning collector may not have the skills nor desire to bring a piece back to life.

The serious, as well as the curious, collector should plan on attending at least one train show to get the feel of what they are all about. Those buying on the East Coast can attend one of the toy, doll, and train shows sponsored by Greenberg Promotions. These frequently feature an auction of toy train material in conjunction with the shows. They are located at 10 different sites from Massachusetts to Florida.

The Great American Train Shows cover such cities as St. Louis, Dallas, Milwaukee, Kansas City, Dayton, and Des Moines. The Train Mart meets monthly at the DuPage County Fairgrounds in Wheaton, Ilinois. With the exception of July, this show features indoor and outdoor sellers as well as tinplate layouts. The Train Mart also sponsors shows in San Francisco at the Solono County Fairgrounds, and in the Los Angeles region at the L.A. County Fair and Expo Center. Twice annually, the Train Collectors Association schedules an enormous toy train meet in York, Pennsylvania.

These train shows frequently run several times a year, but there are shows that are annual or biannual events. Some have just begun to establish themselves, whereas others have been around for many years, such as the Pennsylvania Train Show which is entering its fifteenth year. In addition to the major shows, local train clubs hold swap meets and shows that are open to the public. Before planning to attend any of the shows, it is wise to examine the show calendars. These are listed in the toy train magazines under the calendar of events section. In addition, it is wise to call ahead, especially for club shows. Not all are open to the public at any given time.

Specialized antique toy shows that pop up across the country can be a good source for early material, especially for the tin floor runners and cast iron examples. This also holds true for the general antiques show. This type of show is often overlooked, but at times some unexpected treasures can be found. It is not unusual to find anything from early predecessors to the modern day train set and accessories, depending on the caliber of the show. What

Fig. 19-5. The Great American Train Mart is one of the many arenas for buying, selling, and swapping toy train material.

may appear to be a show of early American antiques could hold a treasure or two for the toy train enthusiast. Therefore general antiques shows should not be dismissed in favor of more specialized shows, but should be part of the full calendar for the collector.

Flea markets can be a wonderful source for material if a collector has patience. Collateral material, such as old advertising examples, signs, and catalogs frequently are hidden in boxes or piles of old magazines. An early Ives or Carlisle and Finch catalog may surface with some diligent searching. The prize makes the effort worthwhile. In addition, the flea market is a good source for individual train pieces such as rolling stock, track, and accessories. A badly damaged piece of rolling stock may turn out to be a source for a needed set of couplers or trucks. Common train sets are offered in a variety of conditions, and unexpected variations from the standard set may be encountered at this type of show. Unlike the antiques shows, the flea market may require a significant amount of time in order to uncover a needed piece. The constantly changing inventory and availability of the flea market make them a natural for the diligent collector.

House sales may contain the "family train" as part of the sale. Usually the rare or unusual sets find their way to dealers, but some good, basic material can be found at such sales. In addition, boxes of old magazines may contain some interesting advertising material, especially examples that date back to the early 1900s. Informa-

tion on little known companies can be gleaned from these examples. Catalogs from companies such as Sears, Penney's, and Montgomery Wards offer a wealth of information, especially on sets that were manufactured for distribution through these outlets. The Fall-Winter Editions are the ones to keep an eye open for as they usually carried a larger toy section for the approaching Christmas season.

Specialized train auctions are few and far between. Occasionally someone's notable collection comes across the block and generates considerable excitement. An example was the "Gasque Collection of Toy Trains" that was auctioned at Christie's East in 1986. This noted collector had assembled a fine array of American and European toy trains in excellent condition. By perusing the catalog and the prices realized, the collector can get a feel for the market as well as observe some rare and unusual specimens.

Toy auctions frequently include toy train examples as part of the inventory, and the number of pieces varies with each auction. It would behoove the serious collector who plans on entering bids in such an auction to examine the material firsthand. It is difficult to determine if a piece has been altered, especially repainted, by examining a photo in a catalog. Many times these items are merely listed with the appropriate manufacturer's catalog number and a brief description of the item. What may appear to be in "fine" condition to one person may actually be in "average" to "fair" condition to another. Rather than making a mistake with an item that is not returnable, attend the auction during the hours scheduled for previewing and examine the examples.

The same criteria holds true for the general auction that occasionally features a small section of toys and trains. Most auctioneers are more knowledgeable in porcelain, furniture, and silver than in American toy trains, and condition can be misleading. Alterations, even of a minor nature may slip by those cataloging the material, and the prospective buyer may find he has purchased something less than what was described. Again, attendance is necessary if significant purchases are contemplated.

Some auctions are by mail bid only. These require the placement of a bid by mail or telephone, but frequently viewing is allowed before the bids are accepted. For those who find it difficult to travel to the area, most auctioneers are helpful in describing the items to the best of their ability. By asking key questions such as wheel type, configuration, coupler type, and presence or absence of surface damage such as scratches, a fairly clear picture of the item can be developed. This requires a good working knowledge on the part of the collector. Homework is the key.

Most communities have a hobby shop of some sort. Frequently these shops deal, to some extent, with scale model railroads, and some expand their merchandise to include present day examples by manufacturers such as Lionel and LGB. The larger this section of the shop, the greater the probability vintage material is included in their inventory. Larger cities with a multitude of hobby shops often cater to the vintage toy train collector and may have extensive inventories of these pieces. In addition, some maintain repair facilities for those who find their sick locomotive needs special attention.

Several magazines cater to the small train enthusiast. *Model Railroading* and *Railroad Modeler* are monthly magazines that emphasize scale model railroading, but feature articles on tinplate and tinplate layouts. Question and answer columns offer hints on repairs and upgrading, and show calendars have listings for major shows, as well as club show events which are detailed by states. Though the emphasis is on the scale models, tinplate is beginning to be featured more frequently. A recent monthly feature in *Model Railroading* examines a classic piece of tinplate in depth and discusses variations and degree of rarity.

The heart and soul of any magazine is its advertising, and this is especially true for model train magazines. In addition to the numerous scale model advertisers, there are dealers who feature both pre- and post-war tinplate trains and accessories. Several dealers specialize in replacement parts for classic tinplate, including missing pieces from action accessories such as milk cans for the automatic dairy cars. Minute items such as replacement marker lights and springs can be found in the classified section in each monthly issue. Collateral material, including actual and reproduction train catalogs are available, as well as reproduction material that may be required to fill out an incomplete set.

A few magazines are a little more specialized in their approach. An example is the *S Gaugian* which features articles on both scale and tinplate in the popular S Gauge. As one might expect, tinplate in this gauge concentrates on the products of the Gilbert-American Flyer Company. Quite thorough in its approach, this type of magazine concentrates its efforts on a specific area and examines the various aspects in considerable detail.

The toy train enthusiast now has a magazine devoted entirely to his field of interest. *Classic Toy Trains Quarterly* is a recent publication dealing with all aspects of toy trains. Feature articles examine hitherto unknown or unrecognized tinplate examples and variations, and they provide basic information for the tinplate nut. One article may examine the many paint variations of a specific tinplate station. Another will discuss the types of loads found on a piece of rolling stock, and the reproduction of these loads that might confuse the collector. In the question and answer forum, some unique examples are brought forth for consideration. Product reports discuss the pros and cons of reproduction items, as well as newly issued pieces from the major manufacturers. Helpful hints are given in articles on repainting, repairing, and restoring vintage tinplate. This magazine is a must for the serious tinplate collector. Classified advertising in this and other specialized magazines offer a marketplace for the purchase or swap of tinplate examples.

General antiques newspapers often feature "Toys For Sale" sections where tinplate examples, either complete sets or individual pieces, can sometimes be found. In addition, the "Miscellaneous For Sale" sections occasionally list tinplate examples, and a sharp-eyed reader may connect in this most unlikely place. Collateral material and catalog reprints are frequently found in these columns. The serious collector should pay attention to these sections. They may pay off with big dividends.

The mecca for the toy train collector is the Train Collectors Association Museum located at Strasburg, Pennsylvania. The museum is open nine months of the year and maintains an extensive collection of classic toy trains, accessories, and collateral material. A research library is on the premises to aid in the further understanding of this interesting subject. TCA boasts a membership of over 20,000 individuals devoted to the subject of collecting American toy trains. It publishes a wonderful magazine devoted to tinplate called *The Train Collectors Quarterly*. For those who like to mingle and discuss operating procedures, the Toy Train Operating Society based in Pasadena, California holds conventions across the country. Several other operating societies devoted to single manufacturers are well-attended by the devotee and curious alike.

Bibliography

General References

Ayers, William S. *The Warner Collector's Guide To American Toys*. New York: Warner Books, 1981.

Divides toys into categories from simple to complex. Good section on American forerunners both trackless and tracked. Weak on trains after turn of the century.

Becher, Udo. *Early Tin Plate Model Railways*. Herts, England: Argus Books, Ltd., 1980.

Heavy emphasis on European trains including Marklin and Bing. Wonderful color plates but very little text. Dates pieces by means of couplers, bumpers, and trucks.

Carlson, Pierce. *Toy Trains*. Philadelphia, PA: Harper and Row, 1986.

Chronological discussion of periods of train production. Discusses the rise and fall by country. Emphasis on German production. Very good photography.

———.*Greenberg's Guide to Lionel Trains 1945-1969 10th Anniversary Edition*. Sykesville, MD: Greenberg Publishing, 1984.

Excellent coverage of Lionel trains from the beginning of the company until World War II. All locomotives and rolling stock examples, along with all sorts of variations.

Greenberg's Guide to Lionel Trains 1945-1969 10th Anniversary Edition. Sykesville, MD: Greenberg Publishing, 1984.

Coverage of Lionel trains from the period after World War II until 1969. A comprehensive listing and study of trains and accessories made during that period.

————.*Model Railroading. A Family Guide*. Englewood Cliffs, NJ: Prentice Hall, 1979.

A good beginner's guide for tinplate railroading including track plans and repair techniques. Mainly discusses Lionel trains and accessories. Good line drawings. Very little in the way of company history.

Heimburger, Donald. A.C. *Gilbert's Heritage*. River Forest, Il: Heimburger Publishing, 1983.

A year-by-year discussion of post-war Gilbert-American Flyer with highlights of each year. Discussions with former workers at American Flyer add to the interest of this softcover book. It also contains a brief discussion of the Erector sets.

Hollander, Ron. *ALL ABOARD! The Story of Joshua Lionel Cowen and His Lionel Train Company*. New York: Workman Publishing Co., 1981.

A very readable, interesting book with lots of personal remembrances about Joshua Lionel Cowen by his family and friends.

Ketchum Jr, William C. *Collecting Toys For Fun And Profit*. Tucson, AZ: HP Books, 1985.

Though the book deals with toys in general, there are good sections on building a train collection. It details where to find and how to care for all toys including trains.

Kimball, Steven H., ed. *Greenberg's Guide to American Flyer Prewar O Gauge*. Sykesville, MD: Greenberg Publishing, 1987.

Continues in the tradition of the Greenberg books with excellent and complete coverage of trains of the period.

Kowal, Case. *Toy Trains of Yesteryear*. Newton, NJ: Carstens Publications, 1987.

A softcover book that covers details of some lesser known companies such as Knapp, Howard, and Dorfan as well as highlights of specific examples from the better known companies.

LaVoie, Roland. *Greenberg's Guide to Lionel Trains 1970–1988 with 1989 Supplement*. Sykesville, MD: Greenberg Publishing, 1989.

Up to the minute information on Lionel through the Fundimensions era and including the present year's production.

Levy, Allen. *A Century Of Model Trains*. New Cavendish Books, 1978.

Large, lavish book with excellent color plates of European trains. Very little text. The picture captions provide the bulk of the text.

Matzke, Eric J. *Greenberg's Guide To Marx Trains 2nd Edition*. Sykesville, MD: Greenberg Publishing, 1985.

A wonderful book which delves into the history, manufacturing techniques, evolution, and variations of these trains. Prices are somewhat dated.

McComas, Tom and James Tuohy. *Great Toy Train Layouts of America.* Wilmette, Il: TM Books, 1987.

Beautiful color photographs of some of the best toy train layouts in America. Brief text discusses fabrication and rolling stock associated with each layout.

McComas, Tom and James Tuohy. *Lionel A Collector's Guide and History to Lionel Trains.* Wilmette IL: TM Productions,
  Volume I: Prewar O Gauge, 1975
  Volume II: Postwar, 1976
  Volume III: Standard Gauge, 1978
  Volume IV: 1970–1980, 1980
  Volume V: The Archives, 1981
  Volume VI: Advertising and Art, 1981

A wealth of information in each volume of all stages of Lionel's growth and development including incredibly detailed listings of trains and accessories made in each period.

McDuffie, Al. *Greenberg's Guide to Ives Trains: 1901–1932.* Sykesville, MD: Greenberg Publishing, 1984.

A complete history of the Ives trains from their inception until the complete takeover by Lionel. Very detailed coverage of examples made by Ives including accessories through the transition periods.

Rosa, Vincent and George J. Horan. *Greenberg's Guide to Lionel HO Trains.* Sykesville, MD: Greenberg Publishing, 1986.

This volume covers HO Gauge from 1957 through 1966 in extensive detail.

Schuweiler, Alan R. *Greenberg's Guide to American Flyer Wide Gauge.* Sykesville, MD: Greenberg Publishing, 1989.

Another fine effort from Greenberg Publishing Company that covers all trains in Wide Gauge plus an extensive section on accessories.

Repair and Restoration Guides

Pauker, Susan, ed. *Greenberg's Repair and Operating Manual For Lionel Trains.* Sykesville, MD: Greenberg Publishing Co., 1983.

Shantar, Stan. *Greenberg's Operating and Repair Manual For Lionel-Fundimensions Trains: 1970–1978.*

Sykesville, MD: Greenberg Publishing Co., 1978.

Smith, I.D. & Richard, ed. *Greenberg's American Flyer Factory Manual.* Sykesville, MD: Greenberg Publishing Co., 1988.

Magazines

Classic Toy Trains, Milwaukee, WI: Kalmbach Publishing,

A bimonthly publication that is a must for the toy train enthusiast. Well researched articles and information sections highlight this magazine. The photography is excellent.

Model Railroader, Milwaukee, WI: Kalmbach Publishing

This monthly emphasizes scale model railroading in all scales, but occasionally visits tinplate layouts. It also features how-to sections, articles on tinplate, and a calendar of shows and events. The Marketplace carries new and used tinplate and supplies.

Railroad Model Craftsman, Newton, NJ: Carstens Publications,

Another monthly with interesting articles on tinplate. Mostly geared for the scale modeler.

S Gaugian, River Forest, IL: Heimburger House Publishing

As the title indicates, this bimonthly deals with the S Gauge both in scale and tinplate.

Price Guides

American Flyer Market Guide, Prewar Edition 1925–1941, Post-war Edition 1946–1966. NY: April Publications, 1988.

Prices for major pieces, brief history and section on variations. Few photographs.

Greenberg, Bruce C. *Greenberg's Price Guide to Lionel Trains and Inventory Checklist, 1901–1941 & 1945–1987*. Sykesville, MD: Greenberg Publishing, 1987.

A great pocket guide listing Lionel examples by number with prices.

Greenberg, Bruce. *Greenberg's Price Guide to Lionel Trains Postwar O and O 27 Trains*. Sykesville, MD: Greenberg Publishing, 1983.

Prices and a comprehensive listing for locos, rolling stock, and accessories from 1945–1983.

Lionel Trains Market Price Guide, Prewar Edition 1925–1944, Post-war Edition 1945–1969. NY: April Publications, 1988.

Prices for major pieces with a brief history and section on variations. Few photographs.

O'Brien, Richard. *American Premium Guide to Electric Trains, 2nd edition*. Florence, AL: Books Americana, 1986.

The only comprehensive price guide presently on the market. Includes some lesser known companies such as Manoil. The photography for the most part is dark and overcrowded. As with most price guides, it should be used as a starting point.

Index